Social Mentality in Contemporary Japan

Quantitative Social Consciousness Studies

Toru Kikkawa

Osaka University Press

Osaka University Press

Osaka University West Front, 2-7
Yamadaoka, Suita-shi, Osaka, Japan
565-0871

Published in Japan
by Osaka University Press
First published 2016

Social Mentality in Contemporary Japan:
Quantitative Social Consciousness Studies
by Toru Kikkawa

Copyright © Toru Kikkawa, 2014
Original Japanese edition published by Yuhikaku Publishing Co., Ltd., Tokyo
English translation copyright © Osaka University Press

All rights reserved. No part of this publication may be
translated, reproduced or transmitted in any form or by any means,
electronic or mechanical, including photocopy, recording,
or information storage and retrieval systems,
without permission in writing from the publisher.

ISBN 978-4-87259-546-8

About the Author

Toru Kikkawa (Ph.D., Osaka University, 1994) is a professor of sociology in the Graduate School of Human Sciences at Osaka University. He leads the Stratification and Social Psychology (SSP) Project based also at Osaka University. He is the author of *Kaisō kyōiku to shakai ishiki no keisei: Shakai ishiki ron no jikai* [Stratification, education, and the formation of social consciousness: The magnetic field in social consciousness studies] (1998) and *Gakureki bundan shakai* [Society of educational disparity] (2009), among other works in Japanese, and has also published several articles in English-language journals. He includes quantitative sociology, social research methodology, sociology of education, social psychology, and social stratification studies among his areas of research, and has a special interest in contemporary Japanese society.

Translator's Note

This book is an English translation of *Gendai Nihon no "shakai no kokoro,"* which was published in 2014 by Yuhikaku Publishing Co., Ltd. As that publication history implies, while the original Japanese version was intended for an *educated* audience it was not necessarily aimed at a *scholarly* audience. Accordingly, numerous asides and turns of phrase in the original text that presumed a non-specialized Japanese readership were recast or eliminated from this translation, which presumes a more specialized global readership. Some are still present as written, however, and the reader's indulgence is asked for in that regard.

Several terms and neologisms appear in the work that are specific to the world of Japanese sociology. Foremost among them is *shakai ishikiron* ("social consciousness studies"), which already has been rendered in various other ways in citations to the author's work that have appeared in English prior to this translation's publication. Every effort had been made when developing translations for these various terms to reconcile any existing English renderings of the relevant or related terminology with the interpretations and wishes of the author. Furthermore, the author closely reviewed the entire translation.

As is customary, Japanese (and as appropriate other Asian) names are presented in the surname-personal name order, while Western names appear in the personal name-surname order.

Carl Freire

Contents

About the Author	iii
Translator's Note	v
INTRODUCTION Quantifying Social Mentality	xi
A Crucial Thing Invisible to the Eye	xi
Survey Data Analysis as Brake	xiv
The Structure of This Book	xv

PART I
REBUILDING SOCIAL CONSCIOUSNESS STUDIES — 1

CHAPTER 1 Approaches to Apprehending Social Consciousness	3
Positioning the Field within the Social Sciences	4
General Concepts of Social Consciousness	7
Stratification, Education, and the Formation of Social Consciousness	10
Social Consciousness Studies in the Postwar Period	12
Establishing Contemporary Social Consciousness Studies	13
Unexpectedly Idled	16
Stratification Consciousness Studies	18
The Pedigree of Social Consciousness Studies	20
CHAPTER 2 The Conduct of Quantitative Social Consciousness Studies	25
The Social Structure Sets Social Consciousness in Motion	25
Observing Contemporary Japanese Society	28
The Horizons Set by Trends and Status-Relatedness	30
Focusing on Society's Middle Ranges	31
Public Opinion Statistics and Quantitative Social Consciousness Studies	32
Analytical Monographs	36
"The Angels' Share"	39

PART II
THE TRAJECTORY OF IDENTIFICATION — 45

CHAPTER 3 Japan in 1985	47
An Age of Subtle Changes	47
Capturing the Eve of Reflexive Modernity	50
The Pinnacle for Shōwa Japan	52
Generational Change and the Human Life-Cycle	55
Positive Reevaluations of the Uniqueness of Japan's Culture: The Age of "Exotic Japan"	57
Social Mentality in the First Modernity	59
Homologies between *Nihonjinron* and the Mass-Middle-Class Phenomenon	61

CHAPTER 4 The Real Nature of the Mass-Middle-Class Phenomenon 65
  The Catalyst that Changed the Debate about Stratification into One about Eras 65
  Curious Consequences 66
  A Point of Debate Consigned to "Galapagos" 69
  The "Phony" Rise of the Mass Middle Class: The Case of the SSM Survey 71
  The "Phony" Rise of the Mass Middle Class: The Case of the Life of the People Survey 76
  The Fiction and Reality of the Mass Middle Class 77

CHAPTER 5 From Mass-Middle-Class Society to Mass-Inequality Society 81
  Redefining Mass Middle Class 81
  Enhancing Causal Explanatory Power 83
  The Quiet Transformation of Status Identification 86
  The Mechanism behind Era Change 87
  What Is the Era of the Mass-Inequality Society Like? 91

PART III
WHAT HAPPENED TO ORIENTATION? 95

CHAPTER 6 The Quiet Retirement of Traditionalism–Modernism 97
  Modern Society and Traditionalism 97
  What Is Authoritarianism? 98
  Self-Direction 100
  The Trajectory of the Authoritarian Attitude 102
  Post-Modernization in Attitudes toward Gender-Role Segregation 109
  Disappearance of the Gradient of Social Mentality 113

CHAPTER 7 The Doctrineless Age 117
  The "Misfire" of Equity Studies 117
  Perception of Inequality Driven by Personal Interest 120
  A Ubiquitous Prosocial Nature 122
  A Meltdown Caused by the Acceptance of Diversity 123
  Searching for a Gradient in the Frequency of Daily Activities 125
  The Consummatory Nature of the Doctrineless Age 131

CHAPTER 8 A Hidden Era-Change in Quality of Life Orientations 137
  Attitudes to Health and the Environment in Contemporary Japan 137
  The Influence of Social Consciousness on the QOL Orientation 139
  Comparative Survey Data from 18 Years Later 144
  An Era Change in the Determinant Structure 146
  From Modernity to Reflexive Modernity 150

EPILOGUE Status Literacy, Consummatory, and Reflexivity 153
  The Described Shape of the Social Mentality 153
  Disembedding from the Collective Consciousness 156
  The Social Mentality of the 1980s 158
  The Social Mentality of Contemporary Japan 161
  The Frayed Influence of Social Attributes 163

Disembedding from Occupation	165
Re-embedding into Education	167
Concluding Remarks	168

Afterword   171

Works Cited   173

Index   183

INTRODUCTION
Quantifying Social Mentality

A Crucial Thing Invisible to the Eye

"Japanese have come to treasure the bonds among people." "No, the connections among people have been lost and everyone feels alone." "Today's young people have lost hope." "No, young people in fact seem to be pretty satisfied with their daily lives."

How do people see the world around them, and what feelings do the things they see arouse? In the broadest sense, the answers to these questions offer us a glimpse of what I call the "social mentality" (*shakai no kokoro*). Social mentality constitutes the software, so to speak, that controls how the social system works. The idea that such a social mentality exists and can be apprehended is attracting renewed interest for its potential as a key to help us unlock the riddles of Japanese society today.

In recent years, the Japanese media has markedly increased its use of psychoanalytic and clinical psychological interpretations to describe events and incidents in the world. Indeed, it has become more common for language (usually with negative connotations) related to mental states like *utsu* ("depression"), *iyashi* ("healing"), *kireru* ("losing it"), *hekomu* ("withdrawing"), *ochikomu* ("feeling down"), and *kokoro ga oreru* ("heart breaks") to be used throughout print and broadcast mediums than ever before. Expressions that emphasize feelings and emotions like "the national sentiment," "public perception," "rumors," and "the sentiment among the people concerned" often function as determinants of whether something is good or bad. The best example of such a phrase from the past decade might be "*kūki o yomu*"—literally, "to read the atmosphere," or more idiomatically "to get the drift."

This tendency is visible when it comes to government policy as well. The criteria used for judging various policy approaches are not such objective facts as "employment," "wages," "welfare," "family," "community," "education," and "punishment," but rather the kinds of feelings people have about them. The rationales offered tend to such statements as "We want to create a society where everyone *feels* happy, rather than one where every member of the society achieves an affluent standard of living," "The way the public *thinks* about gender needs to be changed to achieve equal employment opportunity between the sexes," and "It is more important to pursue decision-making processes that everyone can *agree* to rather than to target urgent changes in policy." For this reason, political scientists, labor economists, pedagogists, and the like all have begun to use social mentality—in the form of such concepts as "hope" (*kibō*), "despair" (*zetsubō*), "happiness" (*kōfuku*), "anxiety" (*fuan*), and "empathy" (*kyōkan*)—as the key concept that underpins their various theories.

Sociologists have described this as the "psychologization" of contemporary society. This trend rapidly grew in conjunction with a shift of emphasis in people's lives toward things deemed to be socially desirable—that is, from the accumulation of material wealth to spiritual richness or improved quality of life. As shall be shown, this development is simply another indicator of a global change from the era of so-called modernity to that of reflexive (*saikiteki*) modernity (second modernity). In the Japanese context, this gradual but definite shift corresponds almost perfectly with the transition from the Shōwa (1925–1989) to the Heisei eras (1989–)—broadly speaking, to the years around the turn of the 20th century.

In more technical language, social mentality is social consciousness (*shakai ishiki*; I will discuss the translation issues involved in Chapter 1). One might expect the fact that the general public being so interested in this topic would provide a welcome tailwind to scholars who have made social consciousness studies (*shakai ishikiron*) their focus. Given that the field is in a position to bridge classic sociological theory and the current interest in social mentality among a non-specialist audience, one could easily be forgiven for expecting it to be "hot" right now.

However, there is nothing to indicate that this is at all the case, for contemporary social consciousness studies has not been able to satisfy what the general public desires of it. There are several reasons why this is so. First, trying to analyze what is reflected in the mentality of a society rather than objective social conditions can be seen as a somewhat peculiar approach to getting at the facts. We can apprehend the general state of a society through any number of objective figures; consider what you can learn, for example, from economic indicators, the real growth rate of the GDP, labor participation ratios, employment rates, the job offer ratio, birthrates, age-based demographics, tertiary education attainment rates, and so forth. In light of this, some will inevitably suspect that intellectuals are merely speaking in riddles because they are trying to convert those facts into that—i.e., a mentality—which expressly cannot be seen.

Moreover, while the way in which social mentality operates can be more or less understood, it is hard to discern its form and make it visible. Empirical sociologists (*keiryō shakaigakusha*) examine it by using yardsticks such as psychological measures. However, this activity is quite different from developing an overall portrait of the social consciousness—the enormous operating system, so to speak—that governs modern society and makes it work. Even if we had several hundred such yardsticks, the number would still be inadequate to the task. Additionally, social consciousness is flexible and shifts with the trends of the times. If we do not establish the contours of the social mentality, the more we try to understand its dynamic character the less traction our explanations of it will have.

That said, the "feel" of this uncertainty that faces us is not something that most non-specialists are likely to perceive. In their view, social consciousness comprises a solid mass of opinions; it can be presented on a bar graph or pie chart in the form of "for/against" or "support/do not support" opinions, or else they anticipate that simple assertions of that sort will eventually be made. Nishiyama Tetsuo argues that when it comes to general scientific knowledge in reflexive modernity, "the more a scientist tries to do their work as a specialist in good faith, the more they will reach conclusions that leave behind some aspects they cannot foresee. It is simply not possible for today's specialists in the sciences to make clear avowals of the sort that laypersons expect" (Nishiyama 2013: 20–21).

If you think about it, it should be easy to recognize that social mentality is not a concept that fits neatly into a box in the ways that, say, "neoliberalism" or "environmentalist" do. The phenomena that social consciousness studies concerns itself with—status identification, authoritarianism, and general life satisfaction—should best be seen as the intermediate terms that sociologists use for turning social survey data into persuasive theories rather than as descriptions of actual conditions. What we truly seek to understand is social mentality as a living, breathing thing that can be learned about through the use of those intermediate terms.

The fact is, however, that there is a vague sense of guilt among empirical sociologists in Japan, for over the course of the past two decades or so they have lost their sense of society's social mentality. Even if they did not actually have a handle on it, through the late 1980s at the end of the Shōwa period (1925–1989) they nonetheless made frequent declarations to the public about what the actual state of social consciousness was. They bandied about certain phrases central to Shōwa-era critical discourse that people of a certain age will recall hearing, like "*Nihonjinron*" (theories of Japanese uniqueness), "*sōchūryū genshō*" (the mass-middle-class phenomenon), and "*hoshu-kakushin no seijiteki ideorogī tairitsu*" (the standoff of political ideologies between conservatism and liberalism).

To get ahead of myself in presenting this book's argument, I believe it was once possible to tell the tale of social mentality in clear terms like this by taking advantage of two "auxiliary lines" that ran through modern Japanese society in the 20th century. One was the time axis of social development, which ran straight from traditional to modern society, while the other was the vertical axis of stratification status. With these two axes, we could generate a two-dimensional plane for apprehending the social consciousness. The power that these axes provided by stipulating something as being "new" or "old," or "upper" or "lower," made it possible to portray various aspects of society in understandable ways. This of course was applicable not only when it came to the mass middle class or someone's attitude toward Japanese tradition, but also to opinions about science and technology policy, views on international relations, nationalism, and attitudes about the family and community.

However, these two lines that had offered such potency in the 20th century are almost completely useless in today's Japan. Many contemporary phenomena and issues—nuclear power and other energy issues, the state of the environment, ethnicity, trade liberalization, non-profit organization activities, grassroots civic movements, the welfare state regime, so-called "herbivore" young men, and young women seeking to become full-time housewives—do not lend themselves to such simple assessments as "That's an old way of thinking" or "That is a bourgeois (or proletarian) value." For that reason, we simply can no longer get a handle so easily on what the social mentality is now. If we do not understand the nature of the operating system that runs society, we cannot ascertain what lies ahead.

Survey Data Analysis as Brake

"If you haven't collected any objective data to support it, then no matter how you argue your point it will still be groundless, right?" Scholars working in fields that are (or see themselves as) close to the natural sciences are likely to immediately draw such a conclusion in the event that such conditions are true. However, while social consciousness studies may be a social science, it is also tinged with the humanities, overlapping as it does with modern thought and cultural studies. As such, specialists in this field simply do not come to the same conclusion about an argument's potential validity. That said, they also should not give up on finding quantitative data to confirm their arguments in favor of relying entirely on unfettered pronouncements about social conditions. Being aware of trends in social survey data is indispensable for getting an undistorted view of the social mentality.

The method used entails measuring what I call the gentle "gradients" that run through society. We do this by asking people throughout the country who are leading quite "ordinary" lives identical questions about their lifestyles and patterns of thinking, and then analyzing the results. This method provides a hard-to-match benefit in that it allows the researcher to move away from a worm's-eye view of how individuals experience daily life and get a bird's-eye perspective on society as a whole.

That said, when putting it into practice, we also find this approach comes with a rigid constraint: the way in which the scholar can develop his or her argument is shackled by scientific "rules" such as those concerning statistical significance. Even just loosening those restraints would markedly expand the degree of freedom to talk about social mentality. Doing so can be tempting, and some studies of contemporary Japanese society in fact have relied on small observations and exaggerated speculations while paying little heed to quantitative data to make specific pronouncements about the state of society. There is a bracing incisiveness to these unrestrained stories; following the facile riddle-solving trajectory laid out therein does produce a certain degree of "oh, now I see" satisfaction.

However, it cannot be said that the grasp they have of the state of Japanese society today is an unerring one. The arguments they present tend to be a hodgepodge with no small amount of armchair speculation based solely on the author's sensitivities. Even those works that carefully adhere to the methods of fieldwork and studies of discourse analysis may make arguments that recklessly clash with the "feel" that we get from the large-scale survey data.

More problematic is the fact that most of their readers do not bring the "literacy," so to speak, needed to discriminate the truth or falseness of arguments. In today's Japan, we frequently see people tapping (figuratively and literally) on the "Like" button without giving it much thought in response to statements about the shared present that critics—whose original purpose was to be mediators of culture—casually toss off without the underpinning of any particular proposition or theory. For example, until quite recently there was much talk of Japan having become a "desperate country," battered by anxiousness about the future and a sense of stagnation. However, it was not possible in the end to uncover any definite evidence in the social survey data—which get at actual conditions in the heart of society—showing Japanese society to be terrorized by risks and consumed with anxiety.

In the meantime, there was a change in political leadership, Tokyo was awarded the Summer Olympics, and the economy recovered slightly. In response, the old discourse was pushed aside and a new one began to take root saying that bright portents were on the horizon. But the social mentality is not something that changes so simply "as expected" like that. The question of what is truly happening remains. Surely everyone would like to know the real story.

Studies of contemporary society supported by survey data tend to be written in the form of a self-evident story; often, their findings are presented as suggesting something that everyone already senses to be the case. Mita Munesuke, the trailblazer in social consciousness studies, once described the difference between quantitative and qualitative studies as follows: "In the case of the former you get analyses that say 'this is definite, but it isn't interesting;' with the latter, you tend to get arguments that say 'this is interesting, but it is not definite'" (Mita 1979: 139). His turn of phrase squarely hits the mark. It is difficult for the researcher to strike a balance between being "interesting" and being "definite." However, precisely because the present age is a confused one, there is still some value to taking on this difficult challenge.

From the discussion thus far, the reader may have developed the following understanding of the state of affairs amid which this book came into being: The degree to which people are coming to see social mentality as meaningful in Japan today is growing stronger in lockstep with a tremendous change in contemporary society. However, sociology grounded in objective survey data does not have the firm grasp on what that mentality is actually like as it did around the end of the Shōwa period. In the field's attempts to get a handle on it, "unfettered" logic has tended to run rampant in a way that turns the lack of verification from quantitative data against itself. As a result, the formal scholarly space once known as social consciousness studies is presenting itself to be something of an "unregulated commons" in contemporary society studies.

If this situation where impressionistic theories about social mentality continues to govern the course ahead, then metaphorically speaking the ship of Japanese society on which we are passengers is going to be steered solely by experience and gut reaction with no one checking the instrument panel. Social consciousness studies that are based on survey data analysis can establish the necessary "oppositional complementarity" (*taikōteki sōhosei*) (Shiobara 1994) to put forth sound arguments about the direction in which the social mentality is headed.

The Structure of This Book

This book is divided into three parts. In Part I, I reconstruct in my own fashion the doctrines and theoretical background of social consciousness and quantitative social consciousness studies. Surprisingly few efforts have been made in these fields to present their research frameworks in an organized fashion. I have organized my thinking in the belief that the style of research should first be made plain so that the reader may better understand the points I am making. Given the somewhat specialized subject matter, the non-specialist reader who wants to know what my specific points are should begin from Chapter 3 by browsing through the figures presented in the first two chapters. They can then be referred back to as necessary to grasp the general sense of my arguments.

Concrete case studies are at the heart of Parts II and III. Using status identification as its core index, Part II traces what contemporary Japanese have perceived their places in society to be from the era of the mass middle class to the present. In Part III, developing my argument in the context of the current state of the conflict between tradition and modernity (referred to in this book as "traditionalism–modernism"[1]), I provide a close reading of the uncertain direction today's Japanese are taking in how they involve themselves with society (their social orientation). In the Epilogue, I link the quantitative social consciousness studies findings presented in this book to the theory of reflexive modernity (second modernity) to illuminate when contemporary Japanese society reached its peak as well as the issues that lay ahead.

NOTES

[1] "Traditionalism–modernism" as I label it comprises a paired construct that informs the social consciousness of Japanese in the postwar period. Japanese during this period judge their own places and those of their peers based on where they were positioned on a spectrum with traditionalism at one end and modernism on the other.

CREDITS

Permission was obtained from the SSP Project to use the SSP-I 2010 (Stratification and Social Psychology Survey, Interview method, 2010), SSP-P 2010 (Stratification and Social Psychology Survey, Postal method, 2010), SSP-W 2013-1st (Stratification and Social Psychology Survey, Web-based, 1st run in 2013) Surveys. The SSM (Social Stratification and Social Mobility) 2005 Study Group gave permission for the use of the data from the SSM 1985, 1995, and 2005 Surveys. Permission was obtained from the Osaka University SRDQ (Social Research Database on Questionnaires) Office to use the Second Monitor Survey data. I thank all the institutions for the permissions.

This book represents the results of research undertaken as part of the Ministry of Education, Culture, Sports, Science and Technology, Japan Society for the Promotion of Science, Grant-in-Aid for Scientific Research (S) 23223002, and Grant-in-Aid for Scientific Research (A) 16H02045 (research representative: Toru Kikkawa). The publication of this book is supported by Management Expenses Grants of Osaka University.

PART I

REBUILDING SOCIAL
CONSCIOUSNESS STUDIES

CHAPTER 1
Approaches to Apprehending Social Consciousness

Quantitative social consciousness studies (*keiryō shakai isikiron*) is a field of research that examines social mentality by analyzing data from large-scale social surveys.[1] That description might make it seem like it is a field devoted to making rough guesses. Indeed, as is the case with many other specialized sociology terms, we are hard put to respond when someone calls that characterization into question.

Social consciousness studies (*shakai ishikiron*) itself may be a term that today has largely fallen off the radar screen, but it once described a discipline that had a certain degree of status in Japanese sociology. Its quantitative counterpart, on the other hand, is a comparatively new field that incorporates methods based on analyzing numerical data; its name, in fact, is a neologism of my own coinage (Kikkawa 1998).

Because of this newness, very few works have discussed exactly where analyses of survey data on matters related to subjectivity fit into studies of contemporary Japanese society. Accordingly, if I am to dissect the social mentality of contemporary Japan in a substantive way, I will first need to make plain the type of research I aim to carry out in this book.

Understandably, this book may be the first time that many non-specialist readers will have heard such terms as "social consciousness," "social consciousness studies," and "quantitative social consciousness studies." Granted, general information about definitions and methods does not contain any substantial information about the actual society involved. Some readers may prefer that I leave the history of this research discipline and my personal ideals for research unspoken and get into the heart of the study without any further ado.

However, I believe that we have lost track of the social mentality not just because it has in reality taken on a new form, but also because there are defects in the framework we use to examine it. I most of all am accountable for explaining what I mean by "quantitative social consciousness studies." In light of the foregoing, please bear with me as I first outline the history and characteristics of this field of research.

Positioning the Field within the Social Sciences

The social sciences today cover a broad spectrum of disciplines. At one extreme sit fields that use objective data to take in the overall shape of their subject matter; examples of this are economics with respect to the nature of industry and market forces, and demography with respect to population dynamics. At the other extreme are such fields as psychology that deal with residual human agency. Sociology sits in the center of these two extremes, and social consciousness studies is positioned within sociology at the edge closest to psychology. The neighborhood is a densely populated one containing mutually overlapping fields that explore psychology, consciousness, culture, and thought; these include such areas as social psychology, behavioral economics, sociology of culture, and modern thought (Figure 1-1).[2] Accordingly, I will begin by enumerating those characteristics of social consciousness studies that set it apart from its neighbors.

First, social psychology uses methods that are almost entirely the same as those of social consciousness studies (and its quantitative peer). Both collect data on individuals in order to develop in quantitative terms an overall picture of attitudes and opinions. In spirit and letter, too, there is a close resemblance between the pairings of "social + psychology" and "social + consciousness." Moreover, from an outsider's perspective the fact that the fields do not differentiate when it comes to deciding which mentality or attitude to focus on makes it appear they are treading similar paths.

However, the two fields clearly diverge in how they are structured when it comes to how "society" is incorporated in their research. As its name indicates, social psychology falls within the framework of psychology. For that reason, it has research traditions that call for precisely measuring the subjectivity it seeks to explain. Additionally, the field is deeply interested in unravelling internal psychological processes; specialists are repeatedly conducting experiments and investigations that have those processes as their issue of concern. Some of the general propositions about human behavior this field develops from even get rerouted to sociology where they provide useful "parts" for that field's own efforts. The theories of conformity and obedience, cognitive dissonance, and relative deprivation come to mind. Furthermore, social consciousness studies itself got its start from adopting approaches to measurement and analyses that social psychology developed.

However, orthodox social psychology is somewhat lacking in one respect from a social consciousness studies perspective: it does not take careful notice of the influence that contemporary Japanese society inherently has on the consciousness of its members.[3] This fact is plainly evident from the nature of the data that social

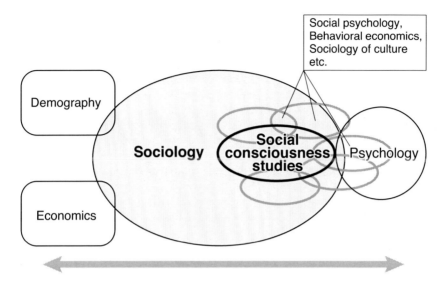

Figure 1-1   The Position of Social Consciousness Studies in Social Science

psychology handles. The social survey data that quantitative social consciousness studies use are collected in such a way as to generate in microcosm an accurate representation of society as a whole. The social attributes of its respondents are varied, the data are distributed in unique ways compared to that from other societies, and there are strong connections within at unexpected points. It would show, for example, that there are more adult women who are junior college graduates than men of the same generation, the youth population of today is considerably smaller than the population of people in their 60s, the population of immigrants born overseas is small, there are few people who believe in religion, and the white-collar worker population is larger in major urban areas. From a sociology perspective, this complex intertwining of various social factors in and of itself comprises the Japanese reality; it is the inherent, essential quality to be read from the social survey data.

Social psychology, on the other hand, seeks to uncover universal tendencies in human behavior. For it, the intertwined factors that social survey data make plain are distortions and biases; they are inconvenient to the purpose of elucidating "real" psychological mechanisms. Accordingly, as often as not social psychology analyses are carried out based on data using research designs meant to narrow the scope of genders, ages, educational attainments, occupations, and so forth of the target population—for example, "female university students between 19 and 21 years old in liberal arts departments at private university X." Selecting respondents in this fashion makes it possible to have a "correct" sample design in the sense that biases and distortions are controlled for from the start. When it comes to the interests of quantitative social consciousness studies, however, the phenomena that social psychology research take up are quite unrealistic—valid, for example, under the rare circumstance that only unmarried university graduate females are gathered together.

The divergence here reflects the different scholarly interests of the two fields. Quantitative social consciousness studies attempts to present an accurate and real portrait of the society concerned, while social psychology seeks to purely abstract the general workings of human behavior. If our only interest was examples of this sort, all we would be left with is an amusing story. However, given that our concern is how to incorporate stratification structure—the central pillar of the social system—into our research, these differences cannot be set aside. The fact is, the key difference with social psychology is that quantitative social consciousness studies examines causal relationships. The field is interested in how much the social mentality might change if some screw, as it were, was adjusted to some degree under actual social conditions.

Meanwhile, over the past decade and a half or so, fields such as behavioral economics, social epidemiology, and public health have come to see the subjective factor of the individual as an important consideration in their empirical analyses. There is a considerable degree of overlap here, too, with quantitative social consciousness studies. Behavioral economics, for example, has recently emerged as a subfield of economics. It uses findings from such adjacent human sciences as psychology, neuroscience, and behavioral genetics to unravel microeconomic phenomena that cannot be explained solely by the premises of rational choice. On that basis, it advances a variety of theoretical constructs about the actual mechanisms that underpin the preferences and choices of *homo economics*—preferences and choices that from the perspective of economic rationalism should have been predictable but in fact are complicated due to the impact of subjective factors (Tomono 2006; Ōtake 2010; Yoda 2010).

Social epidemiology and public health tease out the connections between socioeconomic status and illnesses or physical and mental disorders. Taking those links as primary causal factors, they focus on how individuals perceive their status in society (status identification) and on what the effects are of such positive emotions as satisfaction, happiness, and self-esteem (Kawakami, Kobayashi, and Hashimoto 2006; Kondō 2010). Here, too, the issues are not socioeconomic wealth or poverty themselves, but rather the way such subjective factors function as pivots that inflect causal relationships.

However, these fields of applied social science, too, differ in their orientation from quantitative social consciousness studies. They view social consciousness (subjective factors) as an independent variable (predictor variable) that influences individual behavior and circumstances. Accordingly, the research proposition that interests them is the opposite of that which interests quantitative social consciousness studies, and the causalities on which each focuses are completely opposite—viz., "can social phenomena be explained through social consciousness" (behavioral economics, social epidemiology, public health) vs. "can social consciousness be explained through social factors" (quantitative social consciousness studies). Naturally, this difference also demonstrates that many of the demands in adjacent fields of social science can be met with the findings of quantitative social consciousness studies.

General Concepts of Social Consciousness

Viewing sociology as a field, we see that it brings together a vast array of research findings that analyze the relationships between social attributes and subjectivity. These are generated through such individual disciplines as family sociology, the sociology of labor, urban sociology, political sociology, and welfare sociology.

The object of research for this field of scholarship is "the things of this world" that are familiar to everyone in day-to-day life. Sociology examines this in order to explain the truths hidden in that world, which differ from what the people who live in it can readily see. Social mentality, which despite its invisibility has great power, is almost always involved when we elucidate such hidden mechanisms.

There are countless theories that seek to reveal these hidden truths; we can point to Max Weber's spirit of capitalism, Émile Durkheim's anomie, Robert Merton's relative deprivation, and Erich Fromm's mechanisms of escape. In this light, sociology can be described simply as the social science that speculates on the nature of subjectivity. In fact, it probably would be hard for sociology to accomplish the tasks it sets for itself without any consideration of subjectivity. Consider studies of the family, for example. The legal sciences would focus on matters of civil law related to kinship, genetics and biology on gender and reproduction, microeconomics on household finances and consumption, and pedagogics on childcare. In its attempts to integrate these mutually overlapping issues, for family sociology the indispensable key is the status of subjectivity as seen in love (intimate emotional connection) and role identity.

Not all sociological research that deals with the nature of subjectivity can necessarily be defined as social consciousness studies. Research on the role of consciousness in political participation might also fall within the bailiwick of social consciousness studies, but fundamentally such endeavors come under the mantle of political sociology. Studies of gender role segregation, meanwhile, examine identity through the lenses of gender theory or family sociology; social consciousness studies plays no role here, either.

Still, on further reflection the social mentality intrinsic to contemporary Japan does affect, for example, family structure, labor, minority-majority relations, religious activities, voting behavior, economic behavior, and public health. Research is needed that can ascertain this dynamic sociological phenomenon whose influence is felt universally by all social phenomena and members of that society. Hence, the intrinsic job of social consciousness studies—one that I have likened elsewhere to "measuring the magnetic field" of social consciousness (Kikkawa 1998)—is to supply evidence-based information about the elements that comprise the shared platform that underpins contemporary Japanese society.

In this light, social consciousness can be seen as a term that covers a broad spectrum encompassing those concepts in sociology that deal with the "soul" or "mind." Other terms that work in roughly the same way include "individuality" (*shutaisei*), "subjectivity" (*shukan*), "psychology" (*shinri*), and "national character" (*kokuminsei*). In some cases, social consciousness might even be described as culture (*bunka*). "Social consciousness" itself is not often used as the operative term for research on its own. Rather, it is usually employed as a subordinate concept, and stands as a specialized term with a meaning that is a bit narrowly defined. A list of similar concepts might include ideology, social psychology, ethos, social character, mentality, values and value orientation, identity, types of conformity, and doctrines that reach the status of "isms," a topic that will be the focus of the latter half of this book.

The contexts in which these terms are used are rather predetermined in the sense that they are associated with certain theorists and their respective discourses: Max Weber and ethos, Karl Mannheim and ideology, David Riesman and types of conformity, Pierre Bourdieu and habitus, and so on. Thinking about which word or term to employ leads to making decisions about various modifying nouns or adjectives that can be applied to suit the usage, i.e., the *ideology* of patriarchy, authoritarian *personality*, the Protestant *ethic*, conventional *values*, educational credential*ism*, *attitude* toward gender role segregation, a *sense* of injustice, *degree* of life satisfaction, and so forth. Pairing the wrong terms will quickly produce a combination that lacks meaning. In Japanese, for example, we can talk about satisfaction using such terms as *manzokudo* ("degree of satisfaction") or *manzokukan* ("sense of satisfaction"), but forming expressions like *manzokushugi* ("satisfaction-ism") or *manzoku ideorogī* ("the ideology of satisfaction") represent mismatches.

I do not have the space here to run through in detail the dictionary meanings of scholarly concepts or how the various theories developed. Indeed, this book's readers are not likely to need to know how to use these specialized terms in most real-world situations. What we simply need to bear in mind is that the researcher focusing on social consciousness in a given study will describe in terms of values, feelings, or identity as a result of having made a strategic selection of the appropriate concepts, theories, and terms.

The various modifying nouns or adjectives discussed here—as represented in Japanese by such suffixes as *-ishiki*, *-shin*, *-kan*, *-sei*, and *-taido*—are neutral in the meanings they lend. Hence, there is no limit to the contexts in which they can be used and so are often employed when dealing with survey data. Borrowing an expression coined by Yasuda Saburō, those terms that express the attitudes toward social phenomena can collectively be referred to as "social attitudes" (*shakaiteki taido*) (Yasuda 1973). All the items pegged as dependent variables (explained variables) in actual quantitative analyses—e.g., status identification, authoritarianism, environmentalism, self-esteem, religious devotion, and anxiety—comprise social attitudes. Such modifying terms as *-shugi* ("doctrine" or "-ism") and *-shikōsei* ("orientation") are used to refer when speaking of broader concepts that take one or more of these attitudes under their umbrella.

Summarizing the cluster of terms used in social consciousness studies, these can be categorized based on one of three criteria. First, there are comprehensive higher-order concepts such as social consciousness, individuality, subjectivity, psychology, national character, and culture that indicate the entire object domain.

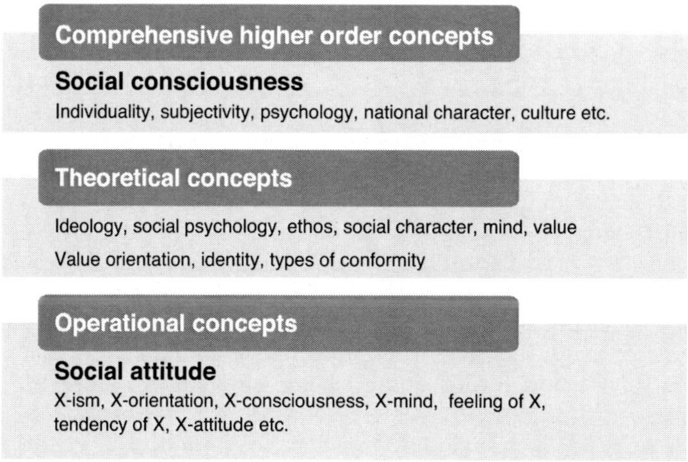

Comprehensive higher order concepts
Social consciousness
Individuality, subjectivity, psychology, national character, culture etc.

Theoretical concepts
Ideology, social psychology, ethos, social character, mind, value
Value orientation, identity, types of conformity

Operational concepts
Social attitude
X-ism, X-orientation, X-consciousness, X-mind, feeling of X, tendency of X, X-attitude etc.

Figure 1-2　The Concepts of Social Consciousness

Next, we have theoretical concepts such as ideology and ethos that have backgrounds associated with doctrines. Finally, there are concrete operational concepts of a lower order (see Figure 1-2). The comprehensive higher-order concepts are equivalent terms of the sort that other disciplines also use when they focus on social consciousness. Theoretical concepts assign distinctive meanings to those higher-order concepts and define the contexts in which they are used. When it comes to undertaking analytical operations, we use social attitudes that are neutral in their import.

Some practical examples will illustrate this last point. Let's say we have a university student who in his or her senior thesis intends to focus on "the nature of subjectivity among residents of Shōnan" (the specific location is unimportant—for example, it could be "of students from X university"). At this point, the student will have to think about whether to speak of this as a "Shōnan-like attitude," "Shōnan consciousness," or even more broadly "Shōnan-ism" or "Shōnan-oriented." Whatever the case, neutrality can be maintained in the context of doing research so long as the student uses such language as "*-sei*" ("-nature"), *-shikō* ("-oriented"), *-shugi* ("-ism"), *-taido* ("attitude"), or *-ishiki* ("-consciousness"). On the other hand, such language as "Shōnan ideology," "Shōnan identity," or "Shōnan-type ethos" changes the nuance completely. Accordingly, the best strategy when attempting to interpret social consciousness quantitatively is to use terminology of this sort that has theoretical connotations. Since its findings are expected to be positioned in sociology, social consciousness studies frequently wields such theoretical concepts in its argumentation. In contrast, social psychology frequently goes no further than using operational concepts with neutral meanings. This point, too, makes apparent the differences between the two disciplines.

Another issue to think about has to do with the identification of such intrapsychological processes as rational choices, value judgements, feelings and emotions, cognition and evaluation, and mental abilities. In psychological disciplines, specialists are expected to give this matter rigorous thought. Quantitative social consciousness studies, however, limits itself to assessing whether a given social attitude is based on feelings or on a rational choice due to whatever situation a given study then goes on to discuss. It rarely gets into developing an understanding of the phenomena themselves.

When it comes to queries related to consciousness in social surveys, the primary consideration is crafting questions that are as easy to answer as possible. Respondents are asked about their actual psychological states in their daily lives. However, it is difficult to control whether the answer is being obtained after having gone through one or another intrapsychological process. Multiple factors may become intermingled. For that reason, making *a priori* judgments that one social attitude is 100% emotion while another is entirely a rational choice would not be appropriate.

For example, the question of how much one is committed to traditional values is certainly the primary mechanism behind authoritarian attitude, but other integral components of that attitude include emotions and feelings such as destructiveness and aggressiveness, and furthermore intellectual ability is also involved (Adorno et al. 1950). To give another example, degree of satisfaction is one type of positive feeling that represents one state of an individual's self-awareness, but it is built upon that person's perception and assessment of the ways in which they are connected to their society. In some respects, it may also be governed by differences in national character. One might expect status identification to be a matter of someone perceiving and assessing their social status, but given that belonging to a group is involved, there are also emotional elements in play. We cannot guarantee that these elements will always intermingle in the same way at different points in time. Aspirations to higher education likewise cannot be understood solely as a rational choice regarding the rate of returns on an educational investment; we must also consider the effects of feelings and emotions, such as passion for a particular area of study and preferences regarding educational attainment. Power of understanding and mental faculties are unavoidably involved when it comes to how people recognize and evaluate political and governmental issues, scientific knowledge, and new technological information. For all these reasons, we must be circumspect about any desire to wholeheartedly specify one or another intrapsychological process—e.g., an "*x*-like value" or "*y*-like feeling"—as being at play with respect to the nature of whatever social attitude is being studied. Careful interpretations are needed that are mindful of the possibility that several processes may be intermingled.

Stratification, Education, and the Formation of Social Consciousness

I will limit my handling of abstract discussions to the foregoing. To see how researchers actually go about quantitative social consciousness studies, I will draw on my work, *Kaisō, kyōiku to shakai ishiki no keisei: Shakai ishikiron no jikai* (Stratification, education, and the formation of social consciousness: The magnetic field of social consciousness studies) (Kikkawa 1998). It is one of the few scholarly works extant that explicitly presents itself as a study in this vein.

In it, I deal with a variety of social attitudes. They include authoritarian traditionalism, which I use to decipher the mass psychology of fascism; conformity to ascribed groups, which is a central topic in *Nihonjinron* (see Chapter 3); status identification, for dealing with the mass-middle-class phenomenon; general life satisfaction; self-esteem; anxiety and related matters of subjective well-being; and environmentalism and health maintenance awareness as concrete, "real world" issues. This is not an exhaustive list, but it covers a broad range of important topics related to social consciousness in contemporary Japan.

The book investigates such stratification variables as educational attainment, occupation, and income, as well as age and gender. It treats them as factors that determine the nature of these social attitudes. I will speak in greater detail about this analytical framework in the next chapter with respect to the social consciousness studies-type regression model; for now, I will say the focus of discussion in a study such as this is on those social attributes that are shared among all respondents.

As to my findings, some theoretical background is in order. Originally, when the social consciousness studies scholar wanted to predict a respondent's patterns of thinking and could ask only one question, that scholar would inquire about the subject's social class or work situation. This was due to the dogma that originated with Karl Marx regarding the relationship between class and hierarchy (social status) on the one hand and social consciousness on the other. However, when I analyzed data from large-scale social surveys carried out in the 1980s and 1990s an unexpected state of affairs became apparent: it was not possible to verify the existence in Japanese society of the definite causal relationship that Marx argued prevailed among class, hierarchy, and social consciousness. Indeed, some social attitudes that reflect emotions and feeling such as self-esteem were changing constantly under the influence of occupational status. Only certain social attitudes were bound to occupation, however. Social identification, social orientation, and intellectual abilities may seem to trend in certain directions under its influence, but the real social factors that produce them are elsewhere.

The real situation that became clear from my analysis of the survey data is of crucial significance, for it shows that social mentality does not change to any significant degree no matter how much the figurative screws that adjust the social structure with respect to industry and the economy are loosened or tightened.

The question still remains, however, as to what is the true determinative factor that has the greatest influence on the social consciousness of the Japanese people. The answer that comes to mind is the significant role played by educational attainment (school education) in Japanese society. Since this gets into the arguments I will be making later in this book, I will refrain from further discussion of the matter here.

Given that my previous work focused on Japanese society in the 1990s, the social backdrop against which it was set is different from the one we face today. With the benefit of hindsight, we can see that a slow but definite transition was then taking place. Furthermore, that book was based on my doctoral dissertation, and so made no big-picture forecasts about the direction in which Japan's social mentality was heading. Still, that work retains a certain significance in that—at a time when few attempts in the vein of social consciousness studies were being made—I turned to empirical research to work on refining some of the arguments about the field's key concern, which is the status-relatedness dimension of social consciousness.

After publishing that work, I went on to conduct research related to the theory of the "education society" (*gakureki shakai-ron*) (Kikkawa 2001, 2006, and 2009; Kikkawa and Nakamura 2012). For that reason, I am often viewed as an educational sociologist. However, my research interest in the Japanese model of an education society had been catalyzed by the fact that I had noticed—rather than consciously searched for—the importance of school education as a determinative factor in social consciousness. This made it necessary for me to investigate the logic of educational attainment, which is of such great significance to Japanese adults today. The foregoing is but one example of how I set up one of my own projects in quantitative social consciousness studies. The scope for how others may set up their own topics of course may be broader.

Social Consciousness Studies in the Postwar Period

With the general nature of this research in mind, I next want to trace the academic history of Japanese social consciousness studies. Unlike most sociological terminology used in Japan, "social consciousness" and "social consciousness studies" are not words "imported" from the West. The term "*shakai ishikiron*" has in the past been translated as "sociological social psychology" or "public opinion studies," but they do not capture all the roles that *shakai ishikiron* plays in Japanese sociology (Mita 1993).

After Japan's defeat in World War II, the nature of individuality and subjectivity among the Japanese people became a topic of national interest. The debate focused on the lag in the modernization and democratization in social consciousness. Ōtsuka Hisao and Hidaka Rokurō respectively argued as follows:

> Is it somehow possible for the people of Japan to throw out the base premodern ethos and hammer out the pattern for a modern, democratic human being? We believe this is the greatest issue today. (Ōtsuka 1948, reprint 1968: 15)

> Democracy constitutes a regime that is properly constructed by the will and initiative of the people. For that reason, the people must be their own men and women. Today the one thing we most need is for the people to improve themselves and become humans who are independent and free. (ibid. 23–24)

> At present [1954], the "conventional consciousness" (*kyūishiki*) is *necessarily* losing its potency, but that of course does not mean that it *automatically* will collapse. The growth of a new consciousness to take on the "conventional

consciousness," and that very development itself, are indispensable conditions for making that collapse occur *inevitably*. (Hidaka 1960: 258) (emphasis in the original)

Maruyama Masao, Kamishima Jirō, Kyōgoku Junichi, and Matsushita Keiichi were among those driving the debate over social consciousness at the base layers of postwar Japanese society. Using such concrete issues as the structure of the family and village community, politics, and labor as reference points, they framed the debate in the context of basically three phenomena: the rivalry between conventional (Japanese tradition) and democratic (Western modernity) values; the survival of nationalism, the emperor system, and the patriarchal system at a grassroots level; and strongly rooted support for conservative political parties. Their arguments pointed out the mismatch (cultural lag) between the social structure and social consciousness. Even if the hardware of the social system had been upgraded, it still could not perform the intrinsic functions of democracy with the software of social consciousness still in its prewar state.

When we turn our attention to 21st century Japanese society, there are no longer many insights to be directly obtained from these postwar examples of social consciousness studies. Even so, we retain both their stance toward using the associations between societal structure and social consciousness as hints for getting a bead on the broader currents of the times (e.g., modernization), and their key concern, which was to think about the nature of the subjective actors who sustain democracy. The direction I take in this book—investigating as it does the two key 20th century concepts of tradition and modernity in social consciousness—likewise wades into the currents that flow from these debates.

Since then, social consciousness studies took root and became a core discipline in Japanese sociology. The experience of defeat and its aftermath was replaced as its principal concern by that of modernization in the form of high-speed economic growth. Specialists in the 1960s pursued their research in a field in which two influential frameworks, Marxist class theory and mass society theory, crossed over.

Establishing Contemporary Social Consciousness Studies

If we were to open an encyclopedia of Japanese sociology today, we would find that the definitions for "social consciousness" and "social consciousness studies" are almost completely the same. Both are based on the ideas set down in the 1960s and 1970s by Mita Munesuke and Miyajima Takashi. Later to become prominent figures in contemporary Japanese sociology, at the time the pair were still just spirited young researchers. Nonetheless, they are the de facto founders of *contemporary* social consciousness studies.[4]

They issued their first declarations as short pieces comprising parts of review articles and commentaries on sociology. These would eventually be woven into full length books: Mita's *Gendai shakai no shakai ishiki* (Social consciousness in contemporary society) (1979) and Miyajima's *Gendai shakai ishiki-ron* (Contemporary theories of social consciousness) (1983).[5] These two books offer us an overall sense of social consciousness studies that they so elegantly established as a core component of sociology in Japan. In his work, Mita defined "social consciousness" and "social consciousness studies" as follows:

> Social consciousness constitutes the mental processes and patterns by which various classes, hierarchies, peoples, generations, and other social groups are defined and formed by the existing conditions respective to each. It sustains those respective existing conditions, or acts as a force for changing them. Social consciousness studies is a field that conducts empirical and theoretical research on the structure and functions of social consciousness, as well as the processes of its formation, development, and sublation. (Mita 1979: 101)

Mita had first developed that definition in 1968, and it has been frequently amended by he and others since its first appearance (e.g., Mita 1976, 1979, 1993; Miyajima 1983; Kikkawa 1998; Kim 2012). The following addition from Mita himself is a well-recognized supplement to his original definition.

> Social consciousness studies is an attempt ... to use the weapon of empirical science to root out the deeper structures of reality, where restrictivity and subjectivity in humans as social beings—i.e., history's inevitability and human freedom—dialectically interact. (Mita 1979: 102)

To untangle the point of his argument, certain expressions here—"defined by existing conditions," "sustain and change existing conditions," "process of formation, development, and sublation," and "the reality where restrictivity and subjectivity dialectically interact"—are terms peculiar to the Marxist theory that demarcated an era. Accordingly, we need to go back further to recall a notable passage from Marx.

> In the social production which men carry on they enter into definite relations that are indispensable and independent of their will; these relations of production correspond to a definite stage of development of their material powers of production. The sum total of these relations of production constitutes the economic structure of society—the real foundation, on which rise legal and political superstructures and to which correspond definite forms of social consciousness. The mode of production in material life determines the general character of the social, political and spiritual processes of life. It is not the consciousness of men that determines their existence, but, on the contrary, their social existence that determines their consciousness. (Marx 1859)

Taking up Marx's argument, Mita put the emphasis on the close relationship between social consciousness and class status. In contemporary quantitative social consciousness studies, this is called the status-relatedness (*kaisōsei*) of social consciousness. If we suppose a subjective-objective relationship between social status and status identity—i.e., people from upper social strata sense that they identify with society's upper echelons, people from middle strata identify with the middle, and people from the lower strata with the lower—then we can probably see how this relationship makes sense. This investigation of status-relatedness in social consciousness is the most important issue to be dealt with in this book.

Next, taking Mita's comment about using the weapon of empirical science as our guide, let us now consider the methods of social consciousness studies. Mita and Miyajima referred to a piece by Kido Kotarō entitled "Shakai ishiki no kōzō" (The structure of social consciousness) (Kido 1970; first published in Kido and Sugi 1954) as the template for actual social consciousness studies.[6]

Kido's work is recognized as the first in Japanese sociology to have employed full-fledged survey data analysis. His aim was to see in what form Hidaka's conventional consciousness survived in what social classes in 1950s Japanese society. The analytical operation employed focused on two social attitudes: "the authoritarian attitude entwined with traditional values" and "the political and economic ideology centered around the desire for socialist problem-solving." As factors forming these attitudes, Kido studied the influence of occupational status primarily, followed by educational attainment, age, and standards of living. In short, his study clearly focused on the two major points of debate in social consciousness studies: the nature of the constituent subjects of democracy and the status-relatedness of social consciousness.

Unfortunately for Kido, his findings did not bear out his postulate. He had assumed that the "structure of social consciousness" would be one in which authoritarians were ideologically conservative and anti-authoritarians (pro-democracy individuals) were oriented toward socialistic problem solving, and that these tendencies were strongly determined by occupational status. However, he had to in all honesty admit that the survey data did not support his preconceptions. Still, in this his study had value in that it was also the first in Japanese sociology to alert its audience that the actual form of society does not correspond to crude hypothetical structures suggested by theory, and in fact is quite complex and hard to grasp.

Be that as it may, what made Kido's study superb lay in the fact that he did not stop with a simple survey report, but went on to skillfully fuse the results of his data analysis with his interests as a critic to present a lucid interpretation of conditions in the postwar period. Furthermore, the procedures he used for his analysis led to the development of what I call in this book the social consciousness studies-type regression model; they have become the primary tool for quantitative social consciousness studies. Even as analytical techniques have improved, the appeal of the manner in which he advanced his argument has not faded.

At any rate, for Mita and Miyajima, the very fact of linking survey data analysis to actual sociological theory (the study of contemporary society) as Kido did was precisely an attempt to root out the deeper structures of reality with the weapon of empirical science. They had great hopes that it would set down the main course to be followed in social consciousness studies.

Unexpectedly Idled

With its definitions and concepts in place, contemporary social consciousness studies as a field seemed ready to start building a store of empirical research for unraveling Japanese society. But instead, after the 1980s, the field entered a fallow period. When I was beginning my own work in the 1990s, numerous studies in all disciplines were taking up social mentality, but none were positioned as belonging to social consciousness studies. Consequently, for a beginner like I was, this scholarly discipline that had been at the core of contemporary sociology and heralded for its outstanding conceptual stipulations alone seemed more like a set of ruins where only a stout cornerstone or two remained.

Quite surprisingly, the primary reason for this unexpected idleness was that the field's owners themselves who had laid the groundwork had done very little research that could be described as social consciousness studies. Three reasons may be surmised for this. First, the remark about "digging into matters using the weapon of empirical science" simply created too high a hurdle for themselves to jump. As the wellspring from which contemporary social consciousness studies had emerged, Kido's research was an outstanding example of the quantitative approach and could not be easily followed. Additionally, given the information technology environment of the time, we can infer that attempting to analyze data derived from theoretical and speculative inquiries about thought and culture rather than from empirical fields such as stratification studies or psychology would have been tremendously difficult.

Second, the leading researchers paid their respects to academic role segmentation. Mita had been caught up in a theoretical debate over qualitative and quantitative methods of data analysis with Yasuda, who in the 1960s and 1970s was a leader in stratification studies (Satō 2011). The debate may not have been the kind that ends with a battle for supremacy, but the pair rarely interacted with one another in its aftermath.[7] For Mita, his estrangement from Yasuda's SSM Survey research group (to be discussed below) apparently had the effect of him keeping the indispensable key concepts of class and stratification at arm's length in his own work.

Third, the term "sociology of culture" had come into play in place of social consciousness studies. Sociology of culture was the term that Miyajima favored for a spell after the 1980s in reference to his own research. Around this time, he was gradually detaching himself from his investigations of social consciousness. He instead shifted his focus toward rereading of Durkheim, the introduction of Bourdieu's theory of cultural reproduction to Japan, and introducing new European social movements and studies of immigrant ethnicity into Japanese society. Mita, meanwhile, having gone through the experiences described earlier, retreated to theoretical and intellectual studies and qualitative data analysis, as typified by his work *Jikan no hikaku shakaigaku* (A comparative sociology of time) (Mita 1981). His desire to separate himself from the very field he had established can be sensed from his use of the penname "Maki Yūsuke" around this time.

Social consciousness studies developed at a time when the sociological perspectives of modernization, Marxist class, and mass-society theory that took center stage in the middle decades of the 20th century remained vital. However, sociology was caught up in a strong contemporary current in academia the goal of which was to disengage from the framework of (first) modern society. Moreover, the subjects that social consciousness studies addressed were consistently limited to those things that humans were "conscious" of, and its field of view was geared toward domestic opinion journalism.

However, if we are to call such research "the sociology of culture," then it is possible to expand the scope of what it analyzes to embrace those cultural phenomena described as practice (*pratique*) and latent inclination—for example, lifestyle and habitus. Furthermore, it should also be possible to take up transnational and global issues related to ethnicity and the public sphere without becoming preoccupied by affairs in a given nation-state. Sociology of culture certainly had aspects that were of greater utility when it came to taking in the new social phenomena that surfaced after the end of the Cold War and the forming of the European Union, as well as the new European theories for understanding them.[8]

The point at which these two fields decidedly differed was in their methodologies. As I earlier remarked, social consciousness studies had great hopes for quantitative methods of analysis, while sociology of culture has no specific methods set down. Survey data analysis is the former field's method for developing a picture of a society in its entirety through amassing information about each of its members. The social mentality is thus apprehended as the summation of individual consciousness. With methodological individualism as its underlying precept, the analytic approach makes it possible to take actual measurements of the social mentality and opens the door to bringing on board approaches from experimental science, such as the concept of statistical significance, to thinking about the issues. There are considerable merits to this approach. However, the downside is that it cannot directly address externalities that are the societal aspects of social consciousness (social facts), such as Durkheim's collective sentiment and collective consciousness.

On that point, if we used a sociology of culture approach, we would be able to view society from the standpoint of methodological collectivism. We could also conduct research through listening and participant observation aimed at deeply knowing microsubjects, or through the textual analysis of newspaper articles and novels. This is because the non-quantitative, speculative approach offers the freedom to move back and forth between the micro and the macro.

Another downside to survey data analysis is its limits in terms of legerity. Inputting data into a computer and analyzing the responses to attitude-related questions given by survey subjects at a certain point in time is a method akin to snapping and developing photos—it is not one that lends itself well to grasping conflicts among social groups or the dynamics of cultural reproduction. Researchers have tried to overcome these limitations in recent years by adopting panel-based surveys and other strategies, but the results are still at best like the experience of watching a video playing one frame at a time; they are not suitable for getting a bead on, say, cultural phenomena or the kinetic processes of organizations and groups with their chameleon-like qualities. It should be noted, parenthetically, that sociology of culture is not without its own inconveniences in this regard.

Does an approach informed by methodological individualism capture more exhaustive evidence? Do researchers get a more agile understanding of social facts once they are freed from the shackles of method? Both quantitative social consciousness studies and sociology of culture have their strengths and weaknesses. However, looking back at Japanese sociology over the past quarter century, it is apparent that survey data analysis has certainly not become a mainstream method (Tarōmaru, Sakaguchi, and Miyata 2009). Studies bringing speculative or qualitative approaches to bear on modern society as it continues to expand across both spatial and conceptual borders have long been ascendant. The path that Mita and Miyajima—leaders in Japanese sociology over those years—took in their own research careers can be said to have lent weight to this trend.

True, with its unrestricted approach the development of sociology of culture did serve to make the analytical character of social consciousness studies more explicit. But the point I wish to emphasize here is that the halting progress of social consciousness studies as an analytical discipline was a proximate cause for our having lost track of the social mentality of contemporary Japanese.

Stratification Consciousness Studies

The foregoing tale certainly does not mean that no work was done in quantitative social consciousness studies after the 1980s. Even during this period, empirical research on the principal concerns in social consciousness studies continued without interruption. In fact, the general public even took notice of them to a considerable degree. However, these were not regarded as social consciousness studies. The reason was simple. The flow of quantitative studies that Kido's work had sparked was absorbed after the 1960s into the stratification studies of Odaka Kunio, and of Yasuda and his collaborators. Their findings accumulated under the label "stratification consciousness" (*kaisō ishiki*). Thus, if we ignore this pedigree, we overlook an important vein in quantitative social consciousness studies.

I will begin with a quick sketch of stratification studies. Individual attributes such as whether a person's occupational status is high or low, whether they are a college, junior college, or high school graduate, and how many millions of yen they earn per year comprise indicators of stratification status (stratification variables) or social status (social attribute variables). They are intimate details that are written down repeatedly in things like resumes and application forms. Stratification studies is a field that focuses on these concrete mechanisms in the social structure. Occupational status of course is regarded as central here, but it mutually overlaps with and is tied to such other factors as financial power, educational attainment, social background, and social clout. The complex of social statuses in modern industrial society is called the stratification structure; to think about its nature is connected to thinking about inequalities and other such factors in the society concerned.

The class structure may be an objectively apparent fact, but there are many things that we cannot understand about the particular combinations of statuses that everyone has within it without asking them directly. Those conditions can be apprehended through large-scale surveys on stratification. Japan's first proper social stratification survey was carried out in 1955 and in 10-year intervals ever since, up to a 60-year track record. It is called the National Survey of Social Stratification and Social Mobility (SSM Survey). The project is a treasure trove for Japanese sociology because of the number of generations and eras it covers. Analyzing its data has been a driving force for empirical sociology in Japan.

The core objectives of the survey have been to investigate the relationship between social attitudes and status, and to understand how "literate" people are when it comes to stratification structure (i.e., what understandings they have about social stratification). That is what stratification consciousness studies does.

It is understood that the differences in the ways people view and think about their society are produced by their current social status and the life experiences they have had. The survey teased out from among various factors the hard-to-uncouple relationship between what sociology calls stratification variables—occupation, educational attainment, and economic power—and the ways people think. Like social consciousness studies, stratification consciousness studies focus on the relationship between this pair of factors.

The main body of stratification studies comprises thorough examinations of the relationships among social status-related variables such as social mobility, inequality of educational opportunity, and job history. Accordingly, stratification consciousness studies are a derivative discipline that applies those findings to social consciousness studies. Incidentally, while one might have expected stratification consciousness studies to occupy a somewhat peripheral position in the parent field, the broad public interest in the mass-middle-class phenomenon (to be discussed later) in the 1970s and 1980s gave it an enormous presence there. Occasionally, even the main body of stratification studies attracted abundant social interest. This is why works that once might have fallen under social consciousness studies instead, in a sense, parasitically attached themselves to stratification studies.[9]

This, in turn, is why stratification consciousness studies remains little more than an umbrella under which a mishmash of survey findings have been collected without a properly developed theoretical framework in place. To give a concrete example, in this field "stratification consciousness in the narrow sense" refers to how someone views the status to which they belong, while "stratification consciousness in the broad sense" refers to research that examines stratum differences for specific values and ideologies. The "narrow sense" and "broad sense," though, are little more than the roughest of distinctions; it is not possible to discern which issues to focus on in a logical way based on them.

However, when reconsidered from the perspective of social consciousness studies, it is possible to easily draw out those items in that accumulated research that are useful. For example, if we give serious thought to the significance of social identification when dealing with the mass-middle-class phenomenon, we notice that the issue here is one that has been crucial since Marx—that of perceiving the

Table 1-1 Characteristics of the Trends of Social Consciousness Studies

	Contemporary social consciousness studies	Sociology of culture
Exponent	Mita Munesuke, Miyajima Takashi	Miyajima Takashi
Time period	Established in the 1960s Idled after the 1980s	Emerged after the 1980s
Primary concern	Dialectical process of the formation and transformation of social consciousness	Broad cultural phenomena (habits and practice)
Approach	Quantitative method as expected ideal	Non-quantitative method
Traits	Succession from the postwar social consciousness studies Based on theoretical backgrounds in the 20th century Domestic concerns Lack of practical research	New tendency of post modernization, coping with transgressive tasks Interpretation of the western theory Open-ended, but diffused issues

relationship between the individual and industrial society. This gives us some purchase toward clarifying the relational processes of dis-embedding and re-embedding that take place between the individual and society that are characteristic of reflexive modernity.

On the other hand, among the cluster of social attitudes addressed under the rubric "stratification consciousness in the broad sense" are such items as authoritarianism and social activities central to social consciousness studies whose importance was ignored or not recognized, like bits of treasure casually tossed into heaps. These materials contain hidden potential and would be useful if they could be brought into social consciousness studies, where they might be employed bundled around ideas like traditionalism–modernism or social orientation to rethink trends in them.

The Pedigree of Social Consciousness Studies

Readers can review the pedigree of social consciousness studies as laid out in this chapter through Table 1-1 and Figure 1-3. The field is one that investigates social mentality as a shared platform in present-day sociology. Research in this area began with thinking about the democratic human subject, which was the most important issue for postwar Japan. Kido paved the road to applying survey data analysis to this study. Mita and Miyajima then put together the theoretical framework for contemporary social consciousness studies, in the process laying the cornerstones for a core component of Japanese sociology.

The field subsequently experienced a fallow period during which few substantial research results were produced. During these years, sociology of culture—a non-quantitative approach with considerable latitude when it came to

Stratification consciousness studies	Quantitative social consciousness studies
Odaka Kunio, Yasuda Saburo	Kikkawa Tōru
Being practiced from the 1960s to present time	Being practiced form 1998 to present time
Status-relatedness of social consciousness (stratification consciousness in the narrow/broad sense)	Status identification and social orientation
Quantitative method	Quantitative method
'Mass middle class" as the central issue Lack of the identification to be social consciousness studies Dependence to stratification studies	Integration of the branched pedigree contemporary sociology in the 21th century

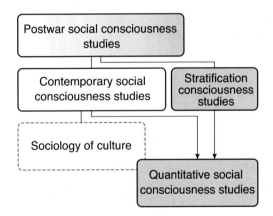

Figure 1-3　The Pedigree of Social Consciousness Studies

methodology—emerged as a concept that could establish a discipline to replace social consciousness studies.

Next came stratification studies. Here, researchers operating in the wakes of Odaka and Yasuda continued to make observations of hierarchies in social consciousness in the name of stratification consciousness studies. They generated an abundance of data that has not adequately examined but likely contains hidden assets for social consciousness studies, including data related to the mass-middle-class phenomenon.

The faint outlines of quantitative social consciousness studies may now be starting to come into view. There are numerous debates regarding the social mentality of the Japanese people that have been left unresolved; examples include the post-war reception of democracy, *Nihonjinron*, and the mass-middle-class phenomenon in the years of high-speed economic growth. Still, though we might be temped to simply argue over whatever new phenomena may arise, it is incumbent upon us to cut the debate and see also how the problems of the present are connected to these old unresolved issues without letting them vanish into the mists of the past. I believe there is an opportunity to make a breakthrough here via frontal assault. The revival of social consciousness studies rooted in a 21st century perspective will help us to see the utility of looking at the past in order to see the present.

NOTES

[1] Numerous terms exist to express sociological research driven by calculations and analyses of numerical data, including empirical sociology, experiential sociology, quantitative sociology, and mathematical sociology. These also overlap to a degree with the terms for methodologies such as social statistics and survey data analysis. Among these, empirical sociology and experiential sociology were used to refer to bundles of methodologies and approaches so large they included all sociology that was neither theory nor theoretical research. In Japanese sociology today, however, it has become most common to refer to sociology that uses survey data analysis as its method as quantitative sociology.

Quantitative sociology is frequently confused with mathematical sociology. Mathematical sociology refers to sociological research that similarly invokes mathematics, but that field's aim is to conduct sociological research that constructs general propositions (axioms) based on deductive thinking. One could say it is a refined form of theoretical sociology.

[2] I will discuss public opinion research—an area that overlaps considerably with social consciousness studies—in greater detail in Chapter 2.

[3] Kitayama Shinobu and other scholars of cultural psychology in North America refined and further developed the ideas of *Nihonjinron* and studied the effects culture has on personality. These developments in social psychology contain possibilities that produce changes in future approaches to quantitative social consciousness studies (Kitayama 1998).

[4] The research of Hidaka Rokurō, Takahashi Akira, and Tsujimura Akira from the 1950s and 1960s can also be seen as a starting point work on social psychology (sociological social psychology) that provided a prototype for social consciousness studies. The focus I have set for my arguments laid out here is on the post-1960s period. Reference could also be made to Kim Myungsoo, who has developed a take on social consciousness from a different perspective (Kim 2012).

[5] In this book, for the reader's convenience, I have as much as possible referred to and cited Mita and Miyajima's remarks in these two books.

[6] Kido Kotarō was the son of noted psychologist Kido Bantarō and a psychologist from the generation between Hidaka and Mita. He died in a mountain accident at the young age of 30, but left behind a variety of manuscripts focusing mainly on practical studies. His research posthumously attracted praise, and his name was given to an incentive award for young sociologists (the Kido Kotarō Prize). Its recipients include a roster of

sociologists from a generation or two ahead of me who were my mentors, including such scholars as Shiobara Tsutomu, Inoue Shun, Yamaguchi Setsuo, and Kōtō Yōsuke.

7   Japanese sociology is generally not viewed as having schools à la the Chicago School or the Annales School. However, when it comes to the perspectives used in social consciousness studies, there are hints of such in the talk of a "Hongō School" and a "Komaba School" regarding qualitative vs. quantitative methodologies. This arises from the contrast between how Odaka and Yasuda at the University of Tokyo's Hongō campus (Department of Sociology, Faculty of Letters) handled social consciousness, and how Mita at the university's Komaba campus (Interdisciplinary Social Sciences, College of Arts and Sciences) did.

Looking back, we can see that just as Tominaga Ken'ichi's stratification research group had begun using the SSM 1975 Survey to chart out the middle strata during the high-speed economic growth years, Mita was using the contrasting approach of closely analyzing the sentiments of a death-row convict to sketch the shape of Japanese society in his article, "Manazashi no jigoku (The hell of gazes)" (Mita 1979; an earlier magazine article version appeared in 1973, and the study was eventually published in book form in 2008). In recent years, Seiyama Kazuo and Satō Kenji have offered their respective views on mixing qualitative and quantitative methods (Seiyama 2004; Satō 2011). However, the fact that scholars believe that such sorting is required for these methodologies speaks to how they are isolated from one another. Be that as it may, we can see that the disconnect between stratum consciousness studies and sociology of culture—two fields that at root might properly be seen as social consciousness studies—developed based on this history.

8   Sociology of culture is a particularly broad term that can subsume any sort of topic if we take it to mean sociological research that deals with culture. In fact, there has been very little discussion that actively seeks to define what "sociology of culture" means. This evasion of a fixed definition is due to the peculiarities that "culture" as a technical term possesses. Today, the rise of such fields as subculture and youth culture studies has expanded further the list of sociological disciplines that discuss culture. Accordingly, while there is something to "sociology of culture," generally speaking we can see that once the research focus is narrowed there is more to social consciousness studies.

9   The isolation that developed between Mita's and Yasuda's work is related to this as well.

CHAPTER 2

The Conduct of Quantitative Social Consciousness Studies

In the previous chapter, I reviewed the path followed by quantitative social consciousness studies in contemporary Japan. In this chapter, I would like to present a number of rules or codes of conduct, so to speak, that I have set down for myself for when I attempt to decipher the social mentality using survey data analysis. This, too, will also serve as an indicator of the direction to be taken by this book.

The Social Structure Sets Social Consciousness in Motion

The first thing to remember is that quantitative social consciousness studies comprises a field whose aim is to unravel the influence that the social structure (the mechanisms of society) has on social consciousness (the social mentality).[1] Figure 2-1 provides an overview of social consciousness studies. Here we see that social structure and social consciousness mutually influence one another. This reciprocal relationship gradually changes shape from era to era. Mita's talk of "the deeper structure of reality where restrictivity and subjectivity dialectically interact" suggests the process by which these two elements cycle back and forth as they transform.

The component elements of the social structure are arrayed on the left of the figure. Some constitute unchanging conditions in Japanese society, while others vary with the times. Whichever the case, these elements influence social consciousness. Among these elements—which might easily be described as the "hardware" of society—is one that has the greatest effect: stratification status (stratification variables). Whether we are talking of theoretical concepts or experience, its impact is indisputable. We should recall here as noted earlier that the social strata comprise

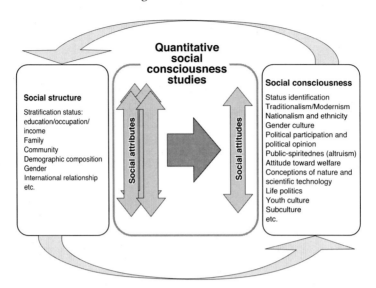

Figure 2-1   Overview of Social Consciousness Studies

a structure that combines stratification variables such as educational attainment, occupational status, and economic power.

The elements comprising social consciousness are on the right. Over the years, I have identified a variety of items as falling under this category, including status identification, conventionality (modernity), nationalism and ethnicity, gender culture, politics and policy, public-spiritedness and altruism, welfare, conceptions of nature and scientific technology, life politics, youth culture, and subculture. Some retain their form for a long time while others change their character, but all draw their power from the right side of the figure. The factors on the left are largely set in stone, but there is considerable latitude when it comes to the issues listed on the right. There are few limits in terms of definitions, with little to disallow one or another attitude as pertaining to social consciousness. Generally, the search for useful indicators is an ongoing process of trial-and-error.

However, there is one existing condition that is necessary for quantitative social consciousness studies: the project must focus on a social attitude that is in a causal relationship deserving of analysis with one of the social attributes on the left (indicated by the large arrow in the center of the figure). Above all, it must be in such a relationship with one or another of the stratification statuses. If this condition is not satisfied, then no matter how elegant the hypothetical proposition the study will be worth little more than a drawing on a page for the purposes of sociological theory. Conversely, if the social attitude being considered is strongly defined by the social structure, then whatever it may be it can become a source of information for understanding the social mentality of that era.

Naturally, this is an extreme case scenario. However, as a review of the unhappy history of empirical research in Japan regarding *class identification* and *feelings of unfairness* reveals,[2] when one gets carried away with theoretical speculations and actually impose them on this framework, you wind up surprisingly frequently with social consciousness of "ideological" sorts that do not function well. Here, bear in mind that in contrast quantitative social consciousness studies was able to use survey data analysis to correct such unrefined theories that preceded it (Kido 1970; Kikkawa 1998).

As the arched arrows on the top and bottom of the figure show, the relationship between social structure and social consciousness comprises a circular system. However, for the purpose of developing theoretical models this is little more than a story. Substantiating this cycle of cause and effect through actual survey data analysis is difficult owing to methodological limitations.

When considering which causal system to emphasize, it is normally thought that social attributes explain (independent variables) and social attitudes are explained (dependent variables). Without an exceptionally strong hypothesis, the researcher cannot work with causal relationships that operate in the reverse direction (from right to left on the figure).[3] This is not to say that social mentality by nature does not work in ways that change society's mechanisms, but in this field the processes through which industry and economy have influenced the ways that people think are the issues that are seen as requiring unraveling. These ways of thinking correspond also to the causal system proposed by Marx, in which social existence defines social consciousness.

This is not to say that social consciousness studies does not conduct research on intrapscyhological causal schema (i.e., using one social attitude to predict and explain others). However, the conditions for formulating such research projects so that they will be particularly meaningful are naturally difficult, for the relationships among social attitudes suggest associations like those between the values implied by a pair of statements like "people deeply interested in politics are more likely to sense injustice" on the one hand and "people with a neoliberal values approve of competition" on the other. Even if you could demonstrate that such intrapsychological processes actually exist, you would still be faced with questions like "what are the educational attainment, occupational background, income, and family background of persons who are deeply interested in politics?" and "what are the people who support neoliberal values like?" All that such pairings show is simply that two similar social attitudes are covariant. They do not get at how much one or another "screw" in the social structure has to be adjusted to change people's senses of fairness or competitive sensibilities. Put another way, they do not get at the question of whether some change in the social structure (hardware) might change the nature of the social mentality (software).

Descriptions of the mechanisms through which social attitudes control expressive behavior, and explications of the processes through which deep-seated values influence surface opinions are limited in their significance to those instances in which causal relationships have been clarified by the researcher having given thought to the mediation that such functions provide. A rare example of such research is the work being done on authoritarianism that I will return to later (see Chapter 6), in which sadomasochistic tendencies comprise the medium being used to shed light on the "black box" of the relationship between fascism on the one hand and stratification status and socioeconomic conditions on the other. Here, too, however, we must not forget that the primary issue of concern is unraveling the associated processes of the social structure and social mentality and not clarifying intrapsychological mechanisms.

Observing Contemporary Japanese Society

My second rule for survey data analysis is to bear in mind that quantitative social consciousness studies is a field that examines Japanese society of the era contemporary to the one in which you are working. This is an unspoken understanding among researchers in this field when they are deciding which period to focus on and the scope of their analytical perspective. Naturally, in light of the fact that "social consciousness studies" is a scholarly term of Japanese coinage, such features were practically a given from the start.

To be able to make predictions about what your analyses might find when it comes to a phenomena that cannot actually be seen like social consciousness, it is imperative for the researcher to have knowledge on par with being firsthand of the era in which the data being used was obtained as well as of that society's atmosphere. To borrow the words of C. Wright Mills, it means being able to use one's sociological imagination (Mills 1959). For example, let's say that I have obtained opinion-survey data related to nationalism in the 1960s from a certain East African society. If I analyze the data, I can perhaps come up with some kind of results. However, given my lack of firsthand experience with that society at that time, I would not be at all prepared to talk about what issues were important in the lives of those people who do have the relevant historical and cultural background and experienced life under whatever type of social system then existed. Accordingly, my analysis would be dependent on the data, and whatever results I obtain solely through that process cannot be understood as representing the social mentality. The sociologist needs to be able to exercise his or her sociological imagination with respect to the society in question, or else the results will be no different than what could be obtained from mechanically analyzing piles of experimental data, say, or corporate financial indicators.

The point I am making here is that the researcher's social being is constrained when they engage in purely objective analysis of survey data, as doing so allows then only a superficial glance of the society under study. What they should be doing instead is actively making the most of their own social being. In my case, I have lived in Japanese society and so to a certain extent I feel confident about proceeding with a study of its social consciousness. But I do not have something to say about other societies like those of India, Finland, or South Africa, for example; for similar reasons, I would find it difficult to focus on a different time period to conduct studies on, say, the social consciousness of ancient Rome or Edo-period Japan. To amplify this train of thought, the empirical sociologist has an obligation of a sort when it comes to analyzing data on his or her own society. Perhaps it is impudent to say so, but very few of our contemporaries are in a position to get a measure from multiple perspectives on data trends and current living conditions in Japanese society today and derive a reasonable logic from what they see. It is just such a self-conceit that prompted me to undertake this book, with its narrowed focus on social consciousness in Japan from the 1980s to the present.

Next, I want to consider the scope of what social consciousness studies takes in. First, in my experience very few research undertakings in the field focusing on particular strata or groups expressly describe themselves as being a "social consciousness study." We see no "study of social consciousness in X Ward of Y City" or "study of social consciousness at a major corporation Z." This is because social consciousness studies is a term that normally had been seen as referring to a broad survey that took in the whole of society. When it comes to data analysis, as you gradually narrow the boundaries of subject (e.g., "parents with children" or "people under 35 years of age"), your perspective will also gradually move away from that of social consciousness studies. You will likely notice that your work is taking on certain aspects of the research being done in other disciplines such as sociology of education or youth studies.

For most people in Japan, hearing the "whole of society" will normally make them think that *Japanese* society is the topic of conversation. The fact that the subject population of a social survey is defined as being part of their society is likewise two sides of the same coin. If we are to think about the trends of an era, even as we refer to findings from previous studies, the scale of the portion of society on which we focus will inevitably grow to take in Japanese society in its entirety. The fact that this overlaps with the Japanese-speaking cultural sphere, or with a Japanese public sphere comprising its political world and mass media, is another reason for this.[4] Finally, recall that the spur for this book to begin with was the sense that our society has lost track of what its own social mentality is and is groping to find the right way forward.

However, this way of thinking—narrow your research interests to issues internal to a particular nation state—is showing signs of vulnerability as globalization progresses. In empirical sociology today, a growing number of researchers are seeking to apply the latest analytical techniques to secondary analyses of data from social surveys that have been carried out on an international scale. Assuming you can just obtain the archival data, from the comfort of your own chair you can work on international comparative research projects of a vastly different scale that may cover from one to several dozen countries, say, using datasets that contain more than 100,000 respondents. Such studies seek to develop universal theories (propositions) grounded in a global perspective or draw comparisons among multiple societies. Naturally, it would not be realistic to pursue any discussions in such analyses that are predicated by understanding the atmosphere in every country covered.

On the other hand, it would also be hard to imagine conjoining social consciousness studies—a field developed as a way to theorize about Japanese society—with analyses of complex datasets based on the latest techniques. In light of all this, at the present stage the notion of "global social consciousness studies" lies beyond the realm of my imagination. Naturally, the question of how to think about this is a matter to be sorted out through careful consideration and discussion.

The Horizons Set by Trends and Status-Relatedness

The third item I keep in mind is that quantitative social consciousness studies is a research discipline that examines the horizons of social consciousness. Those horizons are woven together, with the trends or tendencies that characterize an era (*jidaisei*) providing the warp and status-relatedness providing the woof. The actual method of survey data analysis used in this book entails comparing all survey data from each of the eras between 1985 and 2010 that has a bearing on the relationship between social structure and social consciousness. This is laid out in Figure 2-1. The survey data generates cross-sectional portraits of a particular principal structure, in other words, the hierarchical ordering of statuses in society. Using such multiple cross sections, we can get a sense of the time axis concerned from a broader perspective—more plainly speaking, we can see how conditions change over time.

Furthermore, each data analysis I will undertake incorporates both era-defining trends and status-relatedness into the social structure that explains and the social consciousness being examined. Let us think here about the specific significance of "era-defining tendencies" and "status-relatedness" when they are installed in the concept of social consciousness.[5]

Status identification—meaning, how people view social status and where they position themselves in society—is central to addressing hierarchy in social consciousness. Its "phenotype" has changed over the years. In the postwar period, it began with proletarian consciousness, reflecting a general identification with the lower working class. This was followed by the "mass-middle-class consciousness," "inequality consciousness" (*kakusa ishiki*), and now today one's sense of poverty (*hinkonkan*). Whatever the era, it remains important to ask how people cope with the hierarchical structure of society. Status identity, too, is a social attitude that seems to exhibit "gradients" of social consciousness that reflect stratification status, and is recognized as providing a prototype or template for research in this area.

When we get into the matter of era-defining tendencies in social consciousness, it becomes quickly apparent that conventionality and modernity are the issues central to debate. They comprise an axis that I will refer to as "traditionalism–modernism." In the Japanese context, it would be appropriate to label the axis defined by this pair a "doctrine," one that played a key role in 20th century modern society. In an era of unending social change, traditionalism–modernism provided a shared platform for every issue under the sun, including the family, politics, gender, and labor. For that reason, the feelings that people have of favoring or not favoring such old values rooted in Japanese tradition as "esteem both duty (*giri*) and feelings (*ninjyō*)" or "keep the family going even if you have to adopt" have been monitored as primary indices of how the Japanese national character changes with the times. This axis with conventionality and modernity at each pole has provided a theoretical center for talking about individuality and culture in Western research as well.

That said, the framework built around traditionalism–modernism has been losing its utility for some three decades. This development concurs with the flexing, as it were, that has developed in the viewpoint we bring to grasping such era-defining tendencies as those generated in the transition from (first) modernity to reflexive modernity. The biggest issues before us are how to define the time axis in conceptual terms to replace traditionalism–modernism, and which social attitudes do we use to measure it.

However, at present we have no established indicators for discerning what tendencies may define future eras, and so we are currently groping in the dark. Accordingly, for the moment the task at hand is to carefully observe the conditions under which the framework of traditionalism–modernism that had once been an accepted fact is fading out.

In Parts II and III of this book, I will elaborate on the status-relatedness and era-defining qualities of social consciousness to sort out the key concerns of social consciousness studies using identity and orientation as our touchstones. "Identity" here means the self-awareness that someone has, or evaluations they make about where they fit into society. Thinking that through, it means we are setting our focus on the way individuals are embedded in their society. In this book, status identification in particular provides the core indicator. "Orientation" means how the individual reaches out to and copes with society. Here the goal will be to investigate a wide range of issues—going beyond just social attitudes such as the traditionalism–modernism axis to take in topics like frequency of social activities—in order to grasp the vector that Japanese society will follow in the future.

Focusing on Society's Middle Ranges

Next, I would like to discuss the characteristic traits peculiar to using survey data analysis to examine social mentality. Naturally, these are all tacitly understood among researchers actually working in the field, but I need to make them explicit so that no misunderstandings arise among non-specialist readers.

The first trait to emphasize is that quantitative social consciousness studies demonstrate their utility when coming to grips with social consciousness in the middle ranges of society. Trends that abide latently deep in the heart of society are frequently referred to by such terms as "silent majority." They are what's meant by the "winds" that blow through an election campaign, and represent the true state of "business conditions" or "trends in personal spending" in economic activities. Transformations in social consciousness are given substance by trends in the central stratum. The population of this stratum is large, and it has surprising power. The scale merits and bird's-eye-view aspect of survey data analysis are put to best use when we try to grasp that latent dynamism.

At heart, survey data analysis excels at getting a bead on those trends that develop around the mean (standard value) in which large numbers of people participate. It is not well-suited to drawing a picture of those segments that are other-than-typical in society; phenomena that emerge at edges of response distributions are not good candidates for analysis. In this sense, it resembles the large, heavy equipment, like rollers and bulldozers, used for roadwork. While such equipment is able to efficiently and beautifully handle the job over a wide expanse, it is not effective for tighter spots.

Of course, at an actual paving site, the construction crew does not go about its task using only heavy equipment. Those areas that require more detailed attention such as the side ditches and the spots around the manholes are finished off with manual labor performed by skilled workers. Likewise, in social consciousness studies, researchers get deeper takes on aberrant phenomena and singular cases or firmer grasps on the concrete realities of individual lives using an element of craftsmanship replete with the "humanity" of more qualitative research. Examples include observational methods emphasizing the firsthand perspectives of subject group members, using "clinical" approaches toward real-life examples, and developing interpretations of materials and texts.[6]

For that reason, in those places where we can take advantage of the heavy machinery of survey data analysis, it would not be productive to dig things up by hand non-empirically, nor to run roughshod with attempts at survey data analysis on social phenomena that require delicate probing. If we understand matching subject with method in this way, we recognize that quantitative social consciousness studies and its use of survey data analysis as method are indeed meant to get a handle on the middle stratum (in the broad sense of the word).

During the mass-middle-class era, the middle stratum in Japanese society was the object of intense interest from many. The media and others enthusiastically reported various figures generated by survey data analyses. But by the 2000s when the talk was of an "unequal society" (*kakusa shakai*), while there was no lack of eye-catching journalistic accounts and documentation about realities of life for both the upper and lower classes, the ways in which people in the middle thought and lived lost the capacity to attract interest. It was as though the stratum had slipped into a blind spot. To speak of the "middle class" is to bring up something that in other societies represents the foundations for growth and stability and is even incorporated in the policy programs of the heads of government. Most Japanese today, however, in fact don't really know this. On reflection, it is for that very reason that there is the hidden potential to discover unexpected realities by using survey data analysis to get a bird's eye view of the middle range of society.

Public Opinion Statistics and Quantitative Social Consciousness Studies

We turn next to consider the relationship between data and analytical method. Thanks to the valuable efforts of our predecessors, there is an abundance of large-scale social survey data on Japanese society to serve as research materials for quantitative social consciousness studies. In this book, I will be analyzing mainly the data from the SSM longitudinal project from 1985 onward, as well as face-to-face interview data from a 2010 poll (the SSP-I 2010 Survey) that inherited the stratification consciousness studies aspect of the SSM project.

I will also take up various other surveys related to social attitudes. These include the National Family Research of Japan (NFRJ) Survey conducted regularly by the

Japan Society of Family Sociology; the Institute of Statistical Mathematics' long-running Japanese National Character Survey; the Japanese Value Orientations surveys and International Social Survey Programme (ISSP) cross-national surveys carried out by the NHK Broadcasting Culture Research Institute; the Cabinet Office's ongoing Public Opinion Survey on the Life of the People series; and Osaka University of Commerce's endeavor with its Japanese General Social Survey (JGSS). None of these are one-off (cross-sectional) surveys. All are conducted repeatedly at multiple points in time and contain numerous social attitude questions with an international comparative design.

The subject populations of these Japanese social surveys generally are adult men and women from all around the country, with sample sizes that produce valid responses on the order of 1,000 to 15,000 cases. While there are some exceptions, stratified multistage random sampling is used as the standard object extraction approach. This is regarded as the optimal method for guaranteeing representativeness with respect to the sample population. In terms of survey mode, the standard technique used is that of face-to-face interviews, which provides a high degree of precision.[7] In short, for their rigorousness of design, aptness of method, and history of continuity, we can say that the quality of Japanese social survey data is extremely high.[8]

Accordingly, we can put our trust in that descriptive figure, "response percent," as it appears in this high-quality data, since response percents were widely used as the primary output from surveys, before multivariate analysis was as widely practiced as it is today. I will refer to the method that was used to present survey data through this widely understood approach as "public opinion statistics." A typical example from the Japanese context might be the final tallies released for the various opinion surveys that the Cabinet Office conducts.

In Japanese society, for better or worse, scholars and others have focused on percents such as these and tried to derive findings from them when attempting to grasp the actual state of social consciousness through numerics. The mass-middle-class society discourse that flourished in the 1970s and 1980s—where 90% of the nation's people identified themselves as being part of that group—is the phenomenon that truly symbolizes this faith in percentages. Even today, whenever the totals from official public surveys are announced at press conferences, the mass media gives heavy coverage to the direct connections they make between those tallies and social conditions ("*X* percent of the populace is worried about *Y*!"). However, it should be made perfectly clear that public opinion statistics and quantitative social consciousness studies only seem to be alike.

I do not mean to say that looking intensely at the response percents from various opinion surveys is without value. But to correctly interpret the findings of quantitative social consciousness studies, it would probably be better for any interested parties to put some distance between themselves and whatever controversies may be stirred up based on response percents. The fact is, the final totals embodied in the percents may have been "fixed" at some point in the preparation process.

For starters, bear in mind that the responses to attitude-related questions lack absolute points of reference. The options that are presented take such forms as "positive-negative," "have-do not have," or "support-do not support." Consider general life satisfaction, for example. Do we have and exercise the ability to determine where the completely neutral, neither-satisfied-nor-dissatisfied, "absolute zero of the soul" is located in ourselves? This might bring to mind the Buddhist idea of "being free from all distracting thoughts," but reading "cannot say either way" as a middle response for general life satisfaction as an expression that the respondent is in such a state of *satori* would be too much. We cannot assume that all survey respondents are assessing their respective situations based on an "absolute zero of the soul" standard.

The form of the questions may also vary. Some surveys may ask, "How satisfied are you with your life in general?" while others ask, "On the whole, how satisfying is your life at present?" Likewise, some surveys may use the 4-item format of "satisfied," "somewhat satisfied," "somewhat dissatisfied," and "dissatisfied," while others provide options based on a 5-item format of "extremely satisfied," "satisfied," "cannot say either way," "dissatisfied," and "extremely dissatisfied." Still other surveys may use seven- or ten-item scales to cover the range from "satisfied" to "dissatisfied."

Furthermore, the distribution pattern of the responses will also depend on the survey design: what is the age range of the respondents; what survey mode was used—face-to-face interviews, the leave-and-pick-up and/or mail-in approach, or a telephone or Internet-based method; how precise was the sampling; and were there any of the leading inquiries or carry-over effects that produce biases in the responses?

As should already be clear, we cannot get a reading on the ratio of absolute "positives" and "negatives" in the social mentality from the descriptive statistics (the percents) for the distributions that are publicly announced for such polls. Rather, all we are able to assert is the distribution of responses to question texts (to the wording used) presented to survey respondents as a "yardstick," and the relative positions (deviation) of each respondent within that distribution. Accordingly, when the media reports that "*x* percent of Japanese feel dissatisfied with their lives," we should tamp down our expectations when it comes to trying to discern the social mentality from those numbers.

Naturally, in those cases where the same question is repeatedly asked in ongoing surveys using the same research design, the researcher can show changes in response trends at different points in time. We can safely say that this is the strong point of having accumulated a mass of detailed data on Japanese society from social and public opinion surveys. However, these opinion statistics frequently do not come with sufficient information related to the social structure (stratification status, families, and so forth).[9] That makes them insufficient to the task of knowing whether the vicissitudes in response trends are a product of, for example, a declining birth rate or the popularization of higher education or urbanization. In the long run, they provide only the roughest of narratives about a given era or generation.

As an example, take the fact that general life satisfaction among young adults in their twenties today is high compared to members of the same cohort forty years ago. There is no way for us to know what the reality of this "satisfied young generation" is if we do not investigate how that change is related to, among other things, the rise in per-person incomes following the decline in the number of people who comprise a household, the increase in white-collar young people in urban areas, and how the ratio of people who have completed tertiary education with higher levels of general life satisfaction increased compared to people who only graduated high school. It is not possible to develop an explanatory logic involving the social structure using percents alone by lightly massaging some of the facts that have come to the surface of society. Readers will immediately recognize this once they have read Chapter 4.

On this point, the focus in quantitative social consciousness studies is assiduously on the relations among variables (how consciousness and society are linked) rather than descriptive statistics for social attitudes. This is done in order to provide empirical proof of causal relationships—figuratively speaking, to determine whether turning some "adjusting screw" somewhere in Japanese society to some degree results in changes in the social mentality.

This difference in where emphasis is put expresses itself most glaringly in the different lengths of time spans across which the waves of change in the social mentality are observed. Setting aside certain exceptions such as the Japanese National Character Survey, public opinion statistics produce reports that are detailed but covering only the latest trends. They consider comparatively short time frames, ranging from several months to perhaps three years. Dramatic improvements in recent years in the speed of data collection—for example, the evolution in telephone surveys thanks to the advent of the random digit dialing (RDD) method—has made it possible to issue the results of "flash opinion polls" almost the instant they are taken. Such developments permit us to know about the slightest fluctuations in opinions about government policies, say, or views on business conditions. However, when it comes to why response distributions suddenly change when they do, the magnitude of causal effect can hardly be ascertained just by surmising it was a coincidence.

Quantitative social consciousness studies are largely uninterested in those small fluctuations for which a cause cannot be specified. The field sets its sights instead entirely on major fluctuations that unfold over roughly a decade at a time. The time spans the field is interested in are several decades long, or that correspond to a generation that includes parents and their children. These periods are long enough for fluctuations in the social structure—the popularization of higher education, say, or increased fluidity in the job market, expanded participation by women in the workforce, or falling birthrates paired with an aging society—to cause ongoing changes in the nature of social consciousness.

Figure 2-2 schematically depicts changes over time in social consciousness. Consider it an indicator of the interest people take in national politics. The positions people have regarding politics vary slightly based on such factors as who is in power and how they approach policy, scandals involving Cabinet members, and inappropriate statements that they may make. Cabinet support rate is the epitome of this. Taken practically on a monthly basis, this public opinion statistic

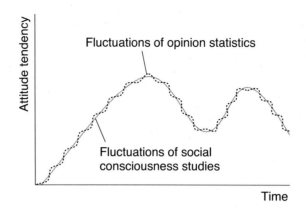

Figure 2-2 Time Trend of Social Consciousness (Hypothetical Model)

constantly fluctuates. It is high when a Cabinet is inaugurated, but gradually drops until matters get to the point that the Cabinet resigns.

The fluctuations in political attitudes that quantitative social consciousness studies gauge, on other hand, have longer wavelengths. Examples include how the so-called 1955 System (named for the year in which it coalesced) grounded in the ideological standoff between conservatives and progressives collapsed, how the populace's distrust in politics rose, and how neoliberalism stated to gain the support of large numbers of people. All these developments were the results of major changes in the social structure of their respective eras. Those major changes would include, for example, declines in the sizes of the farming and self-employed strata, the increased concentration of the population in urban areas, the popularization of higher education, a generational change in the electorate, and changes in the geopolitical environment. Figure 2-2 shows how the minute changes observed in public opinion statistics are generated in the course of the major fluctuations that quantitative social consciousness studies observes. It is difficult to show on the figure, but long-term fluctuations express themselves not only through superficial changes in response percents but are also accompanied by a transformation in the social consciousness. It is explaining this latter fact that quantitative social consciousness studies emphasizes.

Analytical Monographs

The next question is what kinds of analytical methods are appropriate for quantitative social consciousness studies. To put it simply, those methods need to be oriented to the goal of this field of research, which is to produce analytical monographs.

Even for empirical sociology as a whole, the levels of analysis that different methods offer vary widely. The highly descriptive method of ordinary least squares

(OLS) regression analysis is the one most often employed by quantitative social consciousness studies. With newer analytical techniques being developed all the time, there are any number of limitations involved when continuing to rely on a simple, orthodox method that has already been in use for decades. But at least for this field, those limitations can be largely overcome owing to the peculiarities of the data being handled and the research interests involved.

Quantitative social consciousness studies strive to untangle the relationships among multiple social attributes, and to measure the direct effects (their influence once the effects of other contributing factors have been excluded) these have on social attitudes.[10] One could almost say the issues were defined in this way from the start with OLS regression analysis in mind. Moreover, the question of which independent variables (social attributes) this field should investigate was also largely predetermined. Generally speaking, social consciousness studies is not interested in highly personal life experiences that involve only one subset of a society's members, like whether or not someone with a pet has a dog or a cat, or whether someone's children attend public or private schools. Rather, the field is interested in social attributes, which govern the daily lives of all its potential research subjects. Centermost is the influence of stratification variables (occupation, economic power, education), followed by the inseparably connected factors of gender and birth-cohort differences. These comprise the most basic framework for forming social consciousness.

In contrast, community, family, social involvements and relationships, ethnicity, and similar factors are somewhat peripheral to the concerns of survey data analysis. Scholars in other societies direct attention to the effects of such other factors as church attendance and community participation, but the context of contemporary Japanese society, experience suggests that those factors do not have a strong enough influence to sway the state of social consciousness. This is due in part to the fact that the links between social structure and social mentality are weaker in Japan than in other societies. In any case, at the moment these items are not essential to our analytical framework.

Given the above, the OLS regression analysis model most frequently used in this field is of the pattern shown in Figure 2-3. Controlling for the two demographic factors of gender and age as independent variables, we input the three stratification variables of education, occupational status, and economic power to observe direct causal effects (primary causes) on various social attitudes. This, in sum, is the procedure that forms the perennial analytical framework for quantitative social consciousness studies: control in some fashion covariation between *this* and *that* factor, and look for the effects they have.

The causal model that uses these five primary factors to ascertain the contributing factors that form social consciousness will be referred to below as *the social consciousness studies-type regression model*.[11] Kido (from Chapter 1) was the first to use this model to analyze social consciousness in Japanese society. I have followed his example of how to examine the social consciousness formative process using this model quite consistently in my own quantitative studies (Kikkawa 1998, 2000, 2006, 2008, 2011). Hypotheses and propositions premised by use of this model

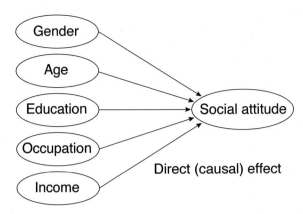

Figure 2-3 The Social Consciousness Studies-type Regression Model

such as "the quiet transformation of status identification" that I take up in Chapter 5 have also appeared in quite a few other studies.

I should note, however, that the results obtained using this model that can be relied upon are limited to those cases in which the data contain few biases (i.e., where residual variances are independent from any other elements). On this point, several new analytical techniques—e.g., multilevel analysis, covariance-based structural equation modeling, and propensity score analysis—were developed premised by the question of how researchers are to infer the causal structures in which they are interested (frequently deemed "the true structures") if the data used contain, for example, considerable distortions, biases, and missing cases.

These techniques can be seen as tools for coping with current conditions, when researchers are frequently forced to deal on a second-hand basis (as a secondary analysis) with compound social survey data that includes various errors and biases. The techniques share an interest in controlling for inconvenient distortions and gaps in the data available at the time of analysis, rather than spending enormous amounts of time and money to mitigate them at the time the data is collected.

These are all superlative statistical techniques, and they likely represent a direction that should be encouraged in future research. However, using the predicted numerics these models produce to test the validity of our operational hypotheses, eventually is reduced to and verified as being a simple "true-false" of the results of a significance test. They instead make it difficult to get a sense of how much "weight" the derived findings carry when it comes to real society.[12]

That said, recall that Japanese society is our focus, we know there already exists a stockpile of high-quality data about it from large-scale social surveys. This gives us the leeway to relax a bit and think about the progressiveness of statistical techniques. In those cases where the precision of the data being analyzed is high enough to assume it contains few biases, we can find meaningful insights through deep examination of the causalities within the data once we distill the essences inherent to the data itself to the extent possible.[13] Accordingly, in this book I will not be employing cutting-edge model-inferring techniques to gather stardust, so to speak, that glimmers only faintly with significance. Rather, I will rely on the simple but robust method of OLS regression analysis so that I can devote my energies toward sorting out the tendencies that appear in Japan's high-quality social survey data.

To put together a quantitative study that prioritizes getting a bead on the properties data show has been described as "sketching an analytical monograph" (*keiryōteki monogurafu o egaku*) (Kikkawa 2001; Ojima ed. 2001; Sugino 2012). In the context of anthropology or regional sociology, the term "monograph" usually refers to a written record based on fieldwork. The analytical monograph, however, refers to a study that is based on the analysis of measured materials (quantities). Such a study describes actual conditions in contemporary society by patiently sorting through the information in social survey data. It is reliant on the quality of the survey data, and it aims to abstract theoretical essences from it.

This is not necessarily the general procedure followed by empirical sociology. In that field, scholars most frequently employ the hypothesis-and-verification approach, emulating the pattern of the natural sciences. Empirical sociology and quantitative social consciousness studies may look the same from the outside, but the fact is analytical monographs seeking to derive theories inductively are on a parallel track to studies that rely on the deductive hypothesis-and-verification approach (Kikkawa 2003).

Let's say we adopted this latter approach. The goals of our data analysis would be fulfilled if we could confirm the existence of our proposition using the same "theory→operationalize→operational hypothesis→measure→test hypothesis" procedure of the natural sciences. This would be the case even if, for example, some subtle latent structure lay buried within some enormous error. In such a case, however, it would be hard to know what impact our proposition might actually have if implemented in Japanese society. In contrast, the analytical monograph emphasizes inductively deriving theories present in whatever propensities may be strongly evinced in the survey obtained (or that should be obtainable) in a way that produces an accurate microcosm of society.

"The Angels' Share"

There are two more supplemental rationales for using OLS regression analysis. First, with this analytical method the social attitudes that operate as dependent variables must be continuous variates with few distortions. When analyzing the social structure, the dependent variables frequently are categorical variates. This enables using a method similar to OLS regression analysis, namely logistic regression analysis. However, given the lack of absolute points of reference, objectively valid thresholds of opinions, or naturally established yardsticks when it comes to social consciousness, there is no need to take the trouble to make categorical measurements. For that reason, quantitative social consciousness studies frequently employs quantitative scales and factor score variables rather than the responses that were chosen themselves. Under these circumstances, a simple regression analysis demonstrates sufficient efficacy. In addition, we can focus our probes on the beta (β) values—the standardized regression coefficient—even when it comes to the magnitude of the effects of the respective dependent variables since there is not necessarily an established scale for them.

The second rationale is more important. The explanatory power of analyses based on the social consciousness studies-type regression model when it comes to explaining social consciousness through social attributes is 20 percent ($R^2 = .200$) at most. Depending on the analysis, it may even stop at roughly around 5 percent ($R^2 = .050$). For the regression model used in this book, the status-relatedness is sufficiently high even with a causal explanatory power of around 10 percent.[14]

Some readers may be doubtful about how small that causal explanatory power is. Even if our intention is to inductively know the actual state of society, such a result would end up treating as much as 80 percent of the information in the data obtained as a measurement error in practically any instance. From a statistical science perspective, there is little leeway for justifying how low this explanatory power is. However, I offer the following assessment in light of the characteristics of social survey data. Imagine an experiment in which two-hundred people controlled for age, gender, and so forth are brought together and are asked to close their eyes. When they open them, some find 2,000 yen has been placed in front of them, others find 1,000 yen, and still others find nothing. Under these conditions, ask each of these subjects about the level of their satisfaction. The causal explanatory power of such an experiment will not be the same as in a case where we observe the effects that annual income has on general life satisfaction for 10,000 respondents in real survey data. Naturally, we can expect the reactions to stimuli under experimental conditions to be vivid, and there will be few measurement errors. However, no matter how exacting the survey method, it is not easy to purely extract from social surveys only the relevant components of people's public perceptions and decisions. Inevitably, you end up capturing only a blur from their responses rather than the picture itself. For example, people's feelings are likely to vary between morning and evening. In polls conducted at the front door of someone's home, response variations not especially relevant to sociological hypotheses invariably will come up. Finally, the respondent's satisfaction might be due to something good that happened to their family, for example, or because they sometimes make good connections on their work commute.

Such "wobbly" responses inescapably are contained in the unexplained portions of the social consciousness studies-type regression model because the causalities are actually mounted on the society. However, these responses are outside the scope of a model that forecasts the state of social attitudes using such important components of society as age, gender, education, occupation, and income. Hence, there is a "glass ceiling" for all practical purposes of about 20 percent on the explanatory power of a social consciousness studies-type regression model, given its exclusive focus on the effects of five primary variables.[15] This, however, certainly does not mean we overlook other important socially prescriptive factors that can explain the remaining parts.

In fact, I have frequently been present for individual face-to-face interview surveys, where one comes face to face with the reality of Japanese society that differs considerably with the image one develops doing data analysis. There are very few instances in which you feel like a fortune teller who has scored a hit. This is so even if the predictions you've made are based on a logic elucidated by some previous study, e.g., "if someone is of this age and gender with this education, their job history will be something like this and their annual income about this, meaning they are going to respond to questions about social attitudes something like this."

Social surveys do not aim to theorize every mechanism in contemporary society. No matter how much the data quality is improved, there will be some elements in the mix that sociological causal explanations will not address. That said, this does not mean that survey data analysis is inadequate. As Seiyama has also argued, "if X then Y" statements are not the sort that are definitely true at any time and in any place (Seiyama 2004). They are descriptive statements about the real world and should more properly be described as (tentative) theories rather than principles.[16]

I have an example I am particular fond of using in this regard. When whiskey is aged, the portion of the alcohol that volatilizes from the cask as the years go by is referred to as "the angels' share." This is not something that is begrudged, since distillers cannot omit losing this portion when it comes improving the quality of the goods they produce.

Similarly, the variations in responses not covered by explanations in the social consciousness studies-type regression model comprise points of individual freedom that cannot be simply prescribed or forecast by social forces. They constitute the element of play that our society needs; without them, contemporary society would comprise rigidly engineered causal relationships. That being the case, such variations can be described as "the angels' share" that cannot be begrudged when distilling and aging theories from survey data.

NOTES

[1] In this book, I use the term "social structure" to refer to the aggregate system comprising social relationships and attributes. "Society's hardware" refers to essentially the same cluster.

[2] Observers have recognized since the 1950s that the ratio of people in Japanese society who see themselves as belonging to the working class is inexplicably large regardless of occupational status. A rather large number of "capitalists" lay claim to a working-class consciousness, for example. It has also long been known that people whose status one might expect would be thought of as unfair do not have a sense of unfairness (see Chapter 7). There has been no end to observers thinking up absent reasons and explanations (in short, the analyst's "excuse") about why a relationship that should exist (the analyst's belief) is not evident between an objective status and the subjective individual (Kikkawa 2003, 2008).

[3] Self-direction as developed by Melvin Kohn and Carmi Schooler rates high marks as one of the few examples of research to demonstrate the existence of reciprocal effects between two parties (see Chapter 6). However, even their work shows that the estimated values of the effect with which the social structure forms social consciousness are several

multiples larger than that of the reverse causal relationships.

4 Asking questions about social consciousness differs from information obtained by asking about categories (mere nouns) such as education or occupation in that the researcher observes the subjective reactions to questions presented in the questioner and respondent's shared language. In that regard, uncertainties arise here when it comes to the equivalence of responses among different countries. For example, saying that "*totemo fuman*" in Japanese is equivalent to "strongly dissatisfied" in English is not necessarily guaranteed from a linguistic perspective (Manabe 2004).

5 The main point of interest for independent variables is the influence of stratification status. However, while occupational status is seen as having a central role to play, its influence in Japanese society is not strong. When measuring the class-based gradients in social consciousness, we will usually very carefully examine a pluralistic class structure configured by economic power, educational attainment, industry and company sizes, and gender.

On the other hand, the birth cohort of respondents is an indicator that includes the time concept as an independent variable. One must be careful here, though, about the fact that three concepts—the effects of the survey period, birth cohort effects, and age effects—are all mixed together.

6 The relationship between qualitative research and survey data analysis is the oldest "new" problem in sociology. I fully understand that the formal conclusions are in a mutually complementary rather than adversarial relationship. However, when it comes to social consciousness studies I believe I should make plain the fact that the relationship between the two is that of a division of labor.

7 This method—in which properly trained interviewers read off questions one by one while showing both the questions and response options to respondents and encouraging them to respond—was established at an early stage after World War II and adhered to for more than 50 years. Although the implementation costs are substantial, it makes it possible to obtain data that is even more precise than self-administered surveys.

8 While they may fall short compared to the General Social Survey (GSS) in the U.S. or various types of panel surveys when it comes to survey continuity, Japanese social surveys have nonetheless built up a large stockpile of high-quality data thanks to considerable expenditures in labor and research funding. We see for example that random sampling using civil registers is not possible in many other countries, compared to Japan where sampling can be done using the Basic Resident Register or voter registration lists. As to survey methods, the self-administered format (collected by mail or leaving) that is easy to implement but offers low response precision is becoming common. Because of this, guaranteeing the possibility when designing a social survey in Japan that cross-time comparisons can be made with previous polls is more difficult than that of making transnational comparisons.

9 Even public opinion surveys report the differences in response distributions for each age cohort, by gender, or by region, very few indeed go on to carry out analyses that drive at social mechanisms (especially the influence of stratification variables).

10 In sociology, for ethical reasons it is difficult to carry out real-world experiments to learn about causal relationships. This should be instantly apparent if you think about the foolhardiness of social experiments and the ethical problems entailed if, for the purpose

of conducting a comparative analysis, a researcher got half of one group of people to get married, got the other half to forego marriage, and then tracked the general life satisfaction of people from both groups for 20 years. We input data collected in a social survey into a computer and apply statistical controls instead of imposing conditions on real society in order to learn about the causal mechanisms present without having to affect the actual lives of the respondents.

[11] This is not particularly novel as an empirical technique; in fact, it is a quite standard regression model.

[12] All these techniques are characterized by the fact that close readings that fit the data become difficult when it comes to the magnitude of the numbers that may be inferred from the model. For that reason, when unseasoned researchers use them, they are liable to chase from start to finish down points on the chart marked with asterisks that indicate statistical significance. Even if the figures can be interpreted accurately, the researcher is limited eventually to drawing rather negative conclusion on the order of "When observing the effects a certain social attribute has on social attitudes, having excluded nonimportant covariations and errors (the total amount of the excluded parts is not normally presented), they are present in a magnitude that viewed statistically cannot be said to be zero." When performing data analysis, the causal relationship that supplies the basis for one's argument must be significant. This is a necessary condition. However, for such analyses, it is not possible to know what issue exactly had however big an effect on the general inclinations of actual society (the total amount of information in the data collected). This also illustrates that more than a few issues in the real world that are little more than trivial affairs get debated on a par with major causal structures.

[13] If the intention is to correct errors from the outset using suppositions based on sophisticated modeling, it will not be necessary to make efforts that inevitably entail spending enormous amounts of money to increase a survey's precision and reduce non-sampling error.

[14] In this book, for causal explanatory power we will look at all the coefficients of determination adjusted for degrees of freedom (referred to hereafter as adjusted R^2). However, because the number of independent variables is fixed there is little difference in the explanatory power of the size of a magnitude relationship from when we looked at unadjusted coefficients of determination.

[15] Based on experience, for the most part we cannot expect to make any tremendous improvements to the explanatory power of a model even if we include further sociological independent variables or consider the interaction effects among independent variables. Please refer also to Note 4 of Chapter 5 regarding experiences related to the size of causal explanatory power.

[16] In those cases where the dependent variable is not a social attitude but rather some social attribute variable like household income, status in terms of employment, or property holdings, the fluctuation in responses gets smaller and causal explanatory power grows because these are objectively clear facts. However, even in that case the causalities shown in the social survey data will be on the order of 40 percent. Propositions whose causal explanatory power exceeds 50 percent represent relationships that are already self-evident even if they cannot necessarily be confirmed through a social survey. An example of such might be the relationship between monthly income and annual income. On

further reflection, the very fact of a causal relationship not being self-evident is what makes it a subject that should be investigated through survey data.

PART II

THE TRAJECTORY OF IDENTIFICATION

CHAPTER 3
Japan in 1985

In Part II of this book, I will consider the changing trends in status identification. I begin in this chapter by inviting readers to briefly cast their minds back 30 years. While those old enough to have lived through that period will find things much as they remember, those born after 1989 (i.e. *Heisei umare sedai*) will not have a firsthand familiarity with the era, and hence will benefit from hearing a bit about the particulars of that time.

An Age of Subtle Changes

There was once a time when the concept of the social mentality carried significant weight in Japan. It was the 1980s, when themes such as the political struggle between conservatism and reform, tradition versus modernism, the mass-middle-class phenomenon, and *Nihonjinron* (to be discussed in depth below) received widespread coverage in the nation's media. Moreover, it was a time when discussion of the social mentality focused overwhelmingly on objective numbers. Everyone from sociologists to policymakers, financiers, historians, and cultural commentators sought to understand the Japan of the day through the prism of public opinion figures suggesting that "X percent of the population held such-and-such an opinion." Though even today opinion polls remain a common feature of the national media, the regularity with which keywords from social consciousness studies peppered the front pages of every newspaper in the 1980s now seems no more than a distant memory.

I would like to propose this golden age of social consciousness and its study of 1985 as a reference point for the comparisons I will be drawing later in this book aimed at achieving an understanding of present-day Japan. I do this in order to reevaluate an age in which there was still a clear grasp of the Japanese social mentality of which we have since lost track.

The "Bubble Years" around 1990 or so might also be worthy of consideration as a proposed benchmark for analysis. That vibrant age is, after all, well known even to those who grew up in the Heisei era, owing to the regularity with which it is referred to in the media. But the era of the bubble economy represents that point when the affluence of Japanese society briefly reached its high-water mark. Using such a period as a benchmark would make all subsequent generations seem by comparison to be mired in an inexorable decline. While that may be a reasonable way of seeing things with regard to industry and the economy, it is likely to give rise to misunderstandings on the topic of changes in the social structure.

I for one do not see the subsequent changes that took place in Japanese society simply as "deterioration" or "decline." Indeed, when seeking a reliable barometer of the prevailing social climate, some would point to the worth in observing the placid surface waters that precede a coming tsunami—in this case, 1985. Not only does this point in time represent the economic phase immediately prior to the bubble years, it also provides a snapshot of Japanese society in the late Shōwa period and thus prior to such major systemic changes as measures to promote deregulation and liberalization, promotion of equal employment opportunities among men and women, and the changes to welfare policy that came in the wake of the so-called "Gold Plan" of the mid-1990s.

It is also true that 1985 comes with a wealth of data generated by that year's installment of the decennial SSM Survey. Moreover, whereas previous surveys had gathered data only on Japan's male population, the 1985 study for the first time also saw women included in its remit. Furthermore, in 2010, as part of the SSP Project[1]—through which my colleagues and I have been working to set up a comprehensive study of social inequality in Japan—the SSP-I 2010 Survey was conducted for an intended comparison with the SSM 1985 Survey. As a result, I have at my disposal a high-quality data set that facilitates comparison of social consciousness over a period spanning a quarter of a century.

A further reason for choosing this year as our starting point is to draw a conceptual distinction from other, earlier periods, i.e.: from what is referred to as "postwar society." Dividing the 70-year period from the end of World War II to the present day into two halves, the latter period somehow seems less significant. Figures 3-1, 3-2, and 3-3 show various indicators of the affluence of society, all of which display steady growth over the first half of this period before leveling off past the halfway mark. The overriding impression of social change in Japan is that the standards of affluence in society rose sharply until the country hit the era of high-speed economic growth, after which they remained on a plateau for a relatively long period of time (Figure 3-4).

When considering the history of contemporary Japan as a single, 70-year block, however, we have a seemingly unavoidable tendency to focus in great detail on the first half of that period. Probably the easiest way to visualize this problem is to consider the example of a soccer match. Imagine a first half in which your team

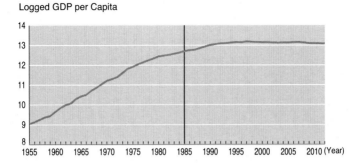

Figure 3-1 The Expanding Trend of GDP per Capita (Kikkawa 2013: 129)

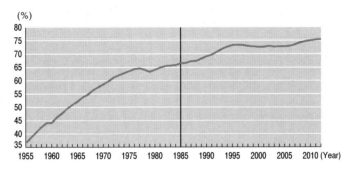

Figure 3-2 The Expanding Trend of Employed Workers (Kikkawa 2013: 130)

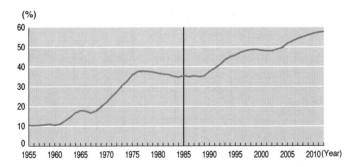

Figure 3-3 The Expanding Trend of Tertiary Education Attendance (Kikkawa 2013: 131)

concedes an early goal but then quickly ties the score, after which comes a second period altogether devoid of scoring chances. When discussing such a match, any observer would naturally be liable to focus mainly on the first half. However, given that most Japanese today are the erstwhile substitutes introduced in the second

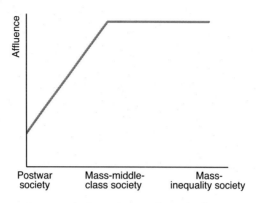

Figure 3-4 Basic Image of Social Change

half of this game, it behooves us to nonetheless get a precise understanding of their contributions no matter how unremarkable they may appear in comparison.[2]

To put it more concisely, before our very eyes, there is a period of some 30 years or more that—although it could reasonably be described as "our age"—we have yet to discuss in sufficient depth. During these years on the plateau, Japanese society experienced a number of complex changes, whose scale and direction can be difficult to grasp. As such, having set our focus on this block of years, it is necessary to set aside the broad yardstick typically used in discussion of the remarkable development of the immediate postwar period, and employ a finer rule for a thorough investigation.

Capturing the Eve of Reflexive Modernity

Although it may seem a somewhat abrupt move, I would here like to introduce the concept of "reflexive modernity" as a means of understanding contemporary society. The term "reflexive modernity" is a means of understanding different eras. It was introduced in the 1980s, principally to describe contemporary conditions in Western societies. This approach contends that contemporary society has arrived at a situation that differs from that of modern society (the so-called "first modernity") that extended to the start of the twentieth century, backgrounded by the rapid and drastic historical developments that occurred in Europe during the latter half of the century, including the end of the Cold War and the formation of the European Union.

Sociological theory is split over how to discuss this change of eras, with one camp describing how we have arrived at an entirely new stage that ought to be termed "post-modern society," while the other sees it as a derivation of modern society in an "evolved" form produced by the "completion of modernity." The British-based sociologists Anthony Giddens (Giddens 1990, 1991) and Zygmunt Bauman (Bauman 2001), along with Germany's Ulrich Beck, approach contemporary society from the latter perspective. This understanding of society is collectively dubbed "reflexive modernity." Although some theorists describe this concept as "second modernity," or use the term "high modernity" to distinguish it from "modernity," in this book I will use "reflexive modernity" as that is the most established term within Japanese sociology.

Suddenly faced here with the term "reflexivity," many readers might find themselves at a loss as to quite what this important keyword might mean. It is true that the term is difficult to explain concisely in a way that leaves no room for misunderstanding. In the final chapter of this book, I will discuss the current state of the Japanese social mentality from the perspective of reflexive modernity as thoroughly as space allows. But for now, let me simply say that it is best to think of the approach as describing a change from a simple, consistent age whose vectors were easily understandable to all, to a more complex, unpredictable, and unfathomable one.

Thanks to the explanatory interpretations of Yamada Mamoru, Mikami Takeshi, and Tomoeda Toshio, this understanding of periodization is already well established in contemporary Japanese sociology (Yamada 2013; Mikami 2010; Tomoeda 2010). However, the social theories surrounding reflexive modernity have themselves long been stalled at the stage of accurately "importing" Western premises into Japanese realities. Moreover, opinion among scholars is divided as to where the focus of such efforts should lie, be it globalization, the rise of information technology, arts and culture, the relationship between society and the individual, and so on.

As a result, from the perspective of survey data analysis—one of the fields that puts such theories to use—two issues remain to be tackled when it comes to the reflexive modernity concept. The first is the continuing lack of a body of evidence to verify whether or not an understanding of periodization that describes reflexive modernity as having arrived is correct. The second is that attempts to apply an in-depth understanding of such theories to studies of contemporary Japanese society remain inadequate.

Throughout my own years studying sociology, the mantra that the modern era ("modernity") has reached its end and that the next era has begun has been repeated ad infinitum with all the hypnotic air of a lullaby. That alone is enough to offer a vague understanding of when the concept of reflexive modernization began to penetrate Japanese sociology. But detailed research applicable when seeking to decipher exactly when and how Japanese society ushered in this era of reflexive modernity remains limited. In Europe, reflexive modernization is typically said to have gradually taken hold over a period of thirty to one hundred years. As such, it surely speaks to the "reality" of a great many people. In Japan and other East Asian societies, however, where a period of rapid, linear social change was followed by a sudden leap into a "post-modern" stage, the notion that the era of reflexive modernity has arrived is to many observers far from a self-evident truth. Accordingly, the issue of how to empirically pinpoint the historical inflection point when it comes to social mentality for Japan remains a significant one.

Many sociologists place this enigmatic juncture either at the turning point from the Shōwa to the Heisei eras or that from the twentieth to the twenty-first century (Imada 1989, Tomoeda 2013). Certainly, postwar theories that placed modernization as a precondition to understanding phenomena can be seen to have started losing their explanatory power around that time. With this in mind, 1985 becomes the eve of this inflection point in historical eras. This timing—which corresponds to the final stages of the era of the mass middle class—makes it possible to discuss this period as what might be termed the climax of the first modernity, or the final phase of modernity itself.

The Pinnacle for Shōwa Japan

Yoshizaki Tatsuhiko has already pulled together a detailed assessment of the social conditions of this time, appropriately titled *1985-nen* (The year 1985) (Yoshizaki 2005). Using his work as a touchstone, let us look back upon the trail of the social mentality of those years. Incidentally, on a personal note 1985 was the year in which I graduated from high school and left my hometown of Matsue, Shimane Prefecture, for the Kansai region, to embark on a new life as a student in a metropolitan area. This left me with a clear and lasting impression of the "adult world" that I was newly confronting.

Shōwa 60 (1985). Japanese society had entered its 40th year since the end of World War II, and with the reverberations from the period of high-speed economic growth still being felt was moving into the bubble years. The signing of the Plaza Accord meant that this was also a key year on the international economic stage. The government of Japan, led by Prime Minister Nakasone Yasuhiro, was still operating under the conservative vs. reformist two-party setup known as the 1955 System (*gojūgonen taisei*).

Turning our attention to the industrial world, one after another state-owned enterprises including Japanese National Railways, Nippon Telegraph and Telephone, and Japan Tobacco and Salt that collectively had been tagged "*oyakata hinomaru*" (essentially, "The government is our boss") were privatized. But despite the creation of new companies that were referred to by their respective romanized acronyms of JR, NTT, and JT, much of industry and the economy continued to dance to the government's tune.

Turning to people's working lives, Shōwa-era norms like long-term employment practices and a seniority-based wage system were still a reality. The SSM Survey provides detailed insight into the employment histories of Japan's citizens. According to these figures, in 1985 the average male had changed jobs 1.16 times in his lifetime, but by 2005 that frequency had risen to 1.46 (Hayashi and Satō 2011). The vertical line that repeats on Figures 3-1, 3-2, and 3-3 represents conditions as they stood in 1985. A glance at these figures reveals that in 1985 some 66.6% of the overall workforce was in full-time employment (as salaried workers), compared to 75.3% in 2013. The proportion of tertiary education attendance was 37.6% as opposed to 55.1% in 2013, while GDP stood at around 70% of its current total. Incidentally, at that time every Saturday was still a work or school day (if only in the morning) while Japan had at least three fewer national holidays per year than we currently enjoy. Although the Japanese of the day were frequently said to be overworked, that was the extent of the extra study or work in which they engaged relative to the present day.

On the cultural front, this was the year of Expo '85, held in the new town of Tsukuba, east of Tokyo. The official name of the event can be translated as "The International Science Technology Exposition" (*Kokusai kagaku gijutsu hakurankai*), and 30 years later Tsukuba is now well established as a hub for the development of the latest technology. However, 1985 also drew a line under the principal theme of science and technology that had underlain the International Expositions since Osaka in 1970. The event returned to Osaka five years later in 1990 reborn as The International Garden and Greenery Exposition (*Kokusai hana to midori no hakurankai*), and the motif of our relationship with nature was continued with the Love the Earth Expo (*Ai-chikyūhaku*) in Nagoya in 2005. It follows that 1985 can therefore also be seen as the eve of a shift in the principle emphasis of Japanese society from science and technology to Earth and the environment.

Another dramatic change—this one related to public-spiritedness—can be seen in smoking habits. In 1985, some 64.6% of men were smokers—roughly two out of every three adult males would light up with scant regard for time, place, or occasion. By 2010, that figure had fallen to 36.6%, a near reversal of the ratio of smokers to non-smokers from 2 : 1 to 1 : 2 (Japan Smoking Rate Survey, JT, 2010). This change has also been accompanied by a remarkable improvement in the nation's smoking etiquette. Thinking back to Japan's streets around the end of the Shōwa era, litter was a vastly more common feature than it is today—not just cigarette butts, but also cans and other carelessly discarded trash. Looking back with today's sensibilities, in those days Japan still had some way to go in terms of social etiquette.

Domestically manufactured automobiles figured among the items most desired by the youth of the day. Not just any old car would do, though: it had to be a two-door coupe modeled after the European supercars of a few years prior. Prominently displayed on the body would be stickers and emblems, proudly proclaiming the presence of various makers' patented high-performance engines, such as Toyota's Twincam 24 Turbo, and the widely used DOHC 20 design. Indeed, many will remember how technology itself became a sort of fashion in this age when faith and hope sprung eternal for the cutting-edge innovation that was driving Japan's major industries. Air quality was much worse than it is today, though, thanks to the exhaust gases those automobiles produced, and Japan's cities were also coated in layers of soot.

Turning to matters related to general convenience and comfort, although the Shinkansen bullet train network had yet to be graced by the Nozomi, Mizuho, and Hayabusa services that we see today, the recent introduction of the then-latest 100 series trains to the Hikari and Yamabiko services had already slashed the journey between Tokyo and Osaka to a mere three hours. Smartphones and the Internet were of course not yet available, but automatic teller machines and the distinctive green of phone-card compatible public telephones were a common sight in most towns, along with a roster of fast food outlets not too dissimilar to the one we see today.

The retail landscape was however rather different. Licenses required for the sale of rice and alcohol meant that 24-hour convenience stores had yet to emerge to offer round-the-clock access to most daily necessities. Shopping malls with their massive selling floors were also a few years off. This was primarily due to the protection afforded to small-to-medium sized retailers by regulations and trade associations. Membership of trade unions was high, and the May Day rallies and *Shuntō* ("spring offensive") wage negotiations loomed much larger in the public consciousness than they do now. It was considered important to abide by the standards and unwritten rules of any organization to which one belonged, from schools to local citizens associations. This was less a matter of legal compliance than of respect for social conventions, enforced by peer pressure. For better or for worse, it was an era when people were deeply woven into the fabric of their society.

On the consumer electronics front, it was around this time that dedicated word processors and home computers first began to rapidly catch on, while microwave ovens and landline telephones were already ubiquitous. The iPod had of course still yet to be invented, but it was possible to listen to music on the move thanks to Sony's portable cassette Walkman. Years before its descendants the Wii and the DS arrived on the scene, Nintendo's *Famicom* ("Family computer," marketed outside Japan as the Nintendo Entertainment System) emerged as a home games console to be connected to the family television, while the portable Game & Watch series offered the chance to enjoy a range of now-well-known titles such as Super Mario anytime, any place.

On the music scene, the genre now known as J-pop had yet to emerge. The rage instead was for so-called "new music." Today's youth would probably chuckle at the term, but at that time the word "new" seemed cool and fresh in a way that may now seem difficult to appreciate.

I may have rambled somewhat on this topic, but these snapshots of 1985 provide a glimpse of the achievements of Shōwa Japan at a time when faith in science and technology and in the economy was absolute. It was a long way removed from the poverty and hardship one normally associates with the label "postwar." But there is no doubt that the overall mood of the times was rather different to how it is now. The changes that would befall Japanese society over the next quarter-century followed a pattern similar to the transition from filament light bulbs, to fluorescent lamps, to LED lighting—the lack of apparent change on a superficial level masked major qualitative strides. Although material affluence did not differ greatly from the standards we enjoy today, standing on the cusp of a major transition from one era to the next—marked by the end of the Cold War and the passage from the Shōwa to the Heisei era—1985 represents a transitional moment in history, one in which the characteristics of the old era and the new one intermingled. Thus, if it were possible to travel back in time and visit those days, for a Japanese it would likely feel rather akin to alighting at an airport in one of Japan's Asian neighbors today, at once familiar yet somewhat peculiar.

Japan in 1985

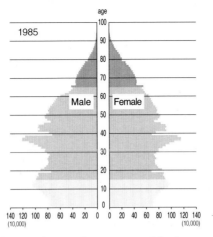

Figure 3-5-a The Population Pyramid for Japan in 1985

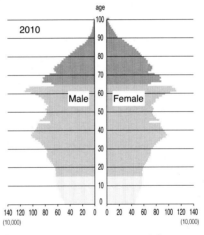

Figure 3-5-b The Population Pyramid for Japan in 2010

Generational Change and the Human Life-Cycle

Let us now continue by considering the people who made up this society. Figure 3-5 compares the population pyramids for Japan in 1985 and 2010 (Source: Ministry of Internal Affairs and Communications, Statistics Bureau website). At first glance the most surprising thing is that Japan's demographic makeup in 1985 retains a clear flavor of the shape suggested by the term "population pyramid." But by 2010, the low birthrate and rapid aging of Japanese society had created a demographic profile rather different from other developed nations, resulting in a spindle-shaped chart that tells the tale of a society that has achieved "maturity."

On the topic of this demographic make-up, it is important to emphasize the fact that the Japanese social mentality of 1985 still bore strong echoes of pre-war and wartime society. The demographic born prior to 1940 (aged 45 and over) that made up the upper portion of the population pyramid for 1985 (Figure 3-5-a) represents a generation that was educated under the pre-war schooling system. Setting aside any evaluation of the quality of that system, Japan's schooling before and during the war is sure to have had a far from negligible influence on shaping the social consciousness of the time. It is a topic that could not be openly discussed until relatively recently, but the fact is the modern Japanese society of 1985 was one that had been built upon a major apostasy in values, for it was the "little citizens" (*shōkokumin*) reared in a system designed to instill an ultranationalist, patriotic mentality who had now taken on the role of "wise elders" in a democratic society. Indeed, the over-60s generation of the time (then known as *rojin* ["the aged"]) had all been born in either the Meiji (1868–1912) or Taishō (1912–1926) eras. From this, we can infer that the vector of the transition from a traditional, feudal society to a modern one was part and parcel of what it meant to live through these years.

Still, the demographic that occupied the largest section of the pyramid for both 1985 and 2010 is the generation born in the late 1940s, Japan's "baby boomers" (*dankai no sedai*). In 1985, this cohort—today in their 60s—were still in their mid-to-late 30s. Many were young parents raising a generation that would be dubbed the "junior boomers" (*dankai jūnia*). Parenthetically, my birth year of 1966 presents a conspicuous slight indentation on the pyramid because of a common superstition about babies born in what was the Chinese year of the horse. As I mentioned earlier, 1985 was the year in which I myself graduated from high school. My birth cohort, having entered the workforce just in time to become an integral part of the thriving industrial boom of the 1990s bubble years, are now the parents of school-age children. Those born in 1985 are themselves now well into their late 20s and are beginning to assume the mantle of the workforce at the backbone of Japanese society and the parents of the next generation.

When thinking in this way about what characterizes an era, it is not sufficient to focus solely on the passage of time; the role played by specific generations as they collectively age (the aging impact) must also be given adequate consideration. In this respect, too, concentrating on a 25-year span works in our favor. This is because we could lose track of the nature of the changes if we were to take the more facile approach of simply comparing ourselves first to our parents' generation and then to that of our children. Conversely, working with an interval of 10 or 50 years would make it rather more difficult to get a sense of the shifts in the generations concerned.

Positive Reevaluations of the Uniqueness of Japan's Culture: The Age of "Exotic Japan"

Let us move on to the ways in which the social mentality of this era was expressed. I would like to start by stressing the fact that in any age a certain amount of predictive debate takes place in the arena of public discourse. The initial stirrings of the era that was to follow can also be detected in the proclamations of 1985. But the social mentality that can be apprehended through data develops in synchrony with such discourse, which trails the former slightly and develops over a more extended period. In light of this, below I will look at explanations of this period that take in a five-to-ten-year timespan and have a consistent grasp of the social consciousness of the age.

First, it is important here to recall a term that in 1985 was crucial to all discussion of the social mentality but which has these days all but disappeared from public discourse. That term is *Nihonjinron*, sometimes called *Nihonbunkaron*—"theories of Japanese national and cultural identity," but most commonly rendered as "theories of Japanese uniqueness." In either case, for brevity's sake I will use the Japanese term *Nihonjinron* below.

Toward the end of the Shōwa era, in tandem with a Japanese economy that was becoming a more and more significant force on the global stage, interest began to grow in the topic of "the essence of Japan." The discussion began to collect around pride in the uniqueness of "Japan." Blended together were a broad range of topics, including behavioral patterns and interpersonal relationships (shame culture, collectivism, and the balance between privately held [*honne*] and publicly espoused opinions [*tatemae*]); distinctive features in the structure and organization of Japanese society (rigid vertical relationships [*tate-shakai*], a clan-based society [*ie-shakai*], and Japanese business and management practices); and unique culture and traditions (bushidō, Zen Buddhism, the tea ceremony, and *wabi-sabi*). This construct was *Nihonjinron*. Prominent writers who participated in this discourse included Nakane Chie (1967); Yamamoto Shichihei (1983); Doi Takeo (1971); Hazama Hiroshi (1971); Murakami Yasusuke, Kumon Shunpei, and Satō Seizaburō (1979); and Yamazaki Masakazu (1984). The era of 1985 was one in which any bookstore would have a section with shelf upon shelf of tomes dedicated to works in the *Nihonjinron* vein.

A few years later, Aoki Tamotsu provided a very concise summing up of the genre (Aoki 1990). Aoki saw the early 1980s as a time characterized by positive evaluation of Japan's uniqueness. Prior to that point, i.e., from the end of the war through to the period of rapid economic growth, the tone of *Nihonjinron* had unanimously emphasized the unique *failings* of Japanese culture. The country's unique history and culture were blamed for Japan taking the wrong path that led down the road to World War II. The postwar years were characterized by the conviction born of stern collective self-reflection that there was a need to leave behind the Japan of old and proceed instead along the route of Westernization. This was seen at the time as an incontrovertible fact. How else was it possible to explain the reality that Japan had lost the war? The starting point for social consciousness studies, which is rooted in that tension between tradition and modernity, was likewise steeped in this mood of negativity concerning Japan's culture.

Yet, by the 1980s, the tone of discourse surrounding Japan's culture had undergone a major shift. Aoki described the phenomenon thusly:

> Studies of Japan broke free from the use of modern Western society as a point of reference that had been evident until that point and moved away from the position that modernization meant Westernization, paving the way for attempts to cultivate an altogether new discipline. Japan's rapid growth had improved the country's global standing to that of an economic superpower and ushered in an age of prosperity. This placed a renewed focus in the nation on attempts to interrogate its identity, i.e., 'What are Japanese, and what potential do they have?' (Aoki 1990: 109)

In this era, it had once again become possible to discuss the social mentality from a position of positivity regarding the uniqueness of Japanese society. Without this change, it would be impossible to account for a situation that Ezra Vogel was already speaking of in 1979 with his title, *Japan as Number One*.

Among the various discussions, perhaps the most definitive was the "contextualism" (*kanjinshugi*) espoused by Hamaguchi Eshun. The "contextual person" (*kanjin*) proposed by Hamaguchi in his foremost work "*Nihon-rashisa" no saihakken* ("Rediscovering Japanese-ness") represented the unique, human-centered outlook of the Japanese people. The main thrust of this concept can be summarized as follows. The Japanese people have absorbed the interpersonal relations characteristic of Japanese society—in short, the context—into their fundamental identity. They are interdependent and have built a society based on mutual trust in one another. Accordingly, they can refer to standards that might change depending on the situation and take whatever actions may be appropriate, even in settings where in a Western society they might be expected to conform to every norm without exception. In recent parlance, this might be termed the ability to "read between the lines" (*kūki ga yomeru*).

Hamaguchi's main premise is that the mechanism by which this is achieved in Japanese society differs from societies founded on individualism in that it is best understood in terms of "the contextual" as opposed to "the individual." From this, Hamaguchi drew the following conclusion.

> It is not that the Japanese are naturally lacking in self-assertiveness, nor do they lack an individual identity. Rather, it is that, in contrast to the frank expressions of personal ego that are acceptable in Western society, such assertions have taken on a socially advanced and refined (read, "sophisticated") form. Interpreted in this way, Japanese—who traditionally display a communal sense of self—have no difficulties when it comes to leading a "modern" lifestyle even without making Western-style individualism their ideal. Indeed, it is even possible to say that, as society steadily becomes more systematically connected, this outlook facilitates an even more functionally superior lifestyle. (Hamaguchi 1977,

reprint 1988: 275)

Considered thusly, such key *Nihonjinron* interests as a society based on rigid vertical relationships (*tate-shakai*), collectivism, dependency, private and public opinion, and Japanese business and management practices begin to seem less the objects of dismissive gazes and instead take on a positive nuance as essential elements of the success of Japanese society. To be sure, by 1985 an increasing number of Japanese were already starting to go cool on this kind of "ultra-Japanism." Even so, there is little doubt that to many at this time, this positive evaluation of the uniqueness of Japanese culture was something that came as second nature.

Incidentally, this was also the time that singer Gō Hiromi had a hit with his memorable piece *Ni-oku yon-sen-man no hitomi, ekizochikku Japan* ("240 million eyes of exotic Japan"), released in 1984. The 240 million figure in the title was apparently intended to reflect the number of eyes (specifically pupils) possessed by a Japanese population that had recently passed the 120 million mark. But thinking anew about the song's repeated "Exotic Japan!" refrain, one realizes that just like Hamaguchi's "*Nihon-rashisa" no saihakken*, it was born of the prevailing mood of looking proudly upon the uniqueness of the society to which we Japanese belong. The fact is, this truly was the era for making flamboyant proclamations about the positive uniqueness of Japanese culture—about "exotic Japan."

Social Mentality in the First Modernity

As Japan entered the 1990s and an increasingly global outlook and sense of cultural relativism began to extend even to the general populace, people began to once more see themselves as "simply Japanese" and discussion of the national identity in an overwhelmingly positive light eventually faded from view. It was the coming of this age of internationalization that prompted Aoki's theories.[3] By the standards of the present day, the tendency of the Japanese to think with uncomplicated favor about our identity as Japanese is further fading from view.

As such, we are now able to analyze the significance of the popular trends in the discourse of those days unburdened by judgments about the actual rights and wrongs of the arguments that *Nihonjinron* once made. In so doing, it becomes apparent that the rise of *Nihonjinron* in the 1980s has the following implications for social consciousness studies.

Firstly, this period presented an opportunity for the society of the day to re-adopt a Japanese sense of traditionalism that had earlier been targeted for rejection as being too conventional. That is not, of course, to say that all Japanese traditions were comprehensively rehabilitated. But at the very least customs seen as "traditional" or "orthodoxly conservative" ceased to be dismissed wholesale as they had previously been, and instead began to be deemed to possess an inherent value that was worthy of preservation.

Secondly, it created an opportunity for Japanese social science and industry to aim at constructing a Japanese-type model that was not an imitation of modern Western society. Rather than view Western (read "modern") offerings—in short, things that were not Japanese—by virtue of their origin as offering the only course that society should pursue, people instead came to explore the possibilities of developing East Asian models (though the Japanese-type model that originated here would once again be rejected as symbolized by the term "Galapagos," evoking evolutionary dead ends developed in isolation in a remote island ecosystem). It should also be stated here that, to keep pace with this cultural relativism, sociological theory was forced to effectively retract so-called modernization theory, which held that a simple convergence on Western models of society was the chief prerequisite for social change.

Thirdly, the very emergence of a *Nihonjinron* that was effectively a rather loose agglomerate of disparate ideas is indicative of vigor at the central foundations of social consciousness. *Nihonjinron* was a construct made up of a series of simple dichotomies. These become apparent in the disparate themes it is necessary to consider when one sets out to explain the notion of "a homogenous society fundamentally different from those in the West, with a unified culture based in a unique tradition;" it had to incorporate a "temporal" dimension (tradition vs. modernity); a "geographical" dimension (Japan vs. the West, or domestic vs. international); and the hierarchical dimension of class in combination with the very make-up of society (multicultural, class-based society vs. monoethnic, homogeneous society).

Ultimately, however, the core axis that unites the social mentality is that comprising the traditionalism–modernism binary. Although the notion of tradition as diametrically opposed to modernity had indeed started to crumble, it abided as a somewhat inflexible premise to which most ideas remained moored and that provided a point of reference for most people. In short, with everyone understanding that their society contained such a self-evident basis for values, Japanese engaged in a constant process of evaluating whether they were being "old fashioned" or "new" based on that standard as they went about their daily lives.

The notion that this conflict in values between tradition and modernity as being unshakably rooted in Japanese society of the time also received evidence-based corroboration from contemporary social consciousness phenomena. Hayashi Chikio utilized a method of his own design to analyze response trends in the Japanese National Character Survey—which he himself had directed for three decades—in order to make plain the "logic" (*kangaekata no sujimichi*) behind the ways Japanese think. According to a succession of studies that Hayashi dubbed "quantitative Nihonjinron," data from answers to a range of yes/no opinion-oriented questions gathered continually since the end of World War II indicated that the period until 1970 clearly adhered to the traditionalism–modernism binary (the tradition-modern mental logic) while from 1980 or thereabouts the tendency towards traditionalism started to become less and less pronounced. At first, it appeared that the younger generation were making efforts to revive certain traditions. But it soon became clear that this mental logic that saw tradition and modernity in opposition was beginning to crumble across a broad age spectrum. Over the next 20 years or so, the traditionalism–modernism axis gradually vanished without a trace. From Hayashi's efforts to convey with some surprise these faint tremors in the mental logic of the late 1980s, it can be reasonably inferred that during this era the default position nonetheless remained a train of thought in which people would keep the conflict between traditionalism and modernism in mind when thinking about the issues at hand and firmly link various opinions to it.

A similar trend of clinging to the vestiges of the traditionalism–modernism axis even as it started to crumble has also been noted in Japanese politics of the time. In his analysis of voter behavior based on value consciousness ("cultural politics"), Watanuki Joji noted a correlation between "traditional" versus "modern" values among the Japanese electorate in the 1960s and their respective preference for either conservative or reformist political parties (Watanuki 1986). But turning to survey data from 1983, we see that the political culture underlying voter behavior is changing to one in which the traditional values that were still extant have begun to meld with industrial values whose basis lies in a faith in science and technology (ibid. 43). This seemingly unlikely union of the traditional and the industrial can be seen as one that evoked a transitional period when the traditionalism–modernism axis was taking on a new form. Still, the framework of the social consciousness of the day was such that the word "tradition" continued to have a strong magnetic attraction; even such concepts associated with "orthodox" modernity as industrialization and the advance of science and technology were drawn into its orbit.

The foregoing illustrates how this period presents a subject that is at once fascinating to analyze and difficult to interpret. It is my belief that both traits arise from deeply ingrained Japanese traditions (and/or the sense thereof) that somehow managed to abide within the advanced industrial society that achieved high levels of economic growth. To rephrase this from the standpoint of contemporary social theory, the Japan of 1985 represented the final moment in which its people were embedded in modern society (society of the first modernity). If that is the case, then Japan's present day reality as a society in reflexive modernization will come steadily into focus once we have grasped the contours of its antecedent.

Homologies between *Nihonjinron* and the Mass-Middle-Class Phenomenon

My fourth and final point is something hinted at by the homologies between the "*Nihonjinron* boom" and the mass-middle-class phenomenon. The people of the age lived through a process that saw their personal circumstances being greatly improved by unprecedented social change. But it was their passage through the decade-long stable period that began in the mid-1970s that gave them a palpable sense that the age of social change had ended and that they had now settled into a prosperous, stable society. This may have been why there was the sense in 1980s Japan of wish fulfilment in that Japanese wanted the images they had of themselves at that moment of arrival to be confirmed in the form of a cultural theory—a "self-reflection" backed with scholarship.

Needless to say, the self-reflection that they expected had to be positive and also so simple that the majority would find it unequivocally compelling. Such a national self-image is something with which it is natural to identify. Against the backdrop of the "*Nihonjinron* boom," people were eager to know what the "standard image" (*hyōjunzō*) of their own society was, and furthermore hoped to find at the heart of this "Japan" something with which they could identify. It is Aoki, in fact, who had the insight to perceive early on that the pivot underpinning the enthusiasm for *Nihonjinron* in the 1980s hinged precisely on this fact.

Furthermore, this tendency for the popular social consciousness to be mobilized en masse in a direction suggested by the intellectual elite dovetails squarely with received 20th century notions of "typical citizens" as depicted in mass society theory. In this regard, too, the prevailing climate of 1985 can clearly be seen to differ from that of the present day.

In any case, from the perspective of this book, the fact that a shift in the social consciousness—a movement defined by people seeking to align themselves with a radiant picture of themselves that came with scholarly backing—was visible is extremely suggestive. That is because the enthusiasm for *Nihonjinron* can be understood in light of the same contemporary trends as the mass-middle-class phenomenon, which was being talked about with reference to stratification consciousness at practically the same time. The latter phenomenon—often also framed as "one hundred million-strong mass middle class," (*ichi oku sōchūryū*)—gained impetus as survey data established "middle class" as the benchmark status of the Japanese with which the citizenry in turn unanimously identified. In this sense, both the *Nihonjinron* boom and the mass-middle-class phenomenon can be seen as efforts to affirm the national self-image that came as a product of the period of rapid economic growth. Accordingly, almost in lockstep both phenomena rapidly tailed off as Japan entered the 1990s.

The very phrase *ichi oku sōchūryū* originated from World War II-era slogans such as *ichi oku hi no tama* ("one hundred million fireballs"), and *ichi oku gyokusai* ("one hundred million honorable deaths"), based on the official estimate of Japan's population provided by the wartime military authorities. Such expressions were clearly intended to symbolize an illusion of unity—of "the whole of Japanese society!"[4] In short, "*ichi oku*" was an expression used when seeking to emphasize the notion of "we Japanese all" (*wareware Nihonjin subete ga*). In much the same way, the postwar years also saw the occasional use of rather more negative expressions such as *ichi oku sōzange* (the penitence of a hundred million) and *ichi oku sōhakuchika* (the madness of a hundred million). The final chapter of the postwar "ichi oku" expressions that had run the gamut from "honorable death" to "penitence" came with "one hundred million-strong mass middle class." Thought of in this way, the interpretation that the mass-middle-class phenomenon and the *Nihonjinron* boom were in closely related contexts becomes much more persuasive.

To close, I would like to look back once again at the 1980s hit song "240 Million Eyes." After the refrain of "exotic Japan," the same phrase suggesting the hearts of one hundred million were all aflutter is repeated over and over almost like the chorus of a classical Greek drama. Reflecting all these years later on this curiously resonant phrase, the fact that this was an age in which the social consciousness of 120 million people became wildly enthusiastic for the positive and unique aspects of Japanese culture (i.e., by "exotic Japan") and in which a normalized image of what it meant to be Japanese possessed a strong pull suddenly becomes clear.

NOTES

1   For further information on the SSP Project, see: http://ssp.hus.osaka-u.ac.jp/
2   I accept the continuing potential for detailed future studies of postwar society to identify as-yet-unrecognized underlying factors that will rewrite scholarly understanding. Such reassessments of existing theories are, however, unlikely to warrant major changes to the overall thrust of my argument here. It is high time that we move beyond to a sociology that remains narrowly focused and continues *ad infinitum* to concentrate on Shōwa-era historical concepts like "postwar" and the "period of rapid economic growth."
3   In 1985, Professor Hamaguchi and Professor Aoki were colleagues at the School of Human Sciences, Osaka University. As a student in this faculty, I myself had the opportunity to study under Hamaguchi. My impression was of a modest and dignified gentleman entering the twilight of his years—something of a contrast with Aoki, who rather daringly moved in international circles.
4   As explained by Oguma Eiji, taking into account the territory under Japan's control at the time of World War II, the figure of 100 million seems somewhat dubious (Oguma 1998). It is, therefore, best seen as an "imagined community" (to borrow from Benedict Anderson) intended to symbolize the Japanese nation state.

CHAPTER 4

The Real Nature of the Mass-Middle-Class Phenomenon

Many writers have already spoken about the visible forms taken by social class from the subjective viewpoint of Japanese in the 1980s. I, too, have offered my own analyses. However, in this chapter so that the reader may grasp the arguments presented in this book unimpeded, I will explore the situation from an angle that established theory does not elucidate.

The Catalyst that Changed the Debate about Stratification into One about Eras

"Mass middle class" (*sōchūryū*) is a well-known term used for describing the social class situation in Japan during the 1970s and 1980s. The focus in this phrase is on the status identification of individuals, i.e., their sense of where they are located if Japanese society has been split into upper, middle, and lower classes.

We measure this based on the trends in responses to those survey questions we sociologists see as pertaining to status identification. The question texts and response options take several different forms, but the most representative one is that provided by the five-level status identification (*go-dankai kaisō kizoku ishiki*) framework. The questions using this form may be categorized as being one of two general types. One is that which has been used in the SSM Surveys from the outset in 1955, while the other is that which the Cabinet Office has used to understand public opinion trends in the Public Opinion Survey on the Life of the People (hereafter, Life of the People Survey) it has been conducting since the 1950s.[1]

The difference is that the SSM Surveys pose the question, "Assuming we can divide present-day Japanese society into five levels, into which of these do you fall in your view? (*Kari ni Nihon shakai zentai o kono hyō ni aru itsutsu no sō ni wakeru to sureba anata gojishin wa dore ni hairu to omoi masu ka?*)" while the Life of the People Survey asks, "From the general perspective of society, where do you think your standard of living fits in ? (*Otaku no seikatsu teido wa seken ippan kara mite kono naka no dore ni hairu to omoi masu ka?*)" Strictly speaking, the SSM Survey question is about status identification, while the one in the Life of the People Survey is about living standards. In addition, the SSM Survey seeks responses from five hierarchically asymmetrical categories—"upper," "*upper middle,*" "*lower middle,*" "upper lower," and "lowest-lower." Meanwhile, the Life of the People Survey presents a straight five categories—"upper," "*upper middle,*" "*middle middle,*" "*lower middle,*" and "lower." Understandably, the ratio for the three middle categories tends to be higher in the latter survey, a result that provided the foundations for "90% of Japanese are middle class."

Status identification is a social attitude that, in Japan, takes in how Japanese understand the class structure of their society and where they position themselves within it. To examine the visible forms that social class takes among subjective actors by taking their pulse with this single measure helps with guiding people toward a basic understanding of industrial and class structures that are complex, subtle, and change ceaselessly. For that reason, this attitude has provided a reference axis for speaking about the nature of society from the end of World War II to the 1980s. For example, Satō Toshiki observed, "I have noted that non-specialists more readily recognize social trends in the distribution of class identifications than in the odds ratios for intergenerational mobility or the Yasuda index" (Satō 2009: 736). He even gave his work *Fubyōdō shakai Nihon* (2000)—which dealt with class structure in its visceral forms—the subtitle, "Farewell to the mass middle class" (*Sayonara sōchūryū*). [2] Status identification research changes the debate about class into a more readily understandable one about what characterizes different eras (*jidairon*). In that light, quantitative social consciousness studies are compelled to investigate the role that this social attitude has played in Japanese society.

Curious Consequences

However, at present there is a considerable gap between the issues that scholars doing research at the cutting edge of the field take up and what the average person understands. I will begin by reviewing how this came to be.

Based on the shift through the 1960s and 1970s that saw "lower" responses replaced by "middle" ones in the majority, scholars reported that status identifications were trending upward. "Middle" responses eventually comprised 70% of the whole in the SSM Survey and 90% in the Life of the People Survey. Given the size of the "middle" response ratios, observers came to speak of status identification in shorthand as "middle-class consciousness" (*chū-ishiki* or *chūryū ishiki*); the rise in the number of respondents who had such consciousness was termed the "mass-middle-class phenomenon" (*sōchūryū genshō*, or *sōchūryū-ka*). The choice of nomenclature is itself indicative. Usually, when a common shorthand name gets assigned to a social attitude, the tendency is to use a term that is strongly positive or negative, e.g., anxiousness, general life satisfaction, or pro-*x* feelings. It is therefore quite singular for a name like this to have been used that further emphasizes the centripetal point in the distribution of responses.

In light of the heightened interest among the general public, various theories were put forth and intense debate ensued in stratification studies about why the numbers of Japanese who self-identified as "middle class" during the period of high-speed economic growth had increased. This was termed the mass-middle-class controversy (*chūryū ronsō*). Status identification trends were such a major topic of interest that this debate played out on newspaper front pages of the day.[3]

Today, however, the distribution of responses to status identification questions no longer attract the interest they once did. One reason is that the notion of a "mass middle class" is now seen as a somewhat antiquated one that smacks of the Shōwa period. Japanese society in the postwar period started from rock bottom amid the ruins of defeat. When people of the day thought about trends in industry and national living standards, the class to which they directed their attention was that of the workers living out their lives at society's lowest levels. Politicians, the press, and academics all focused on the consciousness and activities of the proletariat, a group that identified itself as "We workers!" As the character of the times gradually changed in step with high-speed economic growth, the focus of observers shifted to the social classes in the middle range that had begun to lay their hands on some wealth. The term "mass middle class" arose from this development. If we recall this sequence of events, then it becomes plain to see why no one spoke anymore of the "mass middle class" in the Heisei period—it was simply a term that captured the flavor of the period of high-speed economic growth and no longer had a role to play.

Another reason why status identification no longer attracts societal attention is because there is now a mismatch between the output of the survey data analysis and the way people perceive their era. The response distribution for social attitude-related questions is analytically meaningful only when there are differences in the distribution of responses to questions that have been repeatedly asked in the same format. However, an examination makes it unexpectedly clear that over the past four decades the distribution of responses to status identification questions has changed little.

Figures 4-1 and 4-2 use the past five SSM Surveys and the most recent SSP-I 2010 Survey to show the distribution of status identifications (for men only) at different points in time. Looking at Figure 4-1, the line representing the SSM 1955 Survey reveals that the "lower" ("upper lower" and "lowest lower") responses comprise a majority at 56.3%. This indicates that in the immediate postwar era (to the left of the figure) the distribution was definitely biased downward. A major upsurge in middle-class consciousness for the subsequent era of high-speed economic growth (lasting until 1975) is reflected by the rightward shift in the shape of the graph (the arrows indicate the general nature of these changes). However, Figure 4-2 shows very little change in response distributions for the 35 years from 1975 to 2010; the graph nearly perfectly coincides with the pattern of a normal distribution. In short, the visible form of social strata in Japanese eyes hardly

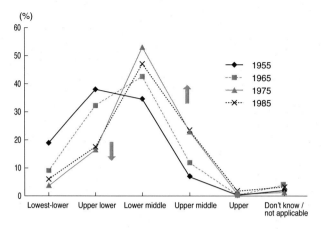

Figure 4-1 Middle Response Trends during the Preriod of High-Speed Economic Growth

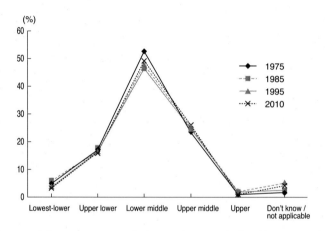

Figure 4-2 Middle Response Trends during the Period of Stable Economic Growth

changed for a quite long period of time.

Thinking back, I recall that the stratum studies scholars who carried out the SSM 1985 Survey were more than a little confused immediately after they had completed their descriptive data analysis. The distribution of responses in the most recent data they had collected did not match their forecasts (expectations) at all. The ratio of "middle" responses had gradually risen over the course of the three previous SSM Surveys, so they naturally had forecast that the ratio for 1985 would be higher than that of 1975. Metaphorically speaking, they had set their net of comparisons between different points of time in the SSM Surveys to capture that particular fish. But when they actually pulled the net up, what they found instead was that the changes had plateaued and the "middle" responses had in fact declined slightly. At the time, the sociological mainstream was awash with arguments that held industrialization would continue to trend upward. Scholars still spoke in university lectures, for example, of the developmental process of postwar Japanese society as a contemporary topic of interest. It is little wonder, then, that these findings were unanticipated. In the official survey report, Hara Junsuke would go on to describe this plateauing of the "middle" response as "'middle class' consciousness saturation" (Hara 1988).[4]

This development that was so shocking for scholars of the day marks the starting point for the discussion in this book. Figure 4-2 shows these later trends. The conclusion we might draw from referring to that graph is that the pattern of status identification distributions remains the same at any point in time. However, in one respect that "reality" simply does not hang together. Despite the fact that people have spoken in volume and at length about changes in class patterns—tossing around such phrases as "the shift from a mass-middle-class to an inequality society," "the split into 'winners' and 'losers,'" "lower-class society," and "poverty society"—it has not been possible to track such changes over time. For that reason, what was once hailed as the latest trend in status identifications (Figure 4-2) and stands at the core of discussions today itself has become something that lacks visible form.

A Point of Debate Consigned to "Galapagos"

Allow me to mention something else here about status identification studies and the mass-middle-class phenomenon that may be unexpected. The fact is, the five-level status identification framework—and above all the ratio of "middle" responses it presents—is an indicator virtually unique to sociology in Japan. It is little used in other countries. Let us quickly review how that came to be.

Almost immediately upon the end of World War II, the general public became interested in various terms with Marxist nuances such as "laborer," "bourgeoisie," and "capitalist." Accordingly, surveys from the 1950s used such names for class and stratum categories as "proletariat" (*rōdōsha kaikyū*), "capitalist class" (*shihonka kaikyū*), "lower class" (*karyū kaikyū*), "lower middle range" (*chūkansō no shita*), and "quasi-bourgeoisie" (*junchūsan kaikyū*). The search for Japanese terms that captured the character of the various classes entailed a process of trial and error.

That task continued in the same way as the public shifted its interest from the proletariat to the middle class. In the 1960s, two key figures behind class surveys of the time, Yasuda and Odaka, engaged in a debate over the precise meaning of "middle class." The key point in contention was which term was the appropriate one to use for labeling the increasingly apparent group of people occupying the middle range. The possibilities included *chūkan kaisō* (literally, "intermediate stratum"), *chūsan kaikyū* (the standard Japanese translation of the Marxism's "bourgeoisie"), and *chūryū kaikyū* (literally "class of the intermediate rank"), among other options. I will refrain from the details here,[5] but the gist is that various words expressing social status got weeded out when theory came face to face with survey data. The terms that still survived by the 1970s became the five options (in the case of the SSM Survey) from which respondents made their self-identification choices—one "upper," two "middle," and two "lower."

The mass-middle-class phenomenon has its origins at this point, and this is the principal reason why the five-level status identification framework stepped into its central role in stratification studies. Repeating the same questions in class surveys has been seen as a critical prerequisite since the 1970s (even though problems may arise when it comes to continuity). Accordingly, this five-level framework for status identifications is one of the few indicators that can facilitate analyses comparing conditions at different points in time over the past half century.

To be clear, I do not mean to say that this indicator lacks real power. To the contrary, it has survived precisely because the way Japanese determined their own statuses has been based on an image of strata that is orderly to a certain degree that this framework grasped. That said, this framework was developed to provide materials for teasing out the contours of a particular point of debate—the mass middle class—in the context of Japanese society during the high-speed growth period. As a consequence, it would be difficult to find an international angle to the arguments and propositions developed based on this framework. In short, both the point being debated and the means for do so are consigned, as it were, to their own Galapagos.

This raises the question of what kind of inquiries are used in other countries related to subjective social status and what issues are in play. To get ahead of myself, most questions may seem similar but they are based on slightly different premises. For example, the GSS Suevey in the U.S. has been asking about class identification for forty years by having respondents choose from among four categories: "upper class," "middle class," "working class," or "lower class." Note that the question here is not about "stratum" but rather "class." Class refers to actual social groups; hence, what people are being asked about is their self-awareness of belonging to a particular group (their class identity). While it may seem similar at first glance, this is quite different from passively choosing from among the strata in Japan that researchers put into a given order. The fact that "working class"—a term that was weeded out from use in Japan—is still being used here speaks plainly to this fact.[6]

In addition to differences in what is being analyzed, there are also major differences in issues at play. As the sudden spikes in talk about topics like "mass-middle-class society" and "inequality society" suggest, what interests the Japanese public about classes and strata fluctuates wildly from era to era. By contrast, in the West the flavor of the times does not color views of this subject in such an extreme fashion. This is because the awareness and self-consciousness of the people in those societies about being working, middle, or some other class is inseparably connected to other matters, including ethnicity, immigration issues, differences in religious denomination and sect, poverty, and community problems. Class is solidly entrenched at the grassroots level as a characteristic upon which social differences are based. In short, the interest in class identity is not of a frivolous sort, quickly rising or subsiding depending on the times. For that reason, it is hard to imagine in the first place that proportions of the responses might change much from era to era. This reminds us again that the mass-middle-class question in Japan focused on characteristics associated with a particular era rather than with their status-relatedness.

The "Phony" Rise of the Mass Middle Class: The Case of the SSM Survey

The foregoing illustrates how tracking five-level status identification question responses and arguing about changes in their distribution as evidenced by the mass-middle-class phenomenon amounted to a sort of game that was popular to play only in Japan over the 1970s and 1980s. Still, the question remains as to why those trends in the distribution of responses so captured the public's imagination at that time. How did those trends capture the atmosphere of those days? I will come back to this in the latter half of the chapter, relying on the dispassionate view that hindsight provides.

Mori Naoto describes that train of thought that sees "mass middle class" as the key concept describing the state of Japanese society as "the mass-middle-class ideology" (*sōchūryū no shisō*). He has speculated about the trajectory followed by this ideology as it took shape after the era of high-speed growth. In his view, the preponderance of "middle range" responses was due to the inquiry having reflected a normal distribution. He writes, "If consciousness of being 'middle' rose during the process of high-speed growth, then perhaps what we really need to be explaining based on these historical trends is why it was so *low* in the 1950s" (Mori 2008: 246). The post-1970s mass-middle-class phenomenon was an ideological one that surprised people because it assigned too much meaning to the operations of normal mechanisms that are not surprising in the first place. He saw that attention should have been directed precisely to the fact that there had been a preponderance of "lower class" responses in the preceding postwar period.

What, then, was the mechanism that caused the distribution of status identification responses to change so dramatically between the immediate postwar period and the 1970s? Mori surmises that the usual mechanisms that would have kept "middle" responses in place as the mode value came to a halt due to the temporary drop in living standards produced by defeat and to the shock that the personal experience of that defeat generated. This caused the proportion of "lower" responses to fleetingly rise in the 1950s. Over the next two decades, the public's inclination to offer "middle" responses gradually returned.

The basis for Mori's reasoning lies in the ratio of "middle" responses by reapondents in the SSM 1955 Survey. Subjects had been asked to look back at which status they identified with around 1935 or so and their sense of status identification after defeat. Mori points out that the "middle" ratio for the retrospective figures stood at 52.9% for 1935 and 41.6% for the immediate post-defeat period (1945). This he then paired with actual measured values of 42.6% for 1955 and 54.9% for 1965. While this offers only a quasi-comparison between different points in time, we can still see that these trends produced a V-shaped trough with a 13.3-point dip in the middle of a 30-year period.

However, what is hard to comprehend is the fact that "middle" response rates remained low even in the SSM 1965 Survey. That survey was carried out the year after the Tokyo Olympics, an event that has been posited as a landmark indicating the end of the "postwar" period. Over the following decade, those rates jumped 21.5 percentage points, from 54.9% to 76.4%. Normally, we might describe such a dramatic change in such a short period as a sign of "a flood into the mass middle class" (*sōchūryūka*), but in any case this trend cannot be explained solely as a consequence of the effects of defeat.

I myself view the notion that the pattern of status identifications changed when this era was reached with some skepticism (Kikkawa 2012). It is my belief that the phenomenon of a trend toward a mass middle class was created in the first place from something of a misreading of survey data. Allow me to sidetrack slightly from the Heisei-era trends that are my ultimate focus to use the benefits of hindsight to say something about the fragile clockwork of the Shōwa-period mass-middle-class phenomenon.

In social survey research, all of the questionnaires on which interviewers write their subjects' responses are themselves treated as source data and are seen as containing genuine information. These forms are carefully preserved based on strict procedures for reference should there be concerns about the electronic data generated from them.[7] I, however, do not completely subscribe to this doctrine of "original-copy supremacy." This is because I have noticed from the many times I myself have carried out face-to-face interviews that the object that provides the interface for communications between investigator and respondent is not the questionnaire itself but rather the groups of small cards showing response options that we call "show cards" (*teiji-kādo*).

Show cards are a tool for visually conveying the options to the respondent, and the investigator will point to them as they read through the questionnaire. For that reason, even if the questionnaires that are the media for the investigator to transcribe information remain identical in format from survey to survey, if some aspect of the show card is changed then the identical question is not being asked. One would expect this to be a crucial point that researchers keep in mind when designing ongoing surveys, but it had been a blind spot in stratification studies in Japan. This fact tends to be overlooked, especially when it comes to using data from earlier surveys.

In that light, I was somewhat surprised to discover that the designers of the SSM Surveys that established the contours of the mass-middle-class phenomenon had not paid attention to maintaining continuity in the show cards for five-level status identification questions. Figure 4-3 presents the card used in the SSM 1955 Survey; project leader Odaka has said (1967) that the same type of card was used for the 1965 Survey (Satō 2009; Kanbayashi 2010b). Figure 4-4 shows the card that has been used in stratification surveys from 1975 to the present.

Just a glance is enough to show that the two show cards are configured quite differently. The old style (1955/1965) card did not simply show possible answers like "lower middle" (*chū no ge*) or "upper low" (*ge no jō*) on their own. Rather, it supplemented them with explanatory phrases and readings of perhaps unfamiliar characters—*chūryū kaisō no shita no hō* ("toward the bottom of the middle class stratum")

The Real Nature of the Mass-Middle-Class Phenomenon

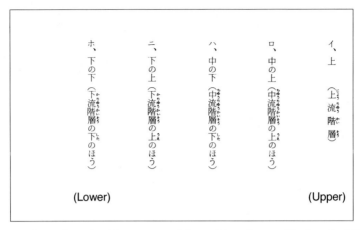

Figure 4-3   Show Card for Five-Level Status Identification Used in the SSM 1955 Survey

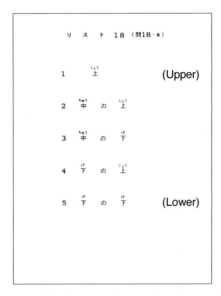

Figure 4-4   Show Card for Five-Level Status Identification Used in the SSM 1975 Survey

and "*karyū kaisō no ue no hō*" ("toward the top of the lower-class stratum"). To wit, they incorporated questions that asked not about "middle" but rather "middle class," and not "lower" but rather "lower class." Furthermore, these options were presented in the Japanese right-to-left reading format based on vertical columns and used the Japanese "*iroha*" ordering system rather than numbers. This, it could be said, emphasized the non-hierarchical character of all the options.

On the other hand, today's (post-1975) show card presents the options in a horizontal, left-to-right format, and assigns them numbers in order from top to bottom. In short, when the SSM Surveys were being pioneered, status identification had characteristics close to those of class categories, but since 1975 the emphasis in these stratification surveys has been on characteristics that allow placing it on a vertically-oriented ordinal scale.

With this in mind, we notice something peculiar when we look at the mass-middle-class phenomenon anew: the middle-range responses surged and "lower" ones plunged in the SSM Surveys between 1955 and 1975. As the bar graph in Figure 4-5 shows, changes in the first half of that period were characterized by a halving in "lowest" responses. In the second decade, "upper lower" responses halved and "upper middle" ones doubled. In terms of the data, the marked growth in the mass middle class actually occurred between 1965 and 1975. Meanwhile, a glance at the data from 1975 onward shows so little change in the distribution pattern as to be nonexistent.

It may be inferred that the following mechanism operated when respondents picked the category to which they belonged. First, from a procedural perspective, "middle" cannot be said to mean the same thing when it appears in a list of options arranged horizontally and tagged with the *iroha* notations as it does when they are arranged vertically and tagged 1 through 5. I cannot speak with absolute certainty about this since it is a matter related to cognitive psychology and hence outside my own field of research, but we cannot deny the possibility that the pattern of responses is more likely to be widely distributed when the options are presented horizontally instead of vertically. Doing so would probably increase the frequency of "lower" responses.

More serious is the issue of changes to the text of the options themselves. The nuances when "*karyū kaisō no ue no hō*" is read aloud in Japanese are more than a little different than those we get from "*ge no jō.*" For example, reading the character for "lower" using the Wu dynasty Chinese-derived reading of "*ge*" somehow gives it a stronger negative connotation than it would have had if the Han Chinese-derived one, "*ka*," had been used. In fact, there are more compound terms including this character that have the nuance of something humble or modest when it is read as "*ge*" than there are when it is read as "*ka*."

In that light, it is possible to imagine that the feelings of resistance toward the "lower" responses were slightly reduced in the SSM 1955 and 1965 Surveys. Supplementing the words in the options offered with parenthetical comments that expanded on their meaning may have been why those surveys had high "upper lower" response rates. Regarding the middle-range responses that are essential here, the supplemental gloss of "middle class stratum" conceivably could have brought a Western-style middle class readily to mind among respondents. They may have judged themselves as not yet being middle class as a result and hesitated to select the option.

To at least partially verify this, in the most recent of these surveys (SSP-W 2013 1st) I asked 2,822 adults of both genders questions with language based

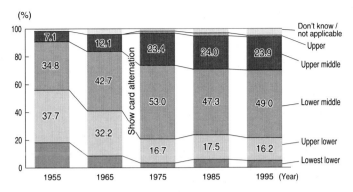

Figure 4-5 Response Distribution of Class identification in the SSM Survey

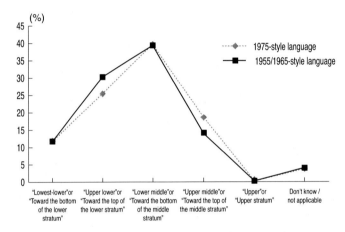

Figure 4-6 Distributions of Responses for 1955- and 1975- Style Language Options

on the post-1975-type SSM status identification options. So that there would be no carryover effects, I pulled 10 of those questions out and configured them to be questions that used the 1955/1965-style language—i.e., offering a range of responses options running from "upper-class stratum" to "toward the bottom of the lower-class stratum" (the Japanese characters appeared without pronunciation guides)—and compared the response distributions (SSP Project 2013). The results have been graphed in Figure 4-6.

The response trends show a statistically significant difference in the patterns of distribution for this style of question. As I expected, the ratio of "upper lower" responses was higher for those questions offering 1955/1965-style options with the word "class" (*ryū*) added in some fashion (25.76% and 30.23%).[8] While this finding is not enough to completely explain the changes in distribution between

1965 and 1975, it does leave open the possibility that the language used had some effect on response trends. Also, aside from differences in the text of response options, the possible effects of differences in horizontal vs. vertical orientation and in the use of the *iroha* system vs. numbering have yet to be examined.

Regardless, the foregoing suggests we cannot completely deny the possibility that the mass-middle-class phenomenon that so stunned the public to some degree originated in a change in the distribution of responses to survey questions, and that this in turn was caused by an alteration to the format of the show cards. If this is the case, then the story behind the explosive growth in middle-class consciousness—a phenomenon that has been regarded as distinctive to Japanese society during the period of high-speed growth—is one that has been told based on somewhat exaggerated data.

The "Phony" Rise of the Mass Middle Class: The Case of the Life of the People Survey

Even if this is the case, how do we explain the increase in "middle" responses for almost the same time period in another ongoing polling project, the Life of the People Survey? In fact, we already know that there were a few fluctuations in the continuity of the questions essential to us here from 1958 through 1970 (Kanbayashi 2010b). The chief concern is that there are blank spots for three years. There are several reasons for this. First, the question text currently in use—"your *standard of living*" ("otaku no *seikatsu teido*")—had yet to be settled on during the early years of the survey. From 1958 to 1961 the survey inquired instead about "your *living circumstances*" (otaku no *kurashimuki*). The responses for these years are shown on the four bars standing apart on the left side of Figure 4-7. Second, no questions were asked about either "living standards" or "living circumstances" in 1962 or 1963. Additionally, minor alterations continued to be made in language even after 1964 (see the six bars in the center of the graph). The centermost category was changed from "middle" to "middle middle" and responses were limited to "head of household or similar" (*setainushi nado*) rather than all respondents.[9] A survey in which such changes have been made does not constitute one that was rigorously repeated. Continuity in the survey questions was not maintained until after the 1970s.

These facts in mind, let us now examine the trends in the Life of the People Survey (Cabinet Office of Japan 2014). As Figure 4-7 shows, the period from 1960 to 1964 when the most striking growth in middle-class consciousness occurred corresponds to the break in survey continuity. A period when 41.0% of responses to the "living circumstances" question were "middle" is followed immediately by one when 50.2% of responses to the "standard of living" question were "middle middle."

Taken together with my earlier discussion, it is plain that the growth in middle-class consciousness in the 1960s and 1970s in both ongoing surveys overlapped with a period when each was changing the way it asked the relevant questions. Cross-checking these facts leads to the suspicion that the mass-middle-class

The Real Nature of the Mass-Middle-Class Phenomenon

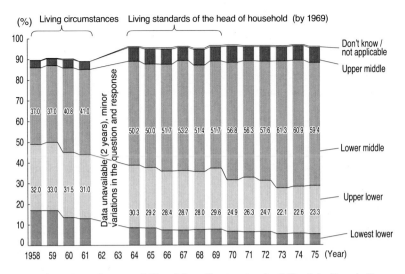

Figure 4-7 Distribution of Class Identification in the Life of the People Survey

phenomenon may not have been the major change that observers have claimed.

Today, it is treated as an "historical fact" that even shows up in Japanese high school history textbooks. However, I am compelled to say that the magnitude of the growth in middle-class consciousness to some degree was—even if unintentionally so—phony. As already noted, no overseas studies have reported any cases in which the distribution pattern of subjective social statuses changed as dramatically as it did during Japan's period of high-speed economic growth.[10] If we also take as fact the likelihood that the continuity of the indicators showing this change fluctuated, then my observation is a conclusive one in every respect.

The Fiction and Reality of the Mass Middle Class

I want to stress that I am not completely rejecting the existence of a "one hundred-million-strong middle class," or attempting to make light of history. To the contrary, I am confident that Japanese during the 1970s and 1980s undeniably lived in an atmosphere in which they were singing their praises of the affluence they were experiencing and the sense that things were only getting better. However, we should consider again the possibility that it was not so inevitable that we would someday be talking about "one hundred million hearts aflutter" in connection with the distribution of responses to queries about status identification. As Sudo Naoki, whose views are similar to mine, puts it: "The important thing is not status identification distribution. Rather, it is whether the contours of what people considered to be 'middle' were clearly defined or not" (Sudo 2010: 185).

That granted, the question remains as to why empirical sociologists of the day did not notice these simple inconsistencies in the data. Perhaps it was because they had already strongly prejudged what they would find before looking at the data; they were certain that the visible form of class that people embraced was changing to keep up with the times.

The story of how the distribution of status identification as an opinion statistic shifted from "lower" to "middle" at first glance dovetails well with various aspects of the social changes that unfolded in postwar Japan. Such aspects include the decline in the number of agricultural workers and increase in that of salaried workers; the fact that a growing segment of the population was able to get jobs that were more stable and better paying than those their parents' generation had held; news reports about the greater competitiveness of Japanese industries and annual increases in the Gross National Product that came in conjunction with bigger paychecks for blue-collar workers; and the fact that the presence of people with diverse status attributes really did increase around society's middle ranges.[11] For that reason, as Mori (2008) has also indicated, it seems likely that Japanese of that era in general, and not just sociologists, projected the spirit of the times—one that mixed affluence, leveling, and equalization among the members of society—onto opinion statistics that were otherwise ordinary. If this is so, then the gap between the reality of social consciousness and the way people talked about it can be seen as an ideological phenomenon that speaks to the wild enthusiasm of the era.

Finally, I want to touch on another caricature concerning status identifications. In the mid-2000s, the phrase "lower-class society" (*karyū shakai*) emerged seemingly overnight and captured the public's imagination. It was the product of a social analysis carried out and presented in a book with that very title by marketing analyst Miura Atsushi (Miura 2005). His argument, roughly speaking, was that the distribution of status identifications was starting to see "lower class" responses increase, coincident with the growth of an economically divided society during the administration of Prime Minister Koizumi Jun'ichirō. Miura warned that Japanese needed to keep a careful watch on this newly emergent social group.

As is plain from a single glance, Miura's claim that status identifications—whose configuration is not something any sociologist would expect to change after all these years—had begun to shift was little more than idle chatter. While the data do appear to show that a lower class was taking shape, viewed more rigorously from a quantitative social consciousness studies perspective we find no evidence other than the "data" that Miura himself obtained that shows a "lower-class society" is at hand (Kikkawa 2009).

In short, Miura's presentation was nothing more than a picture drawn on a lark—a degraded copy of the framework that had described the mass middle class with added embroidery. Stratification studies scholars have not taken it seriously and have dismissed the "lower class society" notion as something to be laughed off.[12]

But the term quickly captured the public spotlight at that time and was on everyone's lips. The general public was more attracted than they could imagine to a story that they seemed to already know. It seemed foreordained in the sense that with everyone already talking about a divided society, it must mean it is divided into winners and losers. What they wanted was a diagram they could understand of this mysterious "divided society" situation that economic liberalization had produced.

The sudden spate of interest in the notion of a "lower-class society" that emerged after the so-called "Lost Decade" of economic doldrums, as well as the spate for "mass middle class" that came after the period of high-speed growth, both contain elements of some value. They represent analyses of society that were developed based on first getting an accurate read on the social mentality at a given point in time. However, both relied on superficial data to present patterns of distribution in status identifications. From the perspective of quantitative social consciousness studies, these are discussions of a dubious sort—like smoke rising from a place where there's no fire. This is what makes these two fads homologous.

The question we are faced with, then, is sorting out what the best way will be for us to examine changes in the trends of the times that have developed in Japanese society in the quarter century since the start of the Heisei period. This matter will be taken up in the next chapter.

NOTES

[1] Other surveys such as the Japanese National Character Survey, the JGSS, and the various opinion surveys conducted by media organizations also repeatedly ask five-level status identification questions using almost equivalent queries and response options.

[2] *Fubyōdō shakai Nihon* is known for having pointed out the strength of inter-generational connections in occupational status, making it the first volley for the "unequal" or "divided" society discourse.

[3] For a detailed recapitulation of the course of the *chūryū* debate, please see Sudo (2010) and Kanbayashi (2012).

[4] These results show that the inflection point between eras came prior to 1975 more or less around the time of the oil shock (1973). Social survey data by nature tend to follow behind actual social realities; when we analyze it, we are verifying conditions a bit after the actual fact.

[5] Kanbayashi (2010a) has laid out the details in his discussion of the matter.

[6] Some comparative surveys conducted on a global scale use a 10-point status identification ladder (number line). Using numbers means the response categories can avoid having to rely on words; as a consequence, this approach is said to be the optimal one for comparing multiple cultures.

[7] Taking the SSM 1965 Survey as an example, the questionnaires were converted into numeric data immediately after the poll was conducted. However, in 1981 the SSM Trends Analysis Study Group led by Tominaga discovered inadequacies in the numeric data and re-coded it using the survey questionnaires that had been saved. Satō Toshiki and Tsuburai Kaoru further re-recoded it around 1994, again using the questionnaires. On each occasion, the aggregate results for the SSM Survey were corrected and in effect the situation at the times they respectively depicted changed. The original questionnaire forms have been saved for a half century now, and I understand there are scholars who would like to code them yet another time. This shows just how much emphasis is placed

on survey questionnaires in their role as the original wellspring for the facts that govern the authenticity of quantitative findings.

⁸ The difference in response distributions is significant by the 1% level under the Wilcoxon signed-rank test.

⁹ The ratio of men increases when responses are limited to "head of household or similar." We know there is a greater tendency for men to identify with lower statuses than women (Sudo 2009). From this, it may be surmised that there were more "lower" responses until 1969.

¹⁰ Michael Hout has examined status identifications in the American GSS Survey across a 20-to-30 year timespan. He did not find any major changes in response distributions across different eras. The same state of affairs persisted, with around 90% of the valid responses indicating respondents who self-identified as either middle or working class (Hout 2008).

¹¹ The gossip that purported these structural changes had produced the mass middle class (*naive realist reflection assertion*) was not supported by the data. Observers have repeatedly suggested that some more complicated mechanism is hiding somewhere (Naoi 1979; Seiyama 1990). The fact is, it was pointed out at a relatively early stage that the relationship between high-speed economic growth and the mass middle class contains puzzles that defy explanation.

¹² *Karyū shakai* was published in 2005, the same year another SSM Survey was conducted. However, the format of response options was changed slightly in the SSM 2005 Survey. This was due to a change from the face-to-face interview method for the status identification survey that had been used for 50 years running to a leaving-self-administrated method. As a consequence, scholars in quantitative social consciousness studies lost the opportunity to show the general public the results of their comparisons between points in time and encourage a correct understanding of them (Satō 2009).

CHAPTER 5
From Mass-Middle-Class Society to Mass-Inequality Society

The phenomenon of a mass middle class—as to be expressed "one hundred million hearts beating as one"—certainly existed in Japan. However, the middle-class consciousness (seen in the distribution of responses to questions about status identification) at its epicenter was not necessarily the appropriate indicator for exhibiting this social consciousness phenomenon. While the specifics of this may be somewhat complicated, this is the conclusion that we arrived at in the previous chapter. Accordingly, in this chapter I will change the yardstick I use for measuring social mentality as we observe how the character of the times changed from the 1980s to the present.

Redefining Mass Middle Class

First, consider the mass middle class as an ideological phenomenon (i.e., false social consciousness). In the 1980s, many Japanese trying to catch a glimpse of themselves in the mirror set their eyes on the data coming out of opinion surveys. Underneath that interest lay their uncertainties about what the current form of a rapidly changing Japanese society was, paired with their desires to sort out where they fit into it. The result was that most people took society in its entirety as their reference group, one with a membership defined by the idea, "I am the same as other Japanese." The spate of *Nihonjinron*-based theorizing that emerged at this time provides evidence that the overall image of an ostensibly ethnically homogeneous society possessing favorable unique characteristics served as the wellspring for Japanese identity.

In such an atmosphere, once academic experts began talking about a "mass middle class" it is not surprising that the populace developed the tendency to self-assimilate in the direction of the standard value (correspondent with mode and median) that reference group presented. Accordingly, people who one might otherwise expect to see themselves as "upper" or "lower" if they were to accurately assess their respective statuses on their own instead tended to suspend judgment and avowed they were in the "middle." Even those who made a point of declaring that they belong to a category such as "upper middle" and or "upper lower" that stands slightly apart from the modal one ("lower middle") may very well have made a judgment based not on an accurate status assessment but rather due to a mechanism skewed by the gravitational pull of "mass middle class."

From our standpoint, demonstrating each and every part of this past process would be unrealistic. However, at the time many researchers had already noticed that something had become a little odd about the state of the social mentality. This was clearly demonstrated by the fierce controversy that broke out over the mass-middle-class phenomenon focusing on the discrepancy between the objective stratification structure and the nature of subjective response.[1]

Among those describing the trend toward the middle range as illusory was Kishimoto Shigenobu. He argued that for everyone to now claim that they were part of the "middle" did not mean a peaceful, rich, leveled, and equal society had come into being, and he warned that all the points being touted mixed both fact and fiction (Kishimoto 1978). The evidence came from various places: the fact that most of Japan's middle strata lived in "rabbit hutch" apartments (the small residences situated in four- or five-story public housing projects) meant they were not comparable to the middle classes in North America or Europe, social disparities persisted unchanged in the postwar period, and inequalities remained deep-rooted in intergenerational relationships and educational opportunities. In the period's waning years, Imada Takatoshi would go on to label the controversy the "fantasy game of middle class" (*chūryū no gensō gēmu*). He opined: "It's not the case that everyone imagined the middle class was real and then determined they, too, were in the 'middle.' . . . People understood from the start that it was a fantasy and knowingly played (or pretended to play) the game" (Imada 1989: 27).

Based on the foregoing, we can redefine the mass middle class (in its guise as social mentality) as presenting a state of affairs in which it is difficult to specify why someone chooses (or does not choose) to describe themselves as being in the "middle." Reframing a social mentality of such uncertainty into a form that would be opperationable through survey data analysis could ease this problem. Using the framework of quantitative social consciousness studies, we can employ a social consciousness studies-type regression model to examine whether the social mentality changes when our metaphorical adjusting screw somewhere in society is turned. We could then set our focus on the relationship between objective stratification variables and subjective status identities. This would permit us to operationalize this otherwise difficult situation, turning it into one where the defining powers (causal explanatory power) that such stratification variables as an advanced education, a high occupational status, and economic power have on status identification are weak.

With that in mind, in this chapter I will shift the analytical focus of status identification from changes in form to changes in causality. By probing just how certain the ties are between objective and subjective status, I hope to explain the mechanisms by which the social mentality shifted from the condition of a mass-middle-class society to that of a mass-inequality society over the next quarter century.[2]

Enhancing Causal Explanatory Power

I will use for my analysis the men and women between 25 and 59 years old who were respondents in the SSM 1985 Survey and the SSP-I 2010 Survey. The method will be an OLS regression analysis, with the dependent variable being five-level status identification. Setting gender (0 for males and 1 for females) and age as control variables, I will look at the influence (direct effects) that the independent variales of educational background (years of schooling), the logarithmic value of ho that the indepedent variables usehold income, and occupational category (using upper class white collar as the reference category, with lower class white collar, self-employed, skilled blue collar, unskilled blue collar, farm worker, and unemployed as dummy variables [Erikson and Goldthorpe 1992]). These are the ingredients for the typical social consciousness studies-type regression model that will be used throughout most of the rest of this book.

Table 5-1 shows the results of the analysis on five-level status identifications for 1985, while Table 5-2 shows those for 2010 (hereafter, unless otherwise explicitly noted, all tables denote statistically significant figures with * at the level of 5%, and ** at the level of 1%). The first thing that catches the eye here is the fact that the coefficient of determination indicating the amount (as a percentage) of causal explanatory power of the entire model grew about 2.5 times over the quarter-century (adjusted R^2 = .068→.173). Looking more closely at the nature of the changes based on the size and significance of the individual regression coefficients, the positive effect of household incomes indicating the wealth of household budgets stands noticeably out (β = .210) in 1985. Adding in the slight positive effect of educational credentials, the effects of occupational status (i.e., an upper-class white-collar individual would have a status identification somewhat higher than that of a skilled blue-collar individual) shows this to be a comparatively simple causal structure.

For 2010, on the other hand, the regression coefficients were all statistically significant with regard to all of the independent variables. Comparing this to 1985, we can see that the effects of economic power remained at roughly the same level while those of educational attainment and category of occupation increased. This contributed to an increase of causal explanatory power.[3] The fact that it became possible to comprehensively evaluate not only economic power but also educational attainment and occupational status suggests that people had become more conversant about and aware of a pluralistic class structure.

Figure 5-1 illustrates this in modal form. We already saw in the last chapter the lack of change in the distribution pattern of status identifications itself between 1985 and 2010, but the determining structure of those identifications changed

Table 5-1 Determinants for Five-Level Status Identification in 1985

	Correlation		Coefficient		Coefficient (standardized)	
	r	Sig.	B	S.D.	β	Sig.
Gender (male = 0, female = 1)	.057	**	.156	.040	.088	**
Age (25–59)	−.013		.000	.002	.002	
Education (years)	.127	**	.021	.008	.065	**
Household income (logged)	.236	**	−.279	.027	.210	**
Upper white (I + II), (reference)						
Lower white (III)	.027		−.089	.056	−.039	
Self-employed (I + Vab)	−.006		−.062	.061	−.024	
Skilled manual (V + VI)	−.047	*	−.110	.060	−.045	
Non-skilled manual (IVc)	−.085	**	−.187	.058	−.083	**
Agricultural (VIIab)	−.004		−.021	.080	−.006	
Unemployed	−.003		−.106	.066	−.044	
Coefficient of determination (R^2)	.071	**	Adj. R^2	.068	**	

*: p < .05, **: p < .01   n = 2590

Table 5-2 Determinants for Five-Level Status Identification in 2010

	Correlation		Coefficient		Coefficient (standardized)	
	r	Sig.	B	S.D.	β	Sig.
Gender (male = 0, female = 1)	.057		.161	.041	.101	**
Age (25–59)	.022		.005	.002	.064	**
Education (years)	.279	**	.069	.011	.175	**
Household income (logged)	.302	**	.198	.023	.218	**
Upper white (I + II), (reference)						
Lower white (III)	.032		−.218	.061	−.107	**
Self-employed (I + Vab)	−.060	*	−.342	.074	−.126	**
Skilled manual (V + VI)	−.052	*	−.235	.072	−.094	**
Non-skilled manual (IVc)	−.191	**	−.449	.067	−.204	**
Agricultural (VIIab)	−.068	**	−.644	.161	−.098	**
Unemployed	−.012		−.209	.064	−.104	**
Coefficient of determination (R^2)	.178	**	Adj. R^2	.173	**	

*: p < .05, **: p < .01   n = 1482

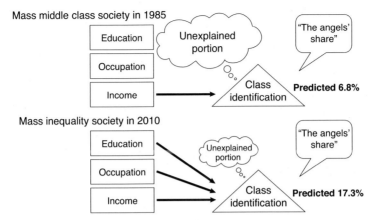

Figure 5-1   Summary of Changes during 25 Years

quietly but considerably during those years. First, for 1985 the total amount of the variation of status identification unexplained by the stratification variables (residual variance in the regression formula) is large. Even if we subtract the fact that this includes a certain amount of variation among the respondents that is difficult to remove from social survey data ("the angels' share"), the situation is still such that the mechanism by which respondents self-identified their status contained distortions and errors (the unexplained portions) to a comparatively large degree.

On the other hand, the total amount of unexplained variation for 2010 was relatively small. Once a researcher heard someone's educational background, occupational status, and household income, they could now make a more definite guess about the stratum with which that individual self-identified.[4]

Naturally, it is difficult to ascertain the characteristics of the social mentality from looking at the situation in 1985 in isolation. Only when viewed in comparison with the situation a quarter century later in 2010 does it become plainly evident that people in that era had no set criteria for self-identifying with one or another status. In short, the situation was we don't really know on what basis people were identifying with the "middle"; that in itself can indeed be said to have been the actual form of that social mentality known as mass-middle-class society.

Furthermore, this cross-time comparison also delineates the characteristic features of the era defined by 2010. In addition to economic power, people expanded their view to also take in educational attainment and occupational status to get an accurate fix on their own statuses in industrial society. The plurality and accuracy of these status assessments is itself the outstanding feature of the social mentality of today's *mass-inequality society*—a label I venture to assign because of the trend toward heightened knowledgeability and awareness of the hierarchy in statuses that presented itself among all respondents.

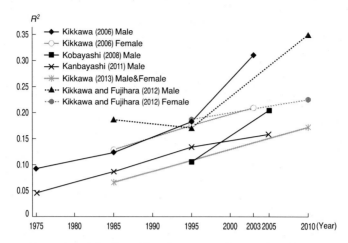

Figure 5-2　The Quiet Transformation of Status Identification (Increase in Coefficients of Determination)

The Quiet Transformation of Status Identification

Over the quarter century when the proportion of people self-identifying with the "middle" did not budge, it was already well-known that the relationship between stratification variables and status identification had strengthened. This proposition was referred to in academic circles as "*the quiet transformation of status identification.*" I first pointed out this transformation in an earlier work, where I drew on evidence from the period from 1975 to 1995 (Kikkawa 1999).[5] Using the effects of economic power as the focal point, I interpreted that 1985—a year right on the eve of the bubble economy—stood at a transitional point where changes in objective stratification variables were becoming more strongly associated with subjective status identifications. I also demonstrated that the contemporary determinant structure—in which individuals are aware of which strata they fit into based on multiple factors, including economic power, occupational status, and educational attainment—had taken shape by the post-bubble year of 1995. In a later work, I showed that the causal explanatory power of this transformation has risen further since the start of the 2000s (Kikkawa 2006).

This quiet transformation has gradually strengthened the causality between stratification variables and status identity. Researchers have subjected it to further examination, adjusting such factors as survey date, respondents, and the numbers and properties of the inputted variables. In all cases, they have confirmed similar transitions, based on as much as 40 years of data for Japan dating back to the 1970s (Kikkawa 2008; Kobayashi 2008; Sudo 2010; Kanbayashi 2010a, 2010b; Tanioka 2012; Kikkawa and Fujihara 2012).

Figure 5-2 collectively shows the growth of the coefficients of determination reported on in those studies. Given the various constraints on time-series data from Japanese social stratification surveys,[6] it is difficult to use the same analytical model to make simple cross-time comparisons among multiple points in time. However, the results of various studies make manifest the fact that causal explanatory power has steadily improved as the years have gone by.

This quiet transformation in status identifications from the era of the mass-middle-class society to that of the mass-inequality society is perhaps not yet widely recognized either among the general public or in global social science circles. Nonetheless, the distribution of "middle" responses that in the previous chapter highlighted the weaknesses of rationales does allow us to see that there has been a definite change in the social mentality across eras. We need not rely only on our impressions to say that the mass-middle-class society has ended and a mass-inequality society has arrived—it is a transformation that can be plotted on a graph and be shown to have definitely grown.

The Mechanism behind Era Change

We turn next to the question of what mechanism caused this quiet transformation to occur. Addressing an issue on the frontiers of research means we lack theories as yet that can offer decisive proof for one or another proposition. Nonetheless, with an adequate accumulation of descriptive facts, drawing inductive corollaries lies within the realm of possibility.[7] Care must also be taken so that any explanations offered that rely on feelings do not duplicate the kinds of mistakes that were made with respect to the mass-middle-class phenomenon. These caveats in mind, I will lay out the series of findings and interpretations that scholars have offered to date.

First, a number of measurable facts have already been identified about this quiet transformation. In my own research, I found that the fluctuations that emerged in the associative structure formed by educational attainment, occupational status, and economic power—that is to say, in the social strata themselves—did not have sufficient influence to sway the determinant structure of status identifications (Kikkawa 1999). The quiet transformation thus was not something that induced changes in patterns on the "hardware" side of society, like a weakening in the cohesiveness among stratification variables or increased inconsistencies in status. Rather, it was a development in which the relation between objective and subjective status themselves became stronger as time went by.

Second, the transformation did not emerge as a result of changes in the birth cohort. Analyses comparing survey results between two points in time focusing on the same cohorts clearly show the transformation was a product of people from the same cohort changing their perceptions of status between eras (Kikkawa 1999, 2006; Kanbayashi 2010b).

Based on this evidence, I am of the view that 1975 marked an era in which the causal explanatory power of status identification was scant; 1985 was one that had an aggregation of prescriptive factors for status identification oriented to the effects of economic power; and 1995 was one in which people used multiple standards for identifying their own status. The situation in 2010 that I present in this chapter shows that this latter era of multiple standards is not yet over; what's more,

Table 5-3 Coefficients of Determination (R^2) of Socioeconomic Status for Subjective Social Status (Multiple Indicator)

	1985	1995	2010	(year)
Japanese Male	.187	.173	.352	
Japanese Female		.187	.226	

	1987	2000	2010	(year)
American Male	.574	.639	.571	
American Female	.455	.518	.497	

Note: The result of multigroup SEM by maximum likelihood estimation, cited from Kikkawa and Fujihara (2012).

the connection between stratification variables and status identification has grown even stronger.

A more recent study used GSS data to compare this cross-time change in Japan with trends over the same period in the U.S. As Table 5-3 shows, that work found that in Japan the status-relatedness of status identification increased over time (for example, among men $R^2 = .187 \rightarrow .352$), but in the U.S.—where status-relatedness was already higher than in Japan—there was almost no change at all (for example, among male $R^2 = .574 \rightarrow .571$) (Kikkawa and Fujihara 2012).

To summarize the findings thus far, the quiet transformation was not the outcome of some fluctuation in the stratification structure or a change of generations. Rather, it was a product of people having changed their ways of thinking as years went on. Furthermore, we have also seen that no such change occurred in the U.S., at least, during this same time period. These are the conditions we must bear in mind, then, as we consider next why people became more conversant—"literate," as it were—about status identity.

At present, the item of greatest interest is the effects produced by the slowdown in social change over the period (an era change in the social structure). I've already noted that the associative structure of independent variables (stratification variables) did not transform much during this period. Now, I want to consider whether or not it was macro structural changes covering society in its entirety, as opposed to the associative structure of social attributes for individuals, that induced conditions that made it easy for people to overlook status positioning.

During the era of the mass-middle-class society, an individual looking back at their youth and at their parents' generation would see that there were huge differences in the standards of affluence. This was apparent whether they considered occupation, income and assets, or educational background. That state of affairs can be observed on Figure 5-3. I simplified the ways in which status is inherited there, depicting it with four arrows; they represent maintaining upper status, moving up, moving down, and stagnating in the lower status. In addition to the rise in their absolute standards for affluence compared to their parents' generation, some people here are smiling especially broadly for they have been able to move from a

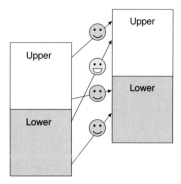

Figure 5-3 Class Identification in the Era of Mass-Middle-Class Society

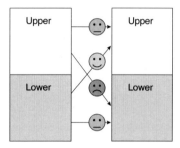

Figure 5-4 Class Identification in the Era of Mass-Inequality Society

lower to an upper status. They were known as the "new middle mass" (Murakami 1984).

In any case, the point we should note in this figure is that not only these "upward movers'" but even people who in comparative terms had stagnated in a lower status or moved downward, still had positive states of mind. The era was one in which few people saw their standards of living decline, since the standards of affluence had risen for everyone. Given the general feeling of well-being, it would have been difficult for someone to pay attention to the fact that their own position was dropping in relative terms. Additionally, with the social structure in constant change it was also possible to feel optimistic about the future, i.e., "I may have not have caught the first boat, but sooner or later my own ship will come in." People working in old-style independent businesses like small shopkeepers and so forth (the old middle class) in 1985 were likely grasping at straws of this ilk.

All told, in an era when affluence had dramatically expanded, figuring out where someone was situated in society relative to someone else was difficult to begin with; furthermore, people just didn't think it was particularly important. We can therefore infer that many people blindly embraced positive images about the statuses they had achieved in vertical comparison with their own past selves ("I'm able to lead a richer life now compared to what I could in the past") rather than by making horizontal comparisons with their neighbors.

The situation today, however, long after the end of the era of rising statuses, is one of leveling out. The gap has shrunk between the standards of affluence from when someone has set out on their life and those of where they have reached now. Those who are maintaining their upper status and those who are stagnating in the lower status are not experiencing many changes in their standards of living as the years go by. As Figure 5-4 suggests, it is difficult to determine if these individuals feel happy to have maintained their status, or if they see not having risen higher as a bad thing. Regardless, what can be said with certainty is that because living standards in society as whole remained almost entirely unchanged, it became possible for people to coolly ascertain their own status identities—i.e., determine where they fit into society—and it also became easier to figure out where others stood as well.

That figure reflects the fact that standards of affluence have been improving in an absolute sense only for those individuals who are moving up to a higher strata, as their smiles suggest. People in the downward-moving strata, on the other hand, are shown to be unreservedly troubled because for the first time they are experiencing a decline in their living standards. Overall, we see two categories of people: one that is troubled, and just one that is smiling. In short, even if the way the four arrows intersect (the composition of inequality) for example were to go unchanged, when the standards of affluence for society as a whole remain largely the same the nature of peoples' consciousness of strata or class will differ radically from that of the previous era.

Indeed, many phenomena today begin to make sense if we compare Figures 5-3 and 5-4: the striking fact that people in lower strata judge themselves to be in a lower class, the fact that people are becoming more vocal with their worries about how their standard of living may drop if they cannot succeed in a divided society, and the fact that the observer gets a very strong sense that the compositions of the upper and lower strata are becoming set in stone or keeping others out.

The foregoing interpretation is one I offered in 2009 in *Gakureki bundan shakai*. Sudo has made a similar observation: "People may find it difficult to get an accurate read on what is happening when society goes through intense changes, but as the situation calms down and society stabilizes doing so tends to become easier" (Sudo 2010: 200). Invoking Sudo, Kanbayashi adopted a similar position. "In a low-growth rate era, changes in a society's economic and living standards slow down. Under such conditions, it is conceivable that as time passes people's class standards become more defined, as they accumulate and share among themselves information about living standards and economic differences. Put another way, in a slow-growth era the more time that passes by the more 'visible' the real state of society becomes. For that reason, the correspondence relationship between status identification on the one hand and socioeconomic status and standards of living on the other is reflected by the actual situation; as a result, it is believed that the relationship between consciousness and objective socioeconomic variables becomes stronger (Kanbayashi 2011: 176)."[8] The view we all share is that the plateau situation that had long prevailed has been replaced by one that has seen us gradually wake up to the image we have of classes and status today.

This can be likened to a footrace in that when everyone is running full out, individual runners tend to have little interest in where they are within that group and are not really giving it much attention anyway. But when everybody stops and remains in place for a while, runners will start to look around to notice what's different about everyone else and get a more specific sense of where they are in the pecking order.

On the other hand, keep in mind also that status awareness remained consistently high in U.S. society. There, people did not experience conditions like those Japan's mass middle class faced, who scarcely had the chance to plant their feet on the ground, so to speak, due to the rapid pace of growth.

The foregoing is largely hypothetical reasoning that will require further investigation. What I can say here is that this is a powerful approach for explaining the mechanisms of the quiet transformation that led from enthusiasm to diversification, and it does so in a form that is not inconsistent with the circumstantial evidence.

What Is the Era of the Mass-Inequality Society Like?

The changes involving status identification presented in this chapter provide significant clues for helping us to understand what the era of the mass-middle-class society was like. They hint also at what that of the mass-inequality society confronting us now will be like.

Japanese frequently look back on the society of 1985 as one wreathed in brightness and a feeling of security. However, stratification survey data do not provide any objective facts that would confirm differences had been leveled or inequalities eliminated to any considerable degree in the 1970s and 1980s. The communal image of having achieved a society that was affluent, leveled, and equal provides a view of what the social mentality was like through and through.

The facts presented in this chapter that allow us to understand conditions during that era show that people of the time were quite interested in their status—meaning the mass middle class—but lacked the necessary literacy for getting a clear read on its form. Regardless, given that so many Japanese were drawn strongly toward the society's center, the way people approached status identification in the mass-middle-class society of 1985 can be defined as a *state of illusory leveling*.

On the other hand, people have been saying for nearly a decade that Japan has become an unequal or divided society. Studies focusing on class structure and microeconomics have not been able to obtain any definite evidence showing that society is becoming unequal or that the divides within it are growing. Research conducted near the turn of the century tell us there was talk that the Gini coefficient representing income inequality was trending upward (Tachibanaki 1998) and that there was a growing tendency for the stratum of the white-collar class to be locked down (Satō 2000). These can be said to be harbingers of the discourse on social inequality. However, subsequent evidence to the contrary has upended both of these claims completely.⁹ As to objective conditions of inequality from 1985 to the present, based on the SSM 2005 Survey the strong understanding currently is that the situation remains that of a plateau (Ishida and Miwa 2011). In short, the inequality society that has been subject of so much noisy discussion also seems to possess aspects of a transmutation in the social mentality; this phenomenon, too, is not accompanied by any objective changes in the stratification structure.

The findings presented in this chapter on this point show the following: it is now possible for Japanese to surmise the status identity of one of their fellows with 2.5 times greater certainty than a quarter century ago if they inquire about their household income, final level of education completed, and occupational status. Simply put, contemporary Japanese are more literate now about the complexly intertwined configurations that status boundaries—i.e., disparities—take; they can now get an unerring grasp of where each person fits in. The variations in status identification that roughly correspond to those of a normal distribution have stabilized into an accumulation of mechanisms for making determinations coolly and without hesitation. The blind pull of centripetal force that once existed is no more. As a result, status identification within Japanese society in 2010 can now be said to be in *a state of disillusioned inequality*.

The present era is one in which we who are alive today must remember that we—having aroused ourselves from the wild but temporary enthusiasms of growth—will have to continue to cope with conditions of inequality, and that their pattern cannot be changed to any considerable degree. Society is now one in which everyone has a grasp on the boundaries and vertical relationships between themselves and their fellows. It is one where those whose status is lower sense that is so, and those whose status is upper similarly are aware of it. This is an ideal society in the sense that everyone understands it. However, living directly faced by inequalities is more difficult than living in an erstwhile mass-middle-class society.

While the mass-middle-class society may have been illusory, you could be happy in it. The mass-inequality society, in contrast, is one with less happiness because there are no illusions. Moreover, it is deadlocked, with conditions like the plateau period that are difficult to modify. Thinking of the situation this way gives rise to fleeting thoughts about which society is more desirable, but regardless, the only choice we Japanese today have is to coolly confront the conditions of our own society.

NOTES

[1] Mori views the mass-middle-class phenomenon as a sort of "normalcy mechanism" that began to operate after Japan recovered from the shock of defeat (Mori 2008). However, I have found no other interpretations that see the mechanisms of normalcy operating in the social mentality of this era.

[2] The issue of quantitative analyses examining the bivariate relationship between status identification and stratification variables was taken up repeatedly from the 1970s to the first half of the 1990s. Naoi Michiko carefully reviewed cross-tabulation tables to tease out the mechanisms by which an individual self-identified as "middle" when objective

class conditions exceeded those of a certain standard, as well as those by which they self-identified as "upper" based on still higher standards. However, she was unable to discover the system by which people made precise strata assessments (Naoi 1979). Mamada Takao followed up on Naoi's work with studies of his own, but he reached no definite conclusion in his analyses, either (Mamada 1990).

Seiyama coined the term "naive realist reflection assertion" (*soboku jitsuzai han'ei-ron*) to describe approaches that attempt to unravel who self-identified as "middle" and why their numbers increased by using such simple measures as objective class and subjective response. He rejects the possibility of its subsistence (Seiyama 1990). Studies attempting to discover such simple rules are all certain to end in failure, which is why the mass-middle-class phenomenon has frequently been deemed an insoluble puzzle.

[3] This reading is not a matter of stating impressions, but rather is based on conclusions obtainable from other analyses (Kikkawa and Fujihara 2012).

Furthermore, when gender differences have been input as a control variable across both points in time, a significant trend emerges in that women identify with higher statuses than men. Sudo (2009) has conducted a detailed investigation of this deeply interesting phenomenon of women identifying with higher statuses despite being in a minority position when it comes to power than men in their majority position do.

[4] While it is not possible to say with certainty just how much of "the angels' share" (the error variance in a social survey that cannot be eliminated) is included here, based on experience the nearly 18% explanatory power of the social consciousness studies-type regression model used to present the analytical results for 2010 is close to the upper limits for quantitative social consciousness studies of Japan. The figures have been created with such substantial explanatory power in mind.

[5] That evidence demonstrated that immediately after the period of high-speed economic growth the causal explanatory power of the stratification variable with respect to status identification was even more tenuous than it was in 1985.

[6] The ideal is to conduct surveys with exactly the same designs repeatedly on a regular basis. However, at some points in time the needed variables were not included, data on women was not collected, the survey modes were different, or the age groups surveyed shifted from year to year.

[7] Given that the quiet transformation was the product of using a simple causal model to create a trend-oriented description about the realities of relationships among variables, the researcher needs to adopt a mathematical approach to develop an "explanation" of the scientific mechanisms present within. That may indeed be the natural tack to take, but the fact is even mathematically deductive theories do not have precision sufficient to "explain" the mechanisms of an actual society the way that, say, the laws of physics predict experimental results (Kōsaka 2000; Hamada 2012). Accordingly, we should see this field in its current state as one in which descriptions of current conditions and theoretical "explanations" mutually supplement one another.

[8] Seiyama (1990) was the first to point out that the standards people use for evaluating their status change with the times.

[9] For details, please see Kikkawa (2006).

PART III

WHAT HAPPENED TO ORIENTATION?

CHAPTER 6

The Quiet Retirement of Traditionalism–Modernism

Pondering the modernity of social consciousness was an omnipresent issue that distinguished the 20th century. Digging further into the significance of this leads one to realize that the focus in fact was on what it meant to be an individual as a constituent subject of democracy, or perhaps on the attitudes that people had toward it. Accordingly, the next task for us to tackle in this book is to think about the social mentality of democracy.

Modern Society and Traditionalism

Modernity is usually understood as the reverse of traditionalism. As a term that refers to the society from the era predating the modern one, traditional society supposes there is an "absolute zero" point somewhere in social change. In theory originating with Max Weber and other Western sociologists, its component elements include conventionalism, a sense of magic or enchantment, ceremonialism, a closed nature, formalism, and a stress on *Gemeinschaft*. These point to social conditions that are consistent but irrational, at the opposite pole to modern industrial society and its pursuit of goal-oriented rationalism.

However, it would be incorrect to say "traditional society" has only one pattern; moreover, no one has ever seen its "real" form in the first place. Traditionalism as conceived in sociology is quite simply an ideal type for suitably understanding the vectors present in contemporary society. The movement that produces distance from the "absolute zero" point as idealized therein is called modernization; the definition of a modern society is a society that lies along that vector.

Accordingly, though it may be a slightly paradoxical way of putting it, the very facts that traditional society explicitly figures as our absolute zero, and that traditionalism is incorporated within the system as an indispensable element, comprise an essential prerequisite for (first) modernity (Giddens 1991). For that reason, we regard the situation where people living in a given era do not refer to, or conform to tradition (which does not necessarily mean affirming its values), as the sign of the arrival of reflexive modernity that lies still further ahead.

In social consciousness studies, investigating traditionalism–modernism has been a major area of interest from the start. The ongoing effort in the contemporary era to ascertain what happened to this reference axis demonstrates the arrival of that era that has been much spoken of in sociological theory, reflexive modernity.

What Is Authoritarianism?

Throughout the world, essentially the same yardstick for measuring attitudes is used when examining the traditionalism submerged in the social mentality of contemporary people. That yardstick is the authoritarian attitude. That being the case, let us examine here what makes authoritarianism appealing as a sociological concept, and explore the role that this yardstick plays in social consciousness studies.

The authoritarian character refers to a personality type that extols and attempts to submit to authority, while simultaneously asking that it, too, can be that selfsame authority and make others submit to it. The question of what kind of authority is the object here deserves careful thought, but in any case in modern society it is traditional authority that is in mind. There are hardly any examples of authority with great power that has not been backed by tradition. The varied labels assigned to this concept have their origin here; they include authoritarian traditionalism, authoritarian conservatism, conventionalism, and even conventionality.

The concept of authoritarianism was extracted from mass psychology theory to explain fascism as the greatest historical fact of the 20th century. Fromm saw the rise of the Nazis in the 1930s as coming out of a deeply submerged sadomasochistic characteristic and psychological factor present among the German masses at the time (Fromm 1941). For a brief spell, the citizens of the Weimar Republic had obtained their freedom as modern individuals cut loose from primary ties (i.e., connections based on status or kinship). However, they also had economic liabilities as citizens of one of the defeated countries of World War I. The modern individual exists in a state where on the one hand they are free, and on the other they are without power, have lost their embedded affiliations, and are isolated. They also cannot escape from the need to continuously think introspectively about right and wrong when it comes to ethical norms, responsibility, and behavioral objectives. That is what it means to be one of the citizens who make up a democratic society, and that in turn is why the freedoms of modernity (democracy) that had been achieved so suddenly were not received as stable or comforting. The Weimar Germans eventually threw away the freedoms they had won and rushed to support Nazism. Their uncritical acceptance of powerful external authority and submission to it (masochism), paired with fierce attacks on others grounded in that authority (sadism), were an attempt to escape from the difficulties of facing up to a complex social environment with their autonomous selves not yet established. This, in sum, was the well-known mechanism of escape.

Fromm's study was superb for its thoroughgoing focus on the social consciousness of the people who had supported Hitler and had not seen Nazism as something that could simply be attributed to his personal insanity. That Fromm had deduced from this the Janus face of modern freedoms with their positives and negatives was a major achievement, as was his exposure of the authoritarianism that lurks in the hearts of millions. The approach that Fromm developed provided a means for understanding much about Japanese militarism despite its different historical and social context. Indeed, the concept of authoritarianism was a keystone for postwar social consciousness studies (Kido 1970).

The historical fact of fascism, which gave rise to authoritarianism research, already lies in the distant past. Nonetheless, the body of study it generated raises a number of issues for us to consider. First is that the concept of authoritarianism is not meant to be used for looking at pre-modernity. Rather, it is a superb *modern* thinking tool for addressing the strong yearnings for traditionalism embedded in 20th century society.

Second, the authoritarian attitude as a measurable operational variable has been refined to a considerable degree as a scale for social psychology. Research based on psychological measurements of authoritarian attitudes began with *The Authoritarian Personality*, produced by the a group of scholars at the University of California, Berkeley, that included social theorist Theodor W. Adorno (Adorno et al. 1950). This comprehensive, social sciences project undertaken in 1940s America showed that even certain clusters of ordinary citizens were easily attracted to antidemocratic propaganda.

The authoritarian attitude scale widely used today is modeled after the psychological indicators developed through a vast amount of trial and error in this and subsequent studies. It measures the strength of the inclinations to be subservient to external authority that lurk in the hearts of many. The method entails asking numerous peripheral questions while avoiding direct references to, say, fascism or xenophobic exclusionism, or bluntly asking reseach participants if they self-identify as authoritarian. The approach provides a means for avoiding bias that the socially desirable position of not seeing authoritarians as good people would otherwise engender. These studies succeeded in teasing out universal points of reference, unbiased toward one or another specific issue, to be found in the depths of the personalities of contemporary persons. Subsequent studies have measured authoritarian attitudes in Europe and East Asia among people of all ages and both genders using almost the same approach that was used in the U.S. This corpus of research confirmed that similar psychological operations are at work in any society.

In both theory and substance, authoritarianism is now regarded as a basic social attitude that strongly affects a range of expressive social phenomena, from nationalism and ethnicity to the patriarchal system and political conservatism. Owing to its central position and general utility, the authoritarian attitude as a tool has become distanced from its initial purpose of elucidating the psychology of fascism.

It now functions as an indicator for grasping the traditionalism in the social mentality that remains strongly rooted in modern society.

Self-Direction

A third characteristic of authoritarianism research that deserves mention is that while the traditionalism–modernism axis may be its primary subject, it has also regularly addressed social status-based differences in personality characteristics. Interest in the status aspects of authoritarianism originates with the historical fact that the strongest supporters of Nazism in German society during World War II were people such as small independent business owners who came from the urban lower-middle class (Fromm 1980). The stage upon which subsequent studies of mass society took place then moved to the U.S., where authoritarian leanings in the working class were a major focus of debate (Lipset 1959). As to contemporary Japanese society, scholars have noted a striking tendency toward authoritarianism among individuals who have completed only compulsory education (Naoi 1988; Kikkawa 1998; Todoroki 2000).

There is one study that has focused on the status aspects to authoritarianism from the standpoint of stratification studies rather based on the previous interest in fascism or traditionalism–modernism. That is *Work and Personality* (1983), a major survey data analysis-based study begun in the 1960s by two American scholars, Melvin Kohn, a sociologist of work and occupations, and his National Institutes of Health-based colleague Carmi Schooler. Also known in English-speaking academic circles as the Kohn-Schooler study, in Japan it is usually tagged "the WP Study" (*WP kenkyū*) (Kikkawa ed. 2007, 2012). The book's main subject was the causal cycle in social consciousness studies. This cycle is centered on the way a person's place in industrial society forms and reshapes their personality in general, and the way that personality in turn controls their social life (refer back to Figure 2-1). However, Kohn and Schooler paid little attention to status identification, the prototypical theoretical construct for this field. Their research interests focused completely on social orientations (intellectual flexibility and value preference), i.e., the degree to which people positively and spontaneously address their living environments as they go about their lives.

The members of a modern industrial society are quite deeply committed to vocational lives; unquestionably, that fact forms the point of contact between individuals and the industrial sector. If an individual is put in an environment where they can make decisions in their vocational life and design their jobs to suit themselves as they deal with complex, constantly changing conditions, it will enable them to mentally prepare themselves to act spontaneously and flexibly. Conversely, when an individual is put into a job situation where the work is quite routine and the actions they take are performed passively under the direction of a superior, there will be a strong tendency for them to be in sympathy with external authorities and established procedures.

Furthermore, differences in the social orientations of such individuals have repercussions in their approaches to how they work throughout their lives. *Work and Personality* clarified how such processes gave the vertical ordering of contemporary society uniform shape in both its hardware and software, and how the influences of these in turn played off one another. This finding is precisely the fundamental issue that social consciousness studies has investigated since Marx.

Self-direction is a key concept in this study. It is used to indicate the true nature of the status-relatedness with respect to both independent (stratification variables) and dependent variables (social attitudes). The concept carries a general idea of being able (and in the right living environment) to make personal decisions about your living situation and actively choose how to orient yourself toward it. At the opposite pole here is conformity, which entails passively submitting to the norms that society dictates and repeatedly making the same stereotypical decisions.[1]

Kohn and Schooler use the expression "self-directed orientation" for the reference axis of subjectivity that resonates with self-direction in working conditions. The concept pulls together those social attitudes (e.g., authoritarian attitude, feelings of alienation, self-esteem, anxiety, morality, and idea of conformity to a group) that have long been seen in sociological social psychology as having status-relatedness. We can think of this as the essence of status-relatedness in social orientation.[2] What they rediscovered to be the most potent indicator of how low someone's tendency toward self-direction was—in short, their tendency toward conformity—was the authoritarian attitude scale that originated in the Berkeley group's research. In keeping with *Work and Personality*, I will refer to this general concept below as authoritarian conservatism.

Given that the essence of rank ordering in the workplace is based on authoritarian human relationships, it is not difficult to imagine that authoritarian conservatism bears a particularly clear correspondence relationship with social status. Meanwhile, as Hans Eyseneck (1954), Milton Rokeach (1960), and then Kohn and Schooler (1983) have pointed out, low levels of flexibility in ways of thinking and in cognitive ability produce authoritarian tendencies in individuals. This is also a major component of status-relatedness in self-direction.

As I have already shown, early authoritarianism research saw an overabundance of conformity to authority among citizens as a pathological predisposition in modern society. The debate was framed from a perspective informed by ideas about the Enlightenment and its legacies, which is why "democratic"—representing the desired societal condition—was positioned with "authoritarian" as its polar opposite. In scholarship since the 1950s, the negative implications of authoritarianism that held it to be equivalent to antidemocratic had lessened, but researchers still used the term with sociopolitical nuances that equated it to a rigid conservative tendency.

What *Work and Personality* did was to drag the rediscovered self-direction concept away from that opposing pole and put it front and center. The study swept aside the concept's historical baggage and political aspects to emphasize only status-relatedness in social attitudes. It described the tendencies of people who lived in environments at society's upper levels where they could design their own lives as "self-direction," while the vague authoritarian tendencies among the people who went along with social conditions as already molded were described as "conformity." Viewed this way, the fact that strata-based differences in the self-direction orientation exist and reciprocally amplify one another does not inevitably mean constructs like "the elite vs. the masses" will arise to obstruct the practice of democracy. To the contrary, it becomes possible to see this merely as a necessary "gradient" that helps to stably maintain the social order.[3]

Thus, the concept of self-direction had an important mediating effect. It made it possible to take the reality discovered by 20th century authoritarianism research that traditionalism and status-relatedness overlap, chip away at that situation to find its more neutral implications, and then smoothly incorporate those in turn into contemporary quantitative social consciousness studies.

The self-direction concept was introduced to Japanese stratification consciousness research in the latter half of the 1970s. The process began with an international comparative survey related to *Work and Personality* (research project leader; Naoi Atsushi) carried out in 1979 by the then-Department of Sociology in the University of Tokyo's Faculty of Letters (Naoi 1987; Kikkawa ed. 2012). In tandem with this project, the members of that department also instigated the SSM 1985 Survey (research project leader: Naoi Atsushi) that provided the data for the first period addressed in this book. Using multiple approaches, these two surveys sought to shed light on the realities that Japan's middle strata faced. They targeted using conceptual axes other than status identification to get a multi-dimensional schime of the social mentality of the society's middle ranges. The expectation was that the questions authoritarian conservatism and the self-direction concept raised would remind specialists of the trends that had developed since the days of postwar social consciousness studies, and provide exactly the tool needed to carve out a new dimension to stratification consciousness (in the broad sense). Since then, Japanese sociologists have deemed this social attitude as providing the most useful perspective for observing the status-relatedness of social consciousness in sociological surveys done in the country (Kikkawa 1998).

The Trajectory of the Authoritarian Attitude

Employing the social consciousness studies-type regression model as I did in the previous chapter, here I have carried out a comparative analysis to see how the place of traditionalism–modernism in society changed from 1985 to the present. Given the limitations regarding the respondents chosen, survey methods, and question design in the poll data I used, I again will not be able to draw cross-time comparisons freely. For example, in the SSM 1985 Survey very few of the social attitude-related inquiries were directed to both men and women; unfortunately, only the men were asked about authoritarian conservatism.[4] Even in the most recent data, there are no signs that adult men and women were asked the battery of questions concerning authoritarian conservatism using the highly precise method of face-to-face interviews in the home; instead, I was forced to use data collected from either mail-in or leaving self-administered surveys.

In light of these circumstances, I decided to use the following procedure to observe cross-time changes in traditionalism–modernism. First, to get a sense of trends at different points of time, I examined data from the SSM Surveys for 1985 (face-to-face interviews in the home) and 2005 (leaving self-administered method) that allowed comparing authoritarian conservatism in male respondents. Next, for supporting evidence of those trends, I crosschecked by looking at changes in authoritarian conservatism among women during these periods, changes in authoritarian conservatism among both adult men and women from 1995 to 2010, and changes in attitudes toward gender-role segregation among women. Finally, I synthesized the results of previous studies to make arguments from a broad perspective about the trajectory that traditionalism–modernism followed over these years.

In this book, I use authoritarian conservatism as a yardstick generated by performing a principal component analysis on the responses to the following four yes-no questions. They constitute inquiries about authority, conservatism, conventionalism, and the tendency to entrust; all were translated from the questions used in *Work and Personality*.[5]

- One should always show respect to those in authority (*Ken'i no aru hitobito ni wa tsune ni kei'i o harawanakereba naranai*)
- It's wrong to do things differently from the way our forefathers did (*Izen kara nasarete kita yarikata o mamoru koto ga saijō no kekka o umu*)
- People who question the old and accepted ways of doing things usually just end up causing trouble (*Dentō ya shūkan ni shitagatta yarikata ni gimon o motsu hito wa, kekkyoku wa mondai o hikiokosu koto ni naru*)
- In this complicated world, the only way to know what to do is to rely on leaders (*Kono fukuzatsu na yononaka de nani o nasu beki ka shiru ichiban yoi hōhō wa, shidōsha ya senmonka ni tayoru koto de aru*)

Table 6-1 shows the results of the analysis for men using the 1985 data. It is important when it comes to the status-relatedness of the authoritarian attitude to know what the actual situation seemed to be—whether authoritarian inclinations were strong among people in all cases—before ascertaining which stratification variable contributes to their formation. If authoritarians are concentrated in a specific stratum of society, then regardless of what caused this it means there is a cluster of people who can be easily mobilized by extreme social movements. In 1930s Germany, for example, due to multiple overlapping social factors the authoritarian personality manifested itself chiefly among the lower middle classes (Fromm 1980).

Looking at this through the correlations (extent of apparent relationships) on the left side of Table 6-1, we see the coefficient between education and authoritarian conservatism is strongly negative ($r = -.317$). For the correlation between an attribute and an attitude to exceed 0.300 in social survey data means that it is so clear people can readily perceive it in the real world. In Japanese society in 1985, it was quite easy to sense that people with low levels of educational attainment (people who had completed only compulsory education) were authoritarians.

In fact, the following mechanisms are known to have been behind the strong

Table 6-1 Determinants of Authoritarian Conservatism in 1985 (Male)

	Correlation		Coefficient		Coefficient (standardized)	
	r	Sig.	B	S.D.	β	Sig.
Age (25–59)	.205	**	.015	.004	.134	**
Education (years)	−.317	**	−.091	.016	−.239	**
Household income (logged)	−.103	**	−.074	.062	−.045	
Upper white (I + II), (reference)						
Lower white (III)	.001		.283	.117	.092	*
Self-employed (I + Vab)	.028		.073	.107	.028	
Skilled manual (V + VI)	.035		.089	.112	.033	
Non-skilled manual (IVc)	.076	*	.161	.115	.059	
Agricultural (VIIab)	.106	**	.366	.168	.080	*
Unemployed	.017		−.124	.262	−.017	
Coefficient of determination (R^2)	.122	**	Adj. R^2	.113	**	

*: p < .05, **: p < .01   n = 834

connection between educational attainment and authoritarianism at the time. Among the birth cohorts (born between 1925 and 1960) being analyzed, there was a strong negative correlation between age and educational attainment. The effects of the rapid educational expansion after the war were such that the younger the person, the more likely they were a graduate of secondary or tertiary education. As a result, differences in birth cohort (the earlier someone was born the stronger their traditionalist orientation) overlapped with the effects of educational background (the less schooling someone had the more authoritarian they were). Additionally, around 10% of the individuals in the prime of life who had completed only compulsory education were from a cohort (born between 1925 and 1934) where the formal education they received before entering adulthood was the extremely militaristic one provided under the old primary education institutions known as "national people's schools" (*kokumin gakkō*). The seasoning that this education provided made authoritarian inclinations especially strong among the less educated persons who grew up before and during the war. On the other hand, the cohort of younger, college-educated persons raised after the war (e.g., individuals who were involved in the various campus conflicts) were quite strongly anti-authoritarian in orientation. Thus, a clear disparity had emerged in terms of educational background and age differences (Kikkawa and Todoroki 1996).

Having verified this gradient in the authoritarian characteristic over these years, I want next to examine the results of a regression analysis to uncover the determinants of authoritarian conservatism. First, the coefficient of determination (adjusted R^2 = .113) shows that there is a causal explanatory power of 11.3% for authoritarian conservatism when the combination of independent variables is adjusted for. This allows us to guess with a predictive power of 10%+ a person's

Table 6-2 Determinants of Authoritarian Conservatism in 2005 (Male)

	Correlation		Coefficient		Coefficient (standardized)	
	r	Sig.	B	S.D.	β	Sig.
Age (25–59)	.045		.004	.004	.035	
Education (years)	−.159	**	−.059	.020	−.138	**
Household income (logged)	−.049		−.087	.078	−.050	
Upper white (I + II), (reference)						
Lower white (III)	−.037		−.046	.137	−.014	
Self-employed (I + Vab)	.099	*	.238	.137	.077	
Skilled manual (V + VI)	.074		.071	.125	.028	
Non-skilled manual (IVc)	−.004		−.092	.131	−.034	
Agricultural (VIIab)	.006		−.018	.294	−.002	
Unemployed	−.033		−.329	.284	−.050	
Coefficient of determination (R^2)	.038	**	Adj. R^2	.024	**	

*: p < .05, **: p < .01   n = 649

authoritarianism score if we know their age, educational attainment, occupation, and income. The status-relatedness in this situation can be said to be relatively high. Incidentally, among men and women at this same (1985) point in time, the coefficient of determination for status identification remained at adjusted R^2 = .068 (Table 5-1).

Looking next at the (standardized) regression coefficients for individual causal effects, the deprivation effects that formal education has on authoritarian attitude—i.e., authoritarian inclinations grow weaker the more years of schooling someone has—are striking ($\beta = -.239$). The direct effect of birth cohort is also apparent in the tendency for someone to be more authoritarian the older they are ($\beta = .134$). A close reading of the significant effects apparent with regard to occupational status shows that being a lower ranked white-collar individual or a farmer strengthens authoritarian inclinations compared to upper class white-collar individuals (management and professionals), who constitute the reference category. While this agrees with the findings of *Work and Personality*, the influence of occupational status in Japan cannot be said to be as strong, relatively speaking.

Table 6-2, on the other hand, shows that the situation in 2005 was quite different. First, while the correlation shows that a slight education-related difference ($r = -.159$) remains, on the whole social attribute-based differences have attenuated. This greatly reduces the causal explanatory power of the model overall, and the coefficient of determination remains at just about 2.4% (adjusted $R^2 = .024$), or less than one-quarter of 1985 levels. Looking at the standardized regression coefficient for formative factors, the only thing that catch our eye is that the correlation between years of schooling and authoritarian attitudes materializes from a direct causal relationship ($\beta = -.138$).

Table 6-3 Determinants of Authoritarian Conservatism in 1982 (Married Female)

	Correlation		Coefficient		Coefficient (standardized)	
	r	Sig.	B	S.D.	β	Sig.
Age (25–59)	.157	**	.008	.006	.078	
Education (years)	−.211	**	−.069	.027	−.164	*
Household income (logged)	−.089		−.171	.092	−.098	
Upper white (I + II), (reference)						
Lower white (III)	.123	*	.263	.242	.126	
Self-employed (I + Vab)	.034		.212	.549	.021	
Skilled manual (V + VI)	−.139	**	−.494	.278	−.151	
Non-skilled manual (IVc)	.046		.025	.256	.010	
Agricultural (VIIab)	.135	**	.322	.286	.091	
Unemployed	−.132	**	−.085	.235	−.046	
Coefficient of determination (R^2)	.111	**	Adj. R^2	.089	**	

*: p < .05, **: p < .01   n = 376

These two sets of results make it plain that the status-relatedness of authoritarian conservatism produced in the 1980s by the synergies between educational effects and birth, compounded by the effects of occupational status, had lost its shape in the mid-2000s. In short, it was no longer easy to see where the authoritarian individuals were in society, and what social forces had produced them. The mention I have made of sociologists losing track of the social mentality refers precisely to this situation.

To be perfectly clear, this does not mean authoritarian conservatism no longer exists. True, findings from earlier research (Todoroki 2000) and opinion statistics have shown that authoritarian inclinations in society have been weakening. But the argument I am making here is based on a different aspect. Simply put, I believe that this social attitude variable has become ubiquitous in society, making it difficult to gauge.

What about women? As I already mentioned, the nature of the data from the SSM 1985 Survey bars us from learning about authoritarian conservatism among women at that time. Accordingly, I will instead use the data on married women from the 1982 *Work and Personality* survey conducted in Japan (Naoi ed. 1989; Kikkawa ed. 2012)[6] and on women in the SSM 2005 Survey (in both cases, women aged from 25 to 29) to make a visual comparison of the analytical results for authoritarian conservatism produced by the social consciousness studies-type regression model.

Table 6-3 shows that for 1982 the causal explanatory power was approximately 9% (adjusted R^2 = .089). The status-relatedness of authoritarian conservatism thus presents itself with relative clarity just as it did among men. Owing to the rather small sample size, the only thing significant about the regression coefficient

Table 6-4 Determinants of Authoritarian Conservatism in 2005 (Female)

	Correlation		Coefficient		Coefficient (standardized)	
	r	Sig.	B	S.D.	β	Sig.
Age (25–59)	−.095	*	−.016	.004	−.168	**
Education (years)	−.115	**	−.081	.026	−.150	**
Household income (logged)	−.065		−.009	.071	−.006	
Upper white (I + II), (reference)						
Lower white (III)	−.053		−.166	.128	−.074	
Self-employed (I + Vab)	.018		.070	.181	.019	
Skilled manual (V + VI)	.045		.164	.209	.037	
Non-skilled manual (IVc)	.040		.041	.150	.016	
Agricultural (VIIab)	.019		.145	.367	.018	
Unemployed	−.007		−.053	.124	−.026	
Coefficient of determination (R^2)	.041	**	Adj. R^2	.025	**	

*: p < .05, **: p < .01   n = 559

was that the less education someone had the greater their authoritarian attitude (β = −.164). Still, it was possible to see a trend largely similar to that revealed by the analyses of male subjects in the SSM 1985 Survey.

The result of the analysis for women in 2005 shown in Table 6-4, meanwhile, demonstrates that the causal explanatory power eventually declined to a considerable degree (adjusted R^2 = .025). Among the direct effects, what stands out is the fact that, if we add in the previously noted negative effects of education, we see that among the women of the present age (born between 1945 and 1980) it is the younger ones who are more authoritarian (β = −.168); at one time, of course, we would have seen an opposite tendency for new values to be replaced by old ones.

The foregoing analysis confirms the weakening in the status-relatedness of authoritarian conservatism to be a trend shared by men and women alike. Just to be sure, I will review the changes to the results of the analyses for authoritarian conservatism between 1995 and 2010 generated by the social consciousness studies-type regression model.[7] The 1995 data come from the SSM Survey (questionnaire B), while those for 2010 are from a national survey of almost the same scale (SSP-P 2010 Survey). The merit of these data sets is that their compositions allow for extracting the same principal component from samples that combine men and women. However, we should also be mindful of a methodological difference in that the former used face-to-face interviews conducted in the homes of subjects chosen by random sampling, while the latter was a mail-in survey sent to a master sample throughout the country (ages from 20 to 59).

Tables 6-5 and 6-6 present the results of these analyses. The transient conditions that existed between 1985 and 2005 can be seen in the results for 1995 whether we look at the coefficient of determination (adjusted R^2 = .058) or the size of the

Table 6-5 Determinants of Authoritarian Conservatism in 1995 (Male and Female)

	Correlation		Coefficient		Coefficient (standardized)	
	r	Sig.	B	S.D.	β	Sig.
Gender (male = 0, female = 1)	−.007		−.048	.056	−.024	
Age (25–59)	.124	**	.009	.003	.082	**
Education (years)	−.216	**	−.067	.013	−.151	**
Household income (logged)	−.115	**	−.130	.045	−.077	**
Farmer (reference)						
Professional	−.078	**	−.035	.153	−.011	
Exective	−.063	*	−.219	.182	−.043	
Clerical	−.079	**	−.074	.139	−.031	
Sales	.036		.111	.147	.036	
Skilled manual	.085	**	.094	.143	.034	
Semi-skilled manual	.047		.043	.148	.013	
Non-skilled manual	.058	*	.196	.177	.039	*
Unemployed	−.006		.002	.142	.001	
Coefficient of determination (R^2)	.065	**	Adj. R^2	.058	**	

*: p < .05, **: p < .01   n = 1523

Table 6-6 Determinants of Authoritarian Conservatism in 2010 (Male and Female)

	Correlation		Coefficient		Coefficient (standardized)	
	r	Sig.	B	S.D.	β	Sig.
Gender (male = 0, female = 1)	.002		−.059	.064	−.030	
Age (25–59)	−.055		−.007	.003	−.071	*
Education (years)	−.116	**	−.061	.015	−.125	**
Household income (logged)	−.042		−.014	.043	−.009	
Farmer (reference)						
Professional	−.004		.076	.124	.025	
Exective	−.069	*	−.151	.154	−.035	
Clerical	−.012		.037	.111	.015	
Sales	−.012		−.007	.132	−.002	
Skilled manual	.011		−.001	.127	.000	
Semi-skilled manual	.044		.120	.147	.029	
Non-skilled manual	.056		.297	.167	.059	*
Unemployed	.010		.063	.115	.026	
Coefficient of determination (R^2)	.026	**	Adj. R^2	.016	**	

*: p < .05, **: p < .01   n = 1227

effects of individual stratification variables. In contrast, the most recent (2010) results show that—even accounting for the differences in survey methods—the causal explanatory power derived from the stratification variable has markedly weakened (adjusted R^2 = .016). The authoritarian inclinations among the younger generation discovered in the analysis of women from 2005 are now apparent in the 2010 data for both men and women as a significant trend (β = -.071).

The weak but nascent tendencies toward traditional values and increasing conservatism among the younger generation will require careful probing in the future. If the 20th century relationship between age and conservatism (the older someone is the more conservative or conventional they are) that family sociology, gender studies, political sociology, cultural studies, and ethnic studies see as self-evident is weakening in the 21st century, then traditionalism's place in the Japanese social mentality must be seen as something that is truly decaying down to its roots.

Post-Modernization in Attitudes toward Gender-Role Segregation

To broadly gauge the course that the values conflict between traditionalism and modernism is taking, I want now to look at the trends in different eras regarding the attitudes in society toward gender-role segregation. This social attitude exists in an area where the family, work, and gender overlap; we can use it to measure the dimensions of the conflict between emphasizing the differences in the male-female roles or emphasizing their equality. Particular attention should be paid to the fact that the "traditional" view of family with gender-role segregation laid the foundations for the existence of the modern family, that being the nuclear family comprising a salaried worker husband and a full-time housewife. This social attitude is a primary indicator for taking stock of traditionalism, which was embedded as an indispensable component of modern 20th century society.

Two questions were used here to get a bead on gender-role attitudes. The first is a yes-no question regarding the opinion, "The man should work outside and the woman should maintain the household" (referred to below as the "inside-outside role" attitude). This is a social attitude that has had a major influence on family sociology in Japan; the very text of the question alludes to the matter of work/life balance that is much-discussed in Japanese society at present. The other is a yes-no question that addresses a way of thinking: "Men play the central role and women play a supporting role" (referred to below as the "master-subordinate role" attitude). Today, in all parts of society the male-female relationship as a question of privilege vs. disadvantage is a topic of debate.

Both questions have been asked in several surveys conducted since the SSM 1985 study. Usually, four response options are offered: "agree," "relatively agree," "relatively disagree," and disagree." I will again use the same social consciousness studies-type regression model for the analysis, with women between 25 and 59 as its subjects. Given the limitations in comparable data, I decided to look at the results of the SSM 1985 and 2005 Surveys with respect to inside-outside attitude, and the results of the SSM 1985 Survey and the SSP-I 2010 Survey with respect to master-subordinate one.[8]

Looking first at the inside-outside attitude, the explanatory power of stratification variables in 1985 as shown on Table 6-7 was comparatively high (adjusted R^2 = .070). Education and birth cohort-effects manifested themselves clearly; the better educated or younger the subject, the more likely they were against gender-role segregation. Furthermore, there was also an occupational effect in that women having upper-class white-collar jobs (the reference category for analysis) tended to be strongly opposed to gender-role segregation. The fact that women's stances toward gender-role segregation vary significantly based on the kind of jobs they do can be said to have a pertinent result in the form of how they think about such segregation. We can also see with respect to the overlap between education and birth-cohort effects that there are homologies with the authoritarian conservatism among male respondents in 1985 that was shown in Table 6-1.

On the other hand, the results of my analysis on the SSM 2005 Survey as presented in Table 6-8 show the coefficient of determination dropping slightly (adjusted R^2 = .043). What's surprising is that the education effect—previously a main determinant—has lost its significance. Moreover, taking its place is a tendency for subjects to be more likely to have a positive (conservative) stance toward inside-outside role segregation the younger they were. This indicates that the progressive, reformist inclination among the younger and better-educated clusters that were once regarded as practically self-evident has disappeared.

Turning next to determinants for the master-subordinate attitude, Tables 6-9 and 6-10 permit a visual comparison of two points in time separated by a quarter century. As expected, the coefficient of determination showing the strength of the stratum factors' overall causal prescriptive force dropped by almost half (adjusted R^2 = .081→.038). Turning next to the effects these various social attributes produce, the 1985 results show a tendency largely resembling the one seen with respect to attitudes toward inside-outside gender-role segregation (positive correlations for age, negative effects for educational attainment, and "non-elite" occupation effect). In contrast, the significant influence that occupational status and age had is gone from the 2010 results. Only an educational background effect can be found—to wit, the more advanced a subject's education the more opposed they would be to master-subordinate role segregation.

As many readers may know, Japanese society during these years saw moves aimed at changing what was socially desirable toward expanding women's rights and rejecting male chauvinism. It is not difficult to imagine that this development weakened the "gradient" that runs the master-subordinate attitude along the traditionalism–modernism axis. The fact that differences due to age or occupational status became less visible speaks precisely to this point. However, among less educated women the values about gender-based role segregation that assign men to a privileged position and women to a disadvantaged one remained as strongly rooted as ever, relatively speaking.

Table 6-7 Determinants of the "Inside-Outside Role" Attitude in 1985 (Female)

	Correlation		Coefficient		Coefficient (standardized)	
	r	Sig.	B	S.D.	β	Sig.
Age (25–59)	.152	**	.008	.004	.071	
Education (years)	–.207	**	–.063	.021	–.126	**
Household income (logged)	–.113	**	–.095	.053	–.059	
Upper white (I + II), (reference)						
Lower white (III)	–.089	**	.314	.158	.118	*
Self-employed (I + Vab)	–.057		.076	.230	.013	
Skilled manual (V + VI)	.007		.389	.198	.090	*
Non-skilled manual (IVc)	.000		.375	.169	.126	*
Agricultural (VIIab)	.080	*	.584	.210	.126	**
Unemployed	.133	**	.630	.153	.272	**
Coefficient of determination (R^2)	.079	**	Adj. R^2	.070	**	

*: p < .05, **: p < .01   n = 914

Table 6-8 Determinants of the "Inside-Outside Role" Attitude in 2005 (Female)

	Correlation		Coefficient		Coefficient (standardized)	
	r	Sig.	B	S.D.	β	Sig.
Age (25–59)	–.074	**	–.008	.003	–.087	**
Education (years)	–.031		–.009	.016	–.018	
Household income (logged)	–.065		–.031	.045	–.021	
Upper white (I + II), (reference)						
Lower white (III)	–.052		.194	.084	.091	*
Self-employed (I + Vab)	.003		.347	.121	.094	**
Skilled manual (V + VI)	.026		.426	.142	.094	**
Non-skilled manual (IVc)	–.038		.217	.100	.082	*
Agricultural (VIIab)	–.015		.223	.235	.028	
Unemployed	.178	**	.530	.082	.265	**
Coefficient of determination (R^2)	.050	**	Adj. R^2	.043	**	

*: p < .05, **: p < .01   n = 1243

Table 6-9 Determinants of the "Master-Subordinate Role" Attitude in 1985 (Female)

	Correlation		Coefficient		Coefficient (standardized)	
	r	Sig.	B	S.D.	β	Sig.
Age (25–59)	.188	**	.007	.004	.067	
Education (years)	−.270	**	−.093	.019	−.194	**
Household income (logged)	−.082	*	−.034	.050	−.022	
Upper white (I + II), (reference)						
Lower white (III)	−.025		.474	.150	.187	**
Self-employed (I + Vab)	−.016		.322	.218	.059	
Skilled manual (V + VI)	.054		.574	.189	.137	**
Non-skilled manual (IVc)	.051		.495	.161	.174	**
Agricultural (VIIab)	.093	**	.606	.200	.136	**
Unemployed	.002		.465	.145	.211	**
Coefficient of determination (R^2)	.091	**	Adj. R^2	.081	**	

*: $p < .05$, **: $p < .01$ n = 903

Table 6-10 Determinants of the "Master-Subordinate Role" Attitude in 2005 (Female)

	Correlation		Coefficient		Coefficient (standardized)	
	r	Sig.	B	S.D.	β	Sig.
Age (25–59)	.061		.001	.003	.011	
Education (years)	−.205	**	−.092	.020	−.176	**
Household income (logged)	−.097	**	−.050	.040	−.045	
Upper white (I + II), (reference)						
Lower white (III)	−.050		.029	.104	.014	
Self-employed (I + Vab)	.024		.111	.145	.032	
Skilled manual (V + VI)	.009		.062	.155	.016	
Non-skilled manual (IVc)	.062		.123	.126	.045	
Agricultural (VIIab)	.047		.383	.292	.047	
Unemployed	.041		.132	.103	.064	
Coefficient of determination (R^2)	.049	**	Adj. R^2	.038	**	

*: $p < .05$, **: $p < .01$ n = 828

Disappearance of the Gradient of Social Mentality

In this chapter, I used the social consciousness studies-type regression model as a framework for comparing the past and the present. Specifically, I examined changes in how traditionalism–modernism is connected to the social structure within the limits that the data allow. Adding the results of Todoroki Makoto's analyses (Todoroki 2000, 2011) of the authoritarian attitude (conservatism) to Figure 6-1, we get a picture of cross-time trends in these studies in the coefficient of determination of authoritarian conservatism and in attitudes toward gender-role segregation. From this we can see that causal explanatory power has been trending steadily downward since the 1980s for any of the cross-time comparisons shown on the figure. Based on this stubborn fact and the changes in the direct effects of each independent variable, we can get the following reading on the trend over those years.

First, in the 1980s the fact that a traditional orientation remained strongly present in particular strata was clearly evident on the surface of society (as a zero-order correlation). However, neither the working conditions that *Work and Personality* stressed nor socioeconomic status (narrowly defined) in terms of household wealth gave status-relatedness to traditionalism (modernity) in Japanese society at this time. Rather, differences in birth cohort set against the context of rapid modernization, overlapped by educational background, are what had a formative effect on social consciousness. Consequently, the sympathetic vibrations between birth-cohort and education effects—linked with the educational meritocracy and the replacement of old industrial sectors with new ones—created a pattern that made it easy to determine at a glance which individuals (e.g., "young, well-educated, white-collar, employable, urban resident" or "prime of life, compulsory education, non-white-collar, rural resident") had which form of social consciousness. The effects of these links among birth cohort, educational attainment, and occupational stratum produced the characteristics distinctive to the social mentality of Japanese from this period—status-relatedness with respect to traditionalism–modernism.

Looking back, it is apparent that the self-direction concept derived from 20th century survey data had grasped the prototypical form of (simple) modern society. In that society, the traditionalism–modernism axis functioned as the ingredient necessary for maintaining the status order. However, a close look at 1980 Japanese society shows that the status-relatedness there was not like that in U.S. society. Rather than occupation as the determinant, it was instead educational attainment (Kikkawa 1998).

That said, when we compare this gradient in the social consciousness (formed by the correlation between birth cohort and education against the popularization of higher education as backdrop) with actual status-relatedness (predicated by the direct effects of occupational status and economic power), we can see it was on unreliable footing. The nature of this unreliability differs from that of the dubiousness of status identification we examined earlier. The dubiousness there was due to its reasoning, since the class-based differences that had been expected to be present could not be detected. In contrast, the status-relatedness visible in

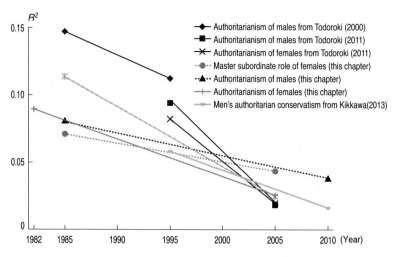

Figure 6-1   The Quiet Retirement of Traditionalism–Modernism
(Decrease in Coefficients of Determination)

traditionalism–modernism stood on shaky legs due to the fact that a status-relatedness originally not expected to have been present in fact put in a pseudo-appearance, emerging from the vestiges of social changes from the 1940s to the 1980s.

Eventually, between the end of the Shōwa period in 1989 and the start of the 21st century the composition of the social consciousness—based on the status-relatedness in traditionalism–modernism that had developed as a result of these acrobatics—became amorphous. As this unfolded, the basic structure itself—one built on the birth cohort differences when it came to traditionalism–modernism—had begun to weaken due to the departure of older generations from the scene and the slowly increasing conservatism of younger ones. On top of that, we should note well the fact that, as the popularization of higher education came to an end, the negative correlation between age and educational attainment dissolved. The overlap in education and birth-cohort effects could no longer be seen (Kikkawa 2006). The correspondent relationship between birth year, education, and stratification status was no longer so close, and it became difficult to gauge the gradient of social mentality—who is traditionalist.

Once that happened, it became difficult to get even a simple sense of which strata supported which perspective; one could no longer state with certainty that one strata harbored many traditionalists and another modernists. Moreover, the shared understanding throughout society about the traditionalism–modernism axis became less certain.

Traditionalism–modernism as a reference axis provided an indispensable "auxiliary line" for understanding all manner of social phenomena in 20th century Japanese society. It worked whether we looked at gender-role segregation (the entry of women into the workforce and the work-life balance question), the Liberal Democratic Party's longtime rule in the political sphere (the 1955 System and its conservative-progressive standoff), or at participation in community and citizen movements. However, as I have shown here, thanks to social changes that had truly become a thing of the past at the turn of the 21st century, traditionalism–modernism became disconnected from the Japanese social structure and quietly stepped away. The loss of this "auxiliary line" has turned the social mentality of contemporary Japan into a thing of chaos.

NOTES

[1] Based on survey data from the 1950s, Kohn discovered that middle-class men tended to value the autonomous orientation while working-class men tended to set store in conforming to norms. He made it his objective to clarify the mechanisms that were at work. His empirical studies renewed research in using job titles as its basic unit to examine the differences in how each person dealt with the vocational lives, which he accomplished by using questions of his own design to measure job conditions (Kohn 1969).

[2] Self-directed orientation is made measurable by using a secondary confirmatory factor analysis in the quantitation operation. Kohn and Schooler used this to derive a definition and significance for the self-directed orientation.

[3] Some have criticized the use of the vertically oriented concept of self-direction to view the magnetic field of social consciousness, seeing it as excessively simplistic (Yoneda 2007). *Work and Personality* focused on American society of the 1960s; the respondents whose life courses were actually tracked were gainfully employed white men who were born in the first half of the 20th century. In that respect, it got right at a basic construct that should be recognized as the prototype for 20th century industrial society. For that very reason, the argument it developed should also be seen as lucid and powerful.

[4] Given that the SSM Surveys did not include women until 1975, for all intents and purposes it is not possible to analyze the social attitudes of both men and women until after the SSM 1995 Survey.

[5] In terms of response options, a three-item method comprising "agree" (*sansei*), "neither agree nor disagree" (*dochira to mo ienai*), and "disagree" (*hantai*) was used in the SSM 1985 Survey. In the surveys of more recent years, however, a five-item Lickert-type scale is used, with responses comprising "agree" (*sō omou*), "modestly agree" (*yaya sō omou*), "neither agree nor disagree (*dochira to mo ienai*)" "modestly disagree" (*amari sō omowanai*), and "disagree" (*sō omowanai*). For that reason, while we know that the comparative possibilities are not complete, almost identical factor structures can be built if the measurement variables are assumed to have a normal distribution and the principal components are extracted.

In this book, all the principal component score variables for authoritarian conservatism were computed using this method. While the results of the principal component analyses differ slightly for each target set, in all cases the patterns they show are roughly the same as those in previous studies. Consequently, in this book I have foregone showing the numerical values for factor loadings and affinities (Kikkawa 2008; Todoroki 2000, 2008).

⁶ The respondents were the spouses of men—in short, married women—chosen through random sampling, who lived in the seven prefectures of the Kantō region. For that reason, it must be kept in mind that the data is not fully reliable in terms of representativeness and sample size.

⁷ Todoroki (2000, 2008) has already presented the results of comparative analyses of the status-relatedness aspect to authoritarian attitudes in 1985, 1995, and 2005. The analysis here was undertaken with reference to those findings.

⁸ The possibilities of performing a strict comparison between the results of the SSM 2005 Survey and those from other points in time have not been secured because the responses to the 2005 survey were collected using the leaving self-administrative method rather than through interviews.

Still, since there were few response options when it came to attitudes toward gender-role segregation and they could be broken down into "yes" or "no" replies, I attempted both multinomial logistic and OLS regression analyses. Given that the trends in the analytical results were largely the same, I used those from the OLS regression analysis with its greater causal explanatory power.

CHAPTER 7

The Doctrineless Age

The analysis in the previous chapters showed on the one hand how today's Japanese are increasing their literacy about status identity, while on the other how the relationship between society's mechanisms and the traditionalism–modernism axis is gradually growing more tenuous.

Here, we now confront a single question: how are we to understand a state of affairs in which two changes that appear to be polar opposites are unfolding simultaneously? We will get to thinking about our ultimate conclusion later, but at the very least, it is reasonable to forecast that the era change in social consciousness will not permit some simple understanding, such as the further increase in inequality or the growing (or declining) power of class.

In this chapter, I would like to bring in some additional ingredients for understanding the contemporary social mentality. In the first half, I will investigate the orientation that has replaced traditionalism–modernism in providing the backbone for social consciousness in contemporary Japan and see what doctrine it constitutes. In the second half, I will outline the current state of the social mentality from a different angle—that of frequency of daily activities.

The "Misfire" of Equity Studies

From the latter part of the 1980s to around 2005, expectations were that "equity" would follow status identification and traditionalism–modernism to become the third indicator of stratification consciousness. At the time, following the mass-middle-class era (which people spoke about as implying wealth, homogeneity, and equality), it appeared this might be the decisive factor for deciphering the nature of the new era.

The unequal distribution of resources and opportunities is intrinsic to the definition of social classes. Just how individuals assess this is a contentious issue that bridges both the objects and subjects of social stratification. "Equity," on the other hand, is a term that also connects to such other terms as fairness and justice. It is regarded as a key concept for thinking about economic theory and policy when it comes to determining the direction in which democracy is headed.

When thinking deductively like this on paper, the importance of examining the relationship between a sense of equity and social class can be acknowledged as largely self-evident (Umino 2000). However, survey data analysis has yet to produce any findings useful to social consciousness studies. The time spent on it thus far has been for nothing.

The old standby yardsticks for equity are a general feeling of unfairness (i.e., "Generally speaking, do you think today's world is unfair? [*Ippanteki ni itte ima no yononaka wa kōheida to omoi masu ka?*]") and feelings of unfairness in certain areas (i.e., "Do you think there is unfairness in Japanese society today as a result of X? [*Ima no Nihon shakai ni wa X ni yoru fukōhei ga aru to omoi masu ka?*]" where X is replaced by some social attribute like race, gender, ancestry, education, age, and so on). However, when attempts have been made to use them for survey data analysis, all that has been discovered among Japanese is the usual tinge of status-relatedness in the sense of equity or unfairness (Umino and Saitō 1990; Oda and Abe 2000; Saitō 2011).

As a typical example, Table 7-1 presents a sampling of the results that Saitō Yuriko and Ōtsuki Shigemi obtained with a multiple indicator for feelings of unfairness using a social consciousness studies-type regression model (Saitō and Ōtsuki 2011). The figure shows the coefficient of determination remained largely in the two-to-four percent range for any point in time after 1985. Such results do not provide the necessary "horsepower" to argue that feelings of unfairness might transform if the adjusting screw in society I have spoken of before were turned the right amount.

I can conceive of two factors as having contributed to this research "misfire." One may be termed the human agency explanation: the expected results could not be obtained because the indicator did not perform well when it came to measuring equity. The other might be termed the real situation explanation: the class-induced "gradient" in feelings of unfairness was not a strong one in the first place. I have spoken elsewhere before about this meager empirical reality behind the feeling of unfairness as "stratification consciousness based on unrealistic speculation," and thought it a failure attributable to the scholars who designed and analyzed the questions asked (Kikkawa 2003). However, when confronted with the opacity now shrouding the whole of Japanese social consciousness, I came to believe that the "misfire" in studies of equity may well have been an omen of a sea change in the nature of contemporary Japanese social consciousness.

Let us first do some soul-searching about problems in question design. First there is the issue of what exactly came to the respondent's mind regarding "fairness" and "unfairness" when they answered social survey questions of the sort I

Table 7-1 Determinants of "Feeling of Unfairness" (Males in the SSM Surveys)

	2005		1995		1985		(Year)
Age	−.107	***	−.119	***	−.027		
Years of education	.092	*	.104	**	.159	***	
Occupational prestige (present job)	.090	*	.027		−.032		
Personal income	−.119	***	−.010		−.055		
Coefficient of determination (*Adj. R*²)	.039		.031		.022		

***: p < .005, **: p < .01,*: p < .05.
Result of OLS regression analysis; Figures represents standardized coefficients.
Extracted from Saitō and Ōtsuki (2011).

mentioned earlier. Most people probably do not give much thought to whether the world is fair or not as they go about their lives, so they won't have an answer readily at hand. The answer a respondent provides on their doorstep to questions about feelings of unfairness may comprise any number of elements. These may include not only some well thought-out value judgments about the desirability of certain social conditions (what the researcher would call justice), but also that person's concept of equality, conservative inclinations (in the sense of being positive about conditions as they are), and on occasion their sense of being dissatisfied (or satisfied) with or inconvenienced (or liberated) by contemporary society.

Here, we might first suspect the inquiry about feelings of unfairness to be the archetype of a vague question, which should be avoided in a social survey.[1] The researcher is anticipating an answer about justice. Even if this agenda setting is handled skillfully, the respondent will still wonder which question to answer: justice in their immediate space (an attitude toward themselves), in the conditions of local government, when it comes to opinions about the government's redistribution policies, or in the international situation (all of these being attitudes toward the society and world around them). Responses will contain a mixture of micro and macro perspectives. Whatever the case, questions about the nature of fairness and justice will always remain a dilemma. Michael Sandel's discussion of justice makes this clear. When we have to choose one of two paths to follow, we don't go out of our way to opt for the just one as being absolutely desirable. Rather, we choose the better of two injustices (Sandel 2009). Of course, this does not mean the sense of unfairness has been swept away just because a more fair alternative was selected.

Talk of the existence of unfair conditions is suitable material for a fiery deliberation. However, when we bring a difficult technical concept like "equity" into a survey's line of sight, the text of the questions themselves will lack specifics when taking daily life into account and, moreover, they will include any number of ambiguous elements. In light of its potential for substandard explanatory power (a multitude of measurement errors), it cannot be denied that operationalizing the concept of equity presents difficulties.[2] Still, in light of this recognition, we should consider the possibility that the analytical results repeatedly generated might actually reflect to some degree actual conditions in contemporary Japanese society.

After all, it is largely impossible to predict based on social attributes who might or might not sense unfairness, which bears evidence to the fact that this social attitude is ubiquitous and latent throughout society.

To be able to describe a certain orientation as a doctrine—an "ism"—with the power to drive society, it should constitute a clear axis running through a conflict in values that represents a social fact everyone knows, and have a specific social stratum shown to be its supporters. Here, equity is not a concept positioned as an "ism" or a subject—it is, rather, nothing more than a feeling. Accordingly, when some person or organization (a politician or political party, say) makes the feeling of unfairness that people might have the focus of their appeals, the people are not likely to be set in motion even if the appeals were aimed at creating some sort of social reforms.

The idea that equity might seem useful from a theoretical perspective despite not being tied to social mechanisms in the real world is still regarded as somewhat incomprehensible. However, taking in the broad social consciousness landscape, we similarly see numerous other instances of social attitudes that may be nothing more than a "sense" or "tendency" that do not function sociologically as a doctrine. Upon reflection, it is now possible to see that the research that led to the equity "misfire" was actually the earliest to grasp the fact that the contemporary Japanese social mentality was becoming opaque.

Perception of Inequality Driven by Personal Interest

At any rate, some studies have seen fit to move forward on the path suggested by the study of equity. One of the problematic aspects of equity studies was the difficulty respondents had with understanding the abstract questions posed. Recalling the process discussed in Chapter 6 by which the authoritarian attitude scale was developed, the success there came from not directly asking respondents if they were "authoritarian." That in mind, perhaps the social mentality could be explored using an approach in which the concept of equity is not directly mentioned. Research on "inequality perception" (*kakusa-kan*) (respondent's understanding of divisions or inequalities in society) emerged from taking equity studies in this direction.

After the Koizumi Administration (2001–2006), there was much discussion in the mass media about government policy relying on terms such as "expanding inequality," "easing of regulations," and "free competition" that quickly attracted public interest. The "game" of thinking about disparities became popular, and such perceptions of inequality became such a concern that they even steered politics. When this happened, the researcher could anticipate that any inquiry mentioning words related to inequality would be met with responses rooted in actual feelings. The fact that "inequality" had entered everyday language in such a major way cleared the way for a new social orientation to take the stage.

The most recently designed SSP-I 2010 Survey inquired about the following four social attitudes. All related to inequality and competition, they were selected from among those taken up in earlier surveys going back as far as 15 years that

Table 7-2 Determinants of "Neoliberal Perception of Inequality" in 2010

	Correlation		Coefficient		Coefficient (standardized)	
	r	Sig.	B	S.D.	β	Sig.
Gender (male = 0, female = 1)	-.215	**	-.392	.054	-.195	**
Age (25–59)	-.126	**	-.011	.003	-.111	**
Education (years)	.217	**	.068	.014	.136	**
Household income (logged)	.173	**	.133	.030	.116	**
Upper white (I + II), (reference)						
Lower white (III)	.021		-.001	.079	.000	
Self-employed (I + Vab)	.013		.001	.097	.000	
Skilled manual (V + VI)	.023		-.017	.092	-.005	
Non-skilled manual (IVc)	-.090	**	-.159	.087	-.057	
Agricultural (VIIab)	-.050		-.390	.209	-.047	
Unemployed	-.107	**	-.086	.083	-.034	
Coefficient of determination (R^2)	.116	**	Adj. R^2	.110	**	

*: p < .05, **: p < .01   n = 1494

produced valid findings. The five-item scale with responses ranging from "agree" to "disagree" was used.

- If opportunities are provided equally, then differences between poverty and wealth through competition are inevitable (*Chansu ga byōdō ni ataerareru nara, kyōsō de hinpu no sa ga tsuite mo shikata nai*)
- Doing away with inequality is more important than protecting free competition (*Kyōsō no jiyū o mamoru yori mo, kakusa o nakushite iku koto no hō ga taisetsu da*) (−)
- I do not mind if inequality becomes more widespread in Japan in the future (*Kongo, Nihon de wa kakusa ga hirogatte mo kamawanai*)
- The inequalities in incomes in Japan today are too great (*Ima no Nihon de wa shūnyū no kakusa ga ōkisugiru*) (−)

(The "−" indicates an attitude with a negative load.)

I have extracted a principal component score from these items to serve as our yardstick.[3] An examination of how these questions work shows the points in contention for each are free competition and where they stand on reducing inequality. Moreover, it should be evident that orientations that support the policy stances of neoliberalism were selected. For that reason, I label this the *neoliberal perception of inequality*.

Table 7-2 displays the results of an analysis regarding these items using the social consciousness studies-type regression model. The coefficient of determination (adjusted R^2 = .110) shows considerable predictive power—three times that for feelings of unfairness.

Looking first at the zero-order correlation, an affirmative inclination toward inequality is linked to being male, having a higher education, being young, having a high household income, and being upper class white collar (the reference category). Of these, those characteristics not tied to occupational status—male, young, university educated, high household income—have positive direct effects (significant regression coefficients) on the neoliberal perception of inequality.

The status-relatedness of inequality consciousness among contemporary Japanese can plainly be seen here. There is a strong tendency to favor the neoliberal perception of inequality among those positioned among society's privileged "majority" (the "winners"), and to desire leveling through redistribution on the disadvantaged "minority" (the "losers") side (Kikkawa 2011). This indicates that the social mentality of Japanese with respect to competition, distribution, and fairness is built upon a calculation of gains and losses based on one's own position in society.

As should be immediately evident, this finding does not undercut what anyone might predict. The status-relatedness of inequality could even be described as a cornerstone of social consciousness. However, the nature of the "interested party" to be found here is some form of egoism; this is rather different from the kind of "auxiliary line"—i.e., a doctrine of some sort—that we hope to discover.

A Ubiquitous Prosocial Nature

This still leaves the question of which orientation to focus on to get a sense of what has become of the social mentality in contemporary Japan. I turn again to the same SSP-I 2010 Survey to examine another social attitude that may help us understand the social orientation of contemporary Japanese.

Ever since the 1995 Hanshin-Awaji Earthquake (or "the Kobe earthquake," as it is more commonly known abroad), there has been considerable interest among the Japanese public in promoting voluntarism and getting people to feel greater concern for others.[4] Volunteer activities are supported by the ideal that everyone should familiarize themselves with those parts of society that tend to be overlooked and be proactive in getting involved for the public good. Inaba Keishin has discussed this new trend in Japan in terms of altruism (Inaba 2008).

That in mind, I have attempted to work this new current in the social mentality—the inclination to proactively engage and connect with society—into the quantitative social consciousness studies framework. I have extracted a principal component, from the following three items, and label the current itself "prosocial nature" (*kōshakaisei*).[5]

- I think more about what I want to do for society than what I want to get from it (*Shakai kara nani ka shitemorau koto o kangaeru yori mo shakai no tame ni nani ka o shitai*)
- We should get away from the gains and losses in own daily lives and place greater value on benefits to society as a whole (*Jibun no hibi no kurashi no*

Table 7-3 Determinants of "Prosocial Nature" in 2010

	Correlation		Coefficient		Coefficient (standardized)	
	r	Sig.	B	S.D.	β	Sig.
Gender (male = 0, female = 1)	−.073	**	−.126	.055	−.064	*
Age (25–59)	.091	**	.011	.003	.108	**
Education (years)	.107	**	.054	.014	.112	**
Household income (logged)	.059	*	.027	.030	.024	
Upper white (I + II), (reference)						
Lower white (III)	−.017		.005	.081	.002	
Self-employed (I + Vab)	.031		.057	.099	.017	
Skilled manual (V + VI)	−.031		−.064	.095	−.021	
Non-skilled manual (IVc)	−.007		.026	.089	.009	
Agricultural (VIIab)	−.051	*	−.461	.207	−.059	*
Unemployed	−.017		.026	.085	.011	
Coefficient of determination (R^2)	.032	**	Adj. R^2	.025	**	

*: p < .05, **: p < .01   n = 1509

sontoku o hanarete shakai zentai no rieki o taisetsu ni subekida)
• I want to know in detail about the workings and events of the world around me (*Watashi wa yononaka no shikumi ya dekigoto o kuwashiku shitte okitai*)

Just how strong is this prosocial nature among people in the different social strata? Table 7-3 presents the results of a social consciousness studies-type regression model analysis for the defining factors of prosocial nature. First, the coefficient of determination is unexpectedly low (adjusted R^2 = .025). As was the case with feelings of unfairness, this result indicates that while it may be possible to make the dependent variable measurable, we cannot identify who in society has a highly prosocial nature. The fact that this prosocial nature is spread evenly throughout society is a favorable tendency for thinking about social movements.[6] But when it comes to the issues this book is interested in, we are forced to conclude that prosocial nature is a social attitude that is not tightly moored at any point to the social structure. It is thus not endowed with a sociological nature that lends itself to being described as a doctrine.

A Meltdown Caused by the Acceptance of Diversity

While this search for some new doctrine—some new "-ism"—in contemporary Japan may only create further confusion, the fact is there indeed is one social attitude that has strong status-related characteristics. To get ideas about what kinds of inquiries to make in the World Values Survey, respondents to the SSP-I 2010 Survey were asked for yes-no opinions about whether they approved of a society

Table 7-4 Determinants of "Acceptance of Diversity" in 2010

	Correlation		Coefficient		Coefficient (standardized)	
	r	Sig.	B	S.D.	β	Sig.
Gender (male = 0, female = 1)	.170	**	.309	.054	.153	**
Age (25–59)	–.270	**	–.024	.003	–.234	**
Education (years)	.144	**	.072	.014	.145	**
Household income (logged)	–.006		–.005	.030	–.004	
Upper white (I + II), (reference)						
Lower white (III)	.087	**	.135	.079	.053	
Self-employed (I + Vab)	–.039		.104	.097	.030	
Skilled manual (V + VI)	–.014		.226	.092	.072	*
Non-skilled manual (IVc)	–.055	*	.115	.087	.041	
Agricultural (VIIab)	–.090	**	–.414	.209	–.050	*
Unemployed	.079	**	.209	.083	.083	*
Coefficient of determination (R^2)	.121	**	Adj. R^2	.115	**	

*: p < .05, **: p < .01   n = 1493

where people with diverse views coexisted, as well as whether or not they endorsed different forms of family. The three social-attitude items were as follows.

- Having a lot of people with different ways of thinking is desirable for a society (*Chigatta kangaekata o motta hito ga takusan iru hō ga Shakai ni totte nozomashī*)
- It is fine for two people of the same gender to love one another (*Dōsei dōshi ga aishi atte mo yoi*)
- It is not absolutely necessary to have children even if two people get married (*Kekkon shite mo kanarazushimo kodomo o motsu hitsuyō wa nai*)

One principal component can be extracted from these that I will label "the acceptance of diversity."[7] Table 7-4 shows the results of my analysis examining the links between this social attitude and society. First, the coefficient of determination shows it has sufficient causal explanatory power (adjusted R^2 = .115). The correlation shows a considerable birth-cohort disparity—the younger the respondent, the more accepting of diverse ways of thinking (r = –.270). Meanwhile, the regression coefficient shows this reflects the direct causal power of the respondent's age ($β$ = –.234). We can probably say this new orientation spread starting with the younger generations.

Two other items deeply interesting as direct effects are the tendency for women to be more accepting of diverse ways of thinking than men, and the tendency for the acceptance of such diversity to rise with a respondent's educational attainment ($β$ = .145). With respect to occupational status, skilled blue-collar workers and the unemployed tend to be more accepting of diversity compared to respondents from the upper-class white-collar reference group; agricultural workers conversely are fairly conservative in their thinking. Economic power (household income), however, has no significant effects. In other words, the connection between social attributes and this social attitude is such that a person is more likely to be accepting of diversity if they are young, female, college-educated, or have a non-elite job or are unemployed. This is an extremely interesting discovery.

Unfortunately, however, this result does not provide the trump card needed for a breakthrough in social consciousness studies. This quickly becomes apparent when some thought is given to what "acceptance of diversity" actually means. Having this social attitude means accepting a condition in which diverse family configurations, diverse modes of living, and diverse value systems are concurrently present. It implies rejecting the very notion of committing to the framework of value conflicts—e.g., male superiority vs. gender equality, traditional family vs. modern (nuclear) family, or conservative vs. progressive—that the society in its entirety shares. Such a way of thinking is frequently required for democracy in the contemporary age. However, it does not constitute the expression of opinions affirming the desirability of something singular; it does not amount to some doctrine we might tag "diversity-*ism*." Accordingly, we cannot think that with this we have discovered a new cornerstone for the social mentality.

Rather, the fact that there are certain social tendencies to the development of this acceptance of diversity paradigm merely indicates that a meltdown in the framework—one in which individuals positioned themselves on the spectrum of various doctrines—is progressing among the young, the female, the highly educated, and the workers in non-elite jobs.

From the foregoing we can see that evidently there are limits on the attempt to discover foundational doctrines akin to those of the 20th century when it comes to contemporary Japan's social mentality. At present, we seem to be facing an era with no overriding doctrines—one without "-isms."

Searching for a Gradient in the Frequency of Daily Activities

While they may not have detected the arrival of this doctrineless age, since the 1990s class survey studies in Japan have been measuring subjectivity using a method that differs from the psychology-derived approach for measuring attitudes to understand how people live their lives. This method entails asking respondents about the frequency of their participation in various activities in daily life. The response options are "frequently do" (*yoku suru*), "sometimes do" (*tama ni suru*), "do not do often" (*amari shinai*), "hardly ever do" (*hotondo shinai*), and "have never done" (*shita koto ga nai*). The approach uses the actual state of someone's daily activities to make conjectures about social mentality as a latent preparatory mental state rather than for grasping the mentality as a subjectivity itself.

Focusing on frequency of daily activities in Japanese class survey studies began with operationalizing Bourdieu's concept of habitus. Eventually, the approach became an extension of quantitative social consciousness studies. Behind this development are Bourdieu's ideas of cultural capital and cultural reproduction

(Bourdieu 1979). Cultural capital—distinct from economic capital—is based on the idea that society's ordering of ranks is created not only by such hardware-related elements as occupational and economic status, but also a hierarchy of subjective, cultural factors. The concept suggests that sophisticated behaviors, interests, sensibilities, and aesthetic tastes really function as a kind of software that indicates how high an individual's status is and produces opportunities and benefits in that person's life. For its part, cultural reproduction refers to how, due to the effects of cultural capital, subjective, cultural factors have hegemony as the framework that structures the ways formal education and occupational status are approached (Kikkawa 2006).

Given that this entails examining the status-relatedness of culture, it plainly comes within the ambit of stratification consciousness research. However, cultural capital is concealed in daily life. Moreover, it possesses a hard-to-grasp-quality in that it has effectiveness to others to demonstrate its latent presence in the pertinent field. Habitus is the word distinctive to Bourdieu that expresses how cultural capital gets embodied in this fashion; that being the case, it is not something easy to operationalize through survey data analysis in the first place.

Nonetheless, Bourdieu himself made an attempt at a quantitative study. His method for operationalization in turn was introduced to Japanese survey-based studies around 1990. The approach taken was to ask respondents about the frequencies of their cultural activities—"Do you listen to classical music?" "Do you read history books or novels?" "Are there things that you practice?"—and examine what class differences that revealed. Ironically, the cultural capital theory for a time built a bridge connecting the long-alienated fields of stratification consciousness studies and sociology of culture. Meanwhile, another concept of capital—that of social capital, which involves the connections between the individual and society (e.g., social participation activities, organizational involvements, networks, and so forth)—was added to the roster of research topics related to frequency of daily activities (Putnam 2001).

The talk that began of a society marked by inequality added still another topic for discussion. The focus of our approach here would be the status-relatedness of such economic activities as consumption, thriftiness, and saving. This is done not due to some complex theory; rather, it is because the causal cycle between objective and subjective has as its chief provision the self-evident relationship between economic power and economic activities. That is to say, it comprises a microeconomic relationship in the narrow sense of an economically affluent person engaging in qualitatively high acts of consumption. If that is our chief provision, then we can certainly see the status-relatedness. However, sociology is not interested in conclusive proof of such a self-evident causality based on economic power. Rather, what is crucial are differences in economic mode based on gender, age, education, occupational status, and the like—in short, observing the modes of cultural consumption.

I again turn to the SSP-I 2010 Survey, this time to look at status-relatedness in the frequency of cultural, social participation, and (cultural) consumption activities. The foci now are on "frequency of museum visits" and "frequency of library

Table 7-5 Determinants of "Museum Visit" in 2010

	Correlation		Coefficient		Coefficient (standardized)	
	r	Sig.	B	S.D.	β	Sig.
Gender (male = 0, female = 1)	.100	**	.249	.051	.127	**
Age (25–59)	.044		.011	.002	.110	**
Education (years)	.316	**	.149	.013	.311	**
Household income (logged)	.160	**	.090	.028	.081	**
Upper white (I + II), (reference)						
Lower white (III)	.085	**	.111	.075	.045	
Self-employed (I + Vab)	.047		.162	.092	.049	
Skilled manual (V + VI)	–.100	**	–.058	.088	–.019	
Non-skilled manual (IVc)	–.107	**	–.052	.082	–.019	
Agricultural (VIIab)	–.083	*	–.619	.192	–.080	**
Unemployed	–.012		–.017	.079	–.007	
Coefficient of determination (R^2)	.146	**	Adj. R^2	.140	**	

*: p < .05, **: p < .01   n = 1516

Table 7-6 Determinants of "Library Visit" in 2010

	Correlation		Coefficient		Coefficient (standardized)	
	r	Sig.	B	S.D.	β	Sig.
Gender (male = 0, female = 1)	.179		.430	.060	.189	**
Age (25–59)	–.095	**	–.004	.003	–.032	
Education (years)	.295	**	.157	.015	.280	**
Household income (logged)	.144	**	.117	.033	.090	**
Upper white (I + II), (reference)						
Lower white (III)	.078	**	.030	.088	.010	
Self-employed (I + Vab)	–.057	*	–.126	.107	–.033	
Skilled manual (V + VI)	–.082	**	.000	.103	.000	
Non-skilled manual (IVc)	–.104	**	–.042	.096	–.014	
Agricultural (VIIab)	–.085	**	–.626	.224	–.069	**
Unemployed	.069	**	.118	.092	.041	
Coefficient of determination (R^2)	.145	**	Adj. R^2	.139	**	

*: p < .05, **: p < .01   n = 1512

Table 7-7 Determinants of "Voting in Election" in 2010

	Correlation		Coefficient		Coefficient (standardized)	
	r	Sig.	B	S.D.	β	Sig.
Gender (male = 0, female = 1)	-.005		.049	.055	.024	
Age (25–59)	.221	**	.025	.003	.244	**
Education (years)	.132	**	.076	.014	.152	**
Household income (logged)	.108	**	.068	.030	.059	*
Upper white (I + II), (reference)						
Lower white (III)	-.028		-.057	.081	-.022	
Self-employed (I + Vab)	.009		-.073	.099	-.021	
Skilled manual (V + VI)	-.058	*	-.121	.095	-.038	
Non-skilled manual (IVc)	-.015		-.016	.089	-.006	
Agricultural (VIIab)	.036		.108	.207	.013	
Unemployed	-.014		-.049	.085	-.019	
Coefficient of determination (R^2)	.084	**	Adj. R^2	.078	**	

*: $p < .05$, **: $p < .01$ n = 1515

Table 7-8 Determinants of "Premium Product Purchasing" in 2010

	Correlation		Coefficient		Coefficient (standardized)	
	r	Sig.	B	S.D.	β	Sig.
Gender (male = 0, female = 1)	.047		.076	.046	.044	
Age (25–59)	-.205	**	-.014	.002	-.158	**
Education (years)	.279	**	.077	.012	.179	**
Household income (logged)	.193	**	.138	.025	.140	**
Upper white (I + II), (reference)						
Lower white (III)	.143	**	.100	.067	.045	
Self-employed (I + Vab)	-.001		.001	.082	.000	
Skilled manual (V + VI)	-.130	**	-.284	.079	-.104	**
Non-skilled manual (IVc)	-.126	*	-.170	.073	-.071	*
Agricultural (VIIab)	-.080	**	-.466	.171	-.067	**
Unemployed	-.036		-.078	.070	-.036	
Coefficient of determination (R^2)	.147	**	Adj. R^2	.141	**	

*: $p < .05$, **: $p < .01$ n = 1512

Table 7-9 Determinants of "Participation in Volunteer/NPO" in 2010

	Correlation		Coefficient		Coefficient (standardized)	
	r	Sig.	B	S.D.	β	Sig.
Gender (male = 0, female = 1)	.018		.095	.054	.048	
Age (25–59)	.105	**	.014	.003	.140	**
Education (years)	.163	**	.071	.014	.147	**
Household income (logged)	.098	**	.041	.030	.036	
Upper white (I + II), (reference)						
Lower white (III)	.022		−.082	.080	−.033	
Self-employed (I + Vab)	.011		−.115	.098	−.034	
Skilled manual (V + VI)	−.061	*	−.201	.093	−.065	
Non-skilled manual (IVc)	−.070	**	−.217	.087	−.080	*
Agricultural (VIIab)	−.027		−.391	.204	−.050	
Unemployed	−.034		−.193	.084	−.078	*
Coefficient of determination (R^2)	.055	**	Adj. R^2	.049	**	

*: p < .05, **: p < .01   n = 1517

Table 7-10 Determinants of "Foreign Travel" in 2010

	Correlation		Coefficient		Coefficient (standardized)	
	r	Sig.	B	S.D.	β	Sig.
Gender (male = 0, female = 1)	−.004		.034	.045	.020	
Age (25–59)	−.030		.003	.002	.030	
Education (years)	.359	**	.122	.011	.288	**
Household income (logged)	.235	**	.139	.025	.142	**
Upper white (I + II), (reference)						
Lower white (III)	.057	**	−.064	.066	−.029	
Self-employed (I + Vab)	−.033		−.186	.080	−.063	*
Skilled manual (V + VI)	−.102	**	−.234	.077	−.087	**
Non-skilled manual (IVc)	−.144	*	−.238	.072	−.101	**
Agricultural (VIIab)	−.059	**	−.486	.171	−.069	**
Unemployed	−.017		−.076	.069	−.035	
Coefficient of determination (R^2)	.164	**	Adj. R^2	.159	**	

*: p < .05, **: p < .01   n = 1514

Figure 7-11 The Consummatory Nature of the Doctrineless Age (Summarized Result)

	Coefficient of Determination (R^2)	Educational Status	Occupational Status	Economic Status	Age	Gender
Equity	0.039				**	
Prosocial nature	0.025	++			+	Male
Neoliberal perception of inequality	0.110	++		++	**	Male
Acceptance of diversity	0.115	++	+		***	Female
Museum visit	0.140	+++	+	+	++	Female
Library visit	0.139	+++	+	+		Female
Voting in election	0.078	++		+	+++	
Participation in volunteer/NPO	0.049	++			++	
Premium product purchasing	0.141	++	++	++	**	
Foeign travel	0.159	+++	+++	++		

Note: +++: Large positive effect, ++: Medium positive effect, +: Small positive effect, ***: Large negative effect, **: Medium negative effect, *: Small negative effect.

visits" for cultural activities; "frequency of voting in elections" and "experience of and frequency of participation in volunteer and non-profit organization (NPO) activities" for social participation activities; and "frequency of purchase of premium goods" and "experience and frequency of foreign travel"—an item that straddles both internationalism and upmarket consumption—for cultural consumption activities.

First, a glance at Tables 7-5 and 7-6 for the status-relatedness of cultural activities based on frequency of museum visits and library usage shows causal explanatory power for both is sufficiently high at around 14% (adjusted R^2 results of .140 and .139, respectively). On closer examination, the direct effects of a more advanced education are shown to be extremely strong, resulting in greater frequency in the usage of such institutions. Economic power and occupational status also influence cultural activities, but their effects are not nearly as great. Furthermore, regardless of these influences, women are more engaged in cultural activities.

We turn next to Tables 7-7 and 7-8 for voting in national and local elections as well as experience and frequency of participation in volunteer and NPO activities (as 53.3% of respondents have no such experiences, the data shown in substance represent "experience and frequency"). From the size of the coefficients of determination, the causal explanatory power for these two behaviors is not as high as it is for other activities (adjusted R^2 results of .078 and .049, respectively). It is also evident that the more education a respondent had, the more likely they were to participate in such activities; the same was true the older a respondent was. Put another way, members of the younger generations or lower social strata who are frequently spoken of as the objects of policies and aid are not so assertive about getting involved with social participation activities.

Looking at these results from the perspective of society in its entirety, a structure emerges marked by a contrast between university graduates in the prime of life who are active in society and non-university graduates in younger generation with low levels of activity. This is a new construct not seen in the 1980s, characterized by an inversion in the relationship between birth cohort and education effects.

Finally, Tables 7-9 and 7-10 show the prescriptive structure of premium product purchasing and experience and frequency of foreign travel (including the 39.5% of respondents who had no such experience). The word "premium" is meant to connote an item that is of a higher grade than a "standard" or "normal" product. The strategy of using that word to differentiate customer bases is a new one in Japan that has become common over the past decade or so. The question of who today responds to this message that a product is not just average ("middle") is deeply interesting not just from a cultural capital perspective, but also for stratification consciousness research. When it comes to experience and frequency of foreign travel, economic power is also in play alongside whether someone has a cosmopolitan outlook or not.

The causal explanatory power indicated by the social consciousness studies-type regression model for both is around 15% (adjusted R^2 figures of .141 and .159, respectively), showing that the social structure and consumption behavior are intimately connected. These results largely support our forecast that, in essence, individuals of higher status will be more active in their consumption in these categories while those from lower strata are less motivated to do so.

However, examining the magnitude of influence that these factors have on each activity, having a household income that suggests considerable buying power is not necessarily the main factor involved (β = .140 and .142, respectively). Being young (β = −.158) or highly educated (β = .179) exhibited considerable predictive power on par with that of economic power when it came to purchasing premium products, while higher education (β = .288) did the same with respect to the experience and frequency of foreign travel. These results allow us to say that cultural consumption is not just a function of economic power; it is also a function of educational attainment (and birth cohort). That overlap is why the status-relatedness here is so clear.

The Consummatory Nature of the Doctrineless Age

In this chapter, I have thus far pursued my data analysis through two procedures: by searching for the new cornerstones of some doctrine—some "-ism"—that might be influencing contemporary Japanese society, and by attempting to discern status-relatedness in the frequency of daily activities. I now bring the results of these analyses together and present them systematically in Table 7-11.

First, let's consider the results of the search for some "-ism" as shown in the upper part of the table. The coefficient of determination is small when it comes to equity and prosocial nature. While it is possible for one or another social strata to induce changes in these social attitudes to some degree if the right opportunity arises, the mechanism involved is not well understood. Furthermore, it is also not precisely clear as to who strongly favors these social attitudes. These are not attitudes tied to the structure of society as would occur when traditionalism–modernism abided—rather, they are freely floating orientations. For that reason, they cannot be seen as functioning as the doctrines we seek.

The neoliberal perception of inequality for its part certainly appears to have linkages with society. However, those amount to an evaluation of gains and losses as the "interested party" (stake holder), which is based on the individual's own status. It does not involve the mediation of some process whereby that individual refers to the criterion of some doctrine ubiquitous in society. To the contrary, we can see that the very fact that an individual's perceptions of inequality comprise the accumulated results of their pursuits of unadulterated self-interest shows how doctrines have lost their influence.

My analyses of the acceptance of diversity, meanwhile, make it clear that this way of thinking that accepts diverse value systems as concurrent realities is gradually beginning to spread, starting with the younger generations, women, and the highly educated. This, too, suggests a further meltdown in the very framework defined by accepting or rejecting one or another doctrine.

To put this all together, we can conclude that the increasingly tenuous status-relatedness of traditionalism–modernism has not been accompanied by people transferring to some other "-ism" as a reference axis. The end has come to the modern-society state of affairs that saw the whole of society pointed in the same direction and its members all relying on standard for how to orient themselves. We are now living in the "doctrineless" age.

This is not to say that being in a doctrineless age means individuals are disconnected from society and behave in ways that are completely without rhyme or reason. The frequency of daily activities shown on the bottom part of the table indicates that the stratification variable has direct effects whether we are talking about cultural, social participation, or consumption activities.

This illustrates that people engage in behaviors that correspond to their respective positions regardless of intermediation by some doctrine. In contemporary sociology, this is what we define as a consummatory situation. To be consummatory—"autotelic" or "self-absorbed" are other descriptives used—in this context means to simply act without goal or reason. This does not mean acting irresponsibly or blindly. Rather, a consummatory activity is one largely constrained by where the individual's place in society. This makes it a mechanism that can be explained sociologically. The "interested parties" of inequality that came up earlier can be properly understood as one aspect of this consummatory shift.

Table 7-11 also offers a suggestion as to what might be important as prescriptive factors for social consciousness. Based on the results of analysis using the social consciousness studies-type regression model, we can say educational attainment—followed by age and economic power—has had a steady influence on social orientation. Educational attainment once held a nodal position. Its effects overlapped with those of birth cohort owing to the influence of the increased popularity of

Table 7-12 Principal Component Analysis for Neoliberal Perception of Inequality

variable	Communality	Loadings
If opportunities are provided equally, then differences between poverty and wealth through competition are inevitable	.410	.640
Doing away with inequality is more important than protecting free competition	.590	-.768
I do not mind if inequality becomes more widespread in Japan in the future	.546	.739
The inequalities in incomes in Japan today are too great (-)	.315	-.561
	Eigenvalue	%
first component	1.861	46.515
second component	.888	22.204
third component	.688	17.192
forth component	.564	14.089

Extraction: Principal Component. Cronback's α = 0.606.

Table 7-13 Principal Component Analysis for Prosocial Nature

variable	Communality	Loadings
I think more about what I want to do for society than what I want to get from it	.600	.774
We should get away from the gains and losses in our own daily lives and place greater value on benefits to society as a whole	.501	.708
I want to know in detail about the workings and events of the world around me	.423	.650
	Eigenvalue	%
first component	1.524	50.796
second component	.820	27.337
third component	.656	21.868

Extraction: Principal Component. Cronback's α = 0.512.

higher education. They also overlapped with other stratification variables owing to the influence of the education-based meritocracy. This is why educational effects provided the backbone in the 1980s for status-related differences along the traditionalism–modernism axis. Educational attainment's direct influence on social orientation—that is to say, the tendencies for the highly educated to be flexible, liberal, and proactive—has been a constant ever since. In contrast, while we can see that economic power has a certain degree of prescriptive influence over daily activities, as was the case in the 1980s the influence of occupational status is feeble at best. Thus, in contemporary Japanese society where it has become difficult to

Table 7-14 Principal Component Analysis for Acceptance of Diversity

variable	Communality	Loadings
Having a lot of people with different ways of thinking is desirable for a society	.161	.401
It is fine for two people of the same gender to love one another	.655	.809
It is not absolutely necessary to have children even if two people get married	.674	.821
	Eigenvalue	%
Factor 1	1.489	49.628
Factor 2	.942	31.395
Factor 3	.569	18.977

Extraction: Principal Component. Cronback's α = 0.483.

predict how someone might think or behave, the most useful question you could use to find out would be how much education (educational attainment) a person has (Kikkawa 2006, 2009).

When it comes to birth cohort, the trend in social participation activities is the younger someone is the less likely they are to have a prosocial nature or be actively engaged. The gentle tendency among younger generations toward conservative revival is a factor here. The fact that there are cohort-based differences in social orientation has been known since the era of rising industrialization. However, closer examination shows that the past construct of younger generations being liberal and active and middle-aged and older generations being guarded and conservative has almost completely disappeared in the past three decades. A reversal of orientations is emerging in its place. The continuity in the education effect and reversal in that of birth cohort are changing a construct defined by a clearness in the contrast between young university graduates and old non-university graduates. In some cases it is flipping the construct over to produce one characterized by a contrast between old university graduates and young non-university graduates.

Finally, a look at gender differences shows that men tend to be more affirmative when it comes to neoliberal perceptions of inequality and a prosocial nature, while women tend to be more affirmative when it comes to cultural activities and acceptance of diversity. While these points require further careful examination, it is possible to see that certain gender differences are emerging: men are attempting to grasp social conditions and be involved while remaining embedded in market principles, while women are acknowledging diversity and possess cultural wealth.

NOTES

[1] Responses to vague questions are distinctive in that their covariance with social attributes tends to become small.

[2] Postwar social consciousness theory was outfitted with a thesis originating in Marx

that served to largely immobilize it: "workers ought to identify with the working class." Much time and effort was expended on the quest to find absolute proof for this hypothesis. However, it eventually became evident that the class affiliations of Japanese were not in a clear objective-subjective correspondence relationship (Misumi 1990). This is another example of scholars not getting the results they expected because they imposed a theoretical concept on people, who do not usually think about the definition of words like "worker."

The lesson here is that if people do not palpably sense as a reality whatever phenomena a theory may propose, then no matter how refined that theory may be it won't generate research results that satisfy the standards of quantitative social consciousness studies. Work in this area should maintain a stance of deriving theories from induction and stay out of the deep furrows such prejudged theories lay (Kikkawa 2008).

3   Table 7-12 shows the results of the principal component analysis for neoliberal perception of inequality.

4   Except for an extremely small group of respondents, this survey was conducted prior to the 2011 Tōhoku earthquake and tsunami.

5   Table 7-13 shows the results of the principal component analysis for prosocial nature.

6   If I had to list statistically significant direct effects, I would note the tendency for respondents with higher education and respondents who are older to be more proactively involved with society. With respect to gender, men tend to have a slightly more prosocial nature.

7   Table 7-14 shows the results of the principal component analysis for acceptance of diversity.

CHAPTER 8
A Hidden Era-Change in Quality of Life Orientations

Having now collected the various fragments needed to identify the social mentality of contemporary Japan, all that remains is to assemble the pieces of this puzzle to gain a more complete picture that will help drive our study of contemporary Japanese society. But to do so, we first require some sense of the overall image we are trying to piece together.

With that in mind, in this chapter I would like to focus on one quantitative study of social consciousness actually undertaken as part of the arguments that make up this book.[1] The various data analysis studies that have been carried out can be likened to boats sailing along the river of history. Selecting one of these boats to study the trails left in its wake can provide constructive hints as to the river's course and how strongly it flows.

Attitudes to Health and the Environment in Contemporary Japan

The major issues in contemporary Japanese society arise from the interplay of improvements in personal quality of life and the sustainable development of society. The May 2013 installment of the Organization for Economic Cooperation and Development's "Better Life Index" counts environmental and health standards among its core components; it regards these variables among the most important indicators of the direction in which contemporary society is heading (OECD 2013).[2] There is an indivisible connection between environmental and health risks. Together, they represent a direct trade-off against such elements idealized by modern society such as economic development and convenience of lifestyles. This trade-off is exemplified by a succession of incidents such as the widespread pollution that accompanied Japan's years of rapid economic development, or the Chernobyl nuclear disaster in the Soviet Union. The societal shockwave felt throughout Japan and around the world in the aftermath of the disaster at the Fukushima Daiichi Nuclear Power Station provided a fresh reminder of how directly and how gravely such issues can affect us.

As I briefly mentioned in Chapter 3, a turning point for health and environmental concerns in Japan can be found in the early 1990s—just a short while after the 1985 date chosen for the purposes of this book as a comparative historical reference point. As the bubble economy finally burst, steady economic growth in both name and substance also became a thing of the past. It was around this time that the shift from simple (first) modernity to a new phase began to make itself felt among the general population. In 1993 Japan passed the Basic Environment Law, a statute that has formed the basis of this country's environmental policy ever since. This was the spur for now-commonplace conservation terms like "environmentally friendly" (*kankyō ni yasashī*), "recycling" (*risaikuru*), and "ecological" (*eko*) to enter the popular lexicon. When it came to health, too, these years marked a crossroads. Vague expressions such as "obesity" (*himan*) and "adult diseases" (*seijinbyō*) gave way to more specific medical terminology like "visceral fat" (*naizō shibō*), "metabolic syndrome" (*metaborikku shōkōgun*), and "lifestyle diseases" (*seikatsushūkanbyō*), stirring fresh interest in health issues.

In this chapter, I will present a comparative analysis of survey data from 1992 and 2010 to trace changes in the awareness of environmental conservation and health maintenance among Japanese throughout this period. As it is used below, the term "environmental conservation awareness" reflects the new attitude of assigning greater precedence on protecting the environment than convenience and comfort. "Health maintenance awareness," meanwhile, indicates a dawning attitude that looking after one's health is important, regardless of the necessary investment in terms of time and money. In light of their shared quest for improved quality of life, I will refer to these social attitudes as the QOL orientation.[3]

In and of itself, a Japanese lifestyle that seeks to take care of the environment and preserve mental and physical well-being is hardly a new thing. When it comes to conservation, we can go back to the Meiji era to see anti-pollution movements and protests against national land development that originated with the environmental disaster at the Ashio Copper Mine in Tochigi Prefecture. In this, we can find the historical roots of citizen movements during the modern era that were predicated on the ideals (ideology) of anti-establishmentarianism and anti-industrialism. Meanwhile, if health maintenance awareness is defined as the orderly habits and avoidance of unhealthy eating implicit in phrases like "eat 'til you're eight-tenths full" (*hara hachibunme*) and "early to bed, early to rise" (*hayane hayaoki*), then such tendencies can be traced back to the Edo-period teachings of Kaibara Ekken (1630–1714), author of *Yōjōkun* ("The book of life-nourishing principles"), and to the emphasis given to such practices in Japan's prewar "moral education." In a testament to the history of environmental conservation and health awareness in the country, such ideals have persisted and are written into the fabric of modern Japan's value system.

Moreover, by looking at the systems by which environmental initiatives (such as modern-day drives to recycle paper, plastic bottles, and aluminum cans; or to save water and electricity), as well as notions like "healthism" and "anti-aging," have taken root and spread, we can also perceive aspects that differ from those of the existing frameworks. Aside from the novelty of such emergent phenomena, they can be interpreted as having arisen from changes in certain deeply submerged drives.

Improving one's quality of life is something that for people today has achieved the status of an unshakeable desire. In the past, the QOL orientation manifested itself in the active engagement among certain sectors of society in various types of activism and advocacy through one or another movement or activity. Today, it should be seen as a gentle gradient that runs throughout society, delineating who is the most strongly committed throughout day-to-day practices based on the idea of improved quality-of-life. At one time, how active people might be was strongly dictated by value systems and ideologies, but at present it may be surmised that the influence of such factors has diminished. In fact, in recent years the term LOHAS—short for "lifestyles of health and sustainability"—has taken root as a way to describe a new mode of living that places a greater emphasis on health and the environment (Pedersen 2006). Given this concept's focus on lifestyles as the name itself suggests, we can infer that it is not underpinned by some doctrine of health and sustainability.

The foregoing suggests that the process by which quality-of-life improvements rapidly took hold in Japanese society was accompanied by the transformation in underlying drives, moving from "activity" that reflected the existing value system to "*habitus*" where the consummatory lifestyle is commonplace. In that light, using social survey data gathered specifically to facilitate a comparison of environmental conservation awareness and health maintenance awareness between two points in time, in this chapter I will consider the underlying sociological factors that define these two social attitudes. Particular attention will be directed toward an era change in how the social consciousness operates. Factors identified elsewhere in this book—including status identification, authoritarian attitude, and general life satisfaction—can be seen as the fundamentals of social consciousness for how they give direction to those opinions and standards for behavior apparent on society's surface. Here, I will seek to use data to substantively ascertain these dynamics.

The Influence of Social Consciousness on the QOL Orientation

One of the earliest analyses of the positions that environmental conservation awareness and health maintenance awareness were claiming in modern Japanese society was a quantitative study I conducted (Kikkawa 1994).[4] Employing data from a nationwide survey conducted in 1992 and using people's psychological attitudes toward health and the environment as yardsticks, it focused on the authoritarian attitude (meaning authoritarian traditionalism) as a factor that has no small influence on this pair of social attitudes.

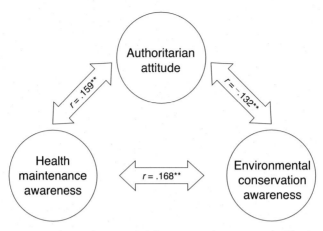

Figure 8-1　Relationship among Three Attitudes in 1992 (Kikkawa 1994)

As stated earlier, the authoritarian attitude had once been a key indicator that took in the central twentieth century theme of the conflict between conventional (traditional) values and modern, liberal ones. My research showed that the influence that this attitude originally had on political conservatism and traditional behavioral patterns had begun to weaken in the Japanese society of the early 1990s, when the threat of fascism had receded and the stage of rapid industrialization lay in the past. However, it also revealed that authoritarian attitude still had influence when it came to the newly emerged social phenomena of environmental conservation and health maintenance.

The structure of that linkage is nonetheless rather complex. First, the partial correlation when controlled for various social attributes reveals a significant positive relationship ($r = .168$) between environmental conservation and health maintenance awareness. Yet, while the authoritarian attitude showed negative correlation with environmental conservation awareness ($r = -.132$), it had a positive relationship ($r = .159$) when it came to the health maintenance one (Figure 8-1).

It may be inferred from the negative relationship between authoritarian attitude and environmental conservation awareness that the latter has a tendency to reject authority or tradition; rather, it is driven by an independent, liberal civic mindedness (self-directedness). Meanwhile, the picture presented by the positive correlation between authoritarian attitude and health maintenance awareness could lead us to conclude that this health maintenance awareness is driven by a stoicism that favors strict observance of a rigid order. These facts portray conditions peculiar to the end of the twentieth century, an era that differed from the one in which the authoritarian attitude provided the psychological basis for the rise of fascism.

Subsequent surveys have continued to shed light on the significance accorded within Japanese society to environmental conservation and health awareness. These have included research into the mechanisms behind waste recycling activities conducted by the Umino Michio-led Working Group on Life and Environment

(Seikatsu kankyō kenkyū kai) (Umino ed. 2007); a comparison with East Asia by Zheng Yuejun and colleagues (Zheng, Yoshino and Murakami 2006); and surveys in the fields of social epidemiology and public health, examining inequality and the connections between social status and health (Kawakami, Kobayashi, and Hashimoto, eds. 2006; Kondō 2010).

Such studies often focus on status identification and general life satisfaction (psychological well-being) as indicators of the social consciousness that dictates activities related to quality of life. Both factors involve recognition or evaluation of one's own lifestyle. They are differentiated by the manner in which status identification rests upon a determination of one's standing in relation to the whole of society, whereas general life satisfaction is generated solely by internal psychological mechanisms and does not involve going through such a reference process.

Taking into account the limitations of the data I will be using,[5] I would here like to consider firstly authoritarian attitude, which reflected twentieth century value systems; and, secondly, general life satisfaction, which is an outlook based on self-fulfillment, as those aspects of social consciousness that influence QOL orientation.[6]

As we have seen so far, the social significance of authoritarian attitude has diminished over the last 20 years or so. Meanwhile, the fact that the more positive mental states (e.g., general life satisfaction and self-esteem) have the effect of actively steering daily life in a prosocial direction has been attracting much attention in recent years (Seligman 2002). The relationship here is easy to grasp. The more subjectively satisfied an individual is, the more likely they will be to aspire to a higher quality of life. If a person is not fulfilled in their daily life, then it will be more difficult for the one to find the mental energy to devote to environmental conservation and health maintenance.

Let's examine the social basis for general life satisfaction, which is often taken as an overall indicator of subjective well-being. Tables 8-1 through 8-4 present analyses of determinants of general life satisfaction from 1985 to 2010, based again on the social consciousness studies-type regression model (SSM 1985, 1995, 2005 surveys and the SSP-I 2010 Survey, using figures on respondents of both sexes from the 25–to–59 age group). These tables show firstly that the causal explanatory power of the social attribute variable when it comes to general life satisfaction lies in the 5–8% range regardless of when the survey was conducted. In other words, these social attitudes are less strongly rooted in social structure than might be imagined. Secondly, aside from the trend towards higher general life satisfaction among women and slight differences in the relationship between satisfaction and age,[7] the primary factor at any point in time behind raising one's level of satisfaction appears to be household income. This tendency is well known in the field of economics. Here, Figure 8-2 graphs trends in the adjusted coefficient of determination. In contrast to how status identification strengthened status-relatedness and authoritarian attitude weakened status-retatedness, general life satisfaction remains loosely tied to the social structure mainly based on economic determinism. The reason is the factors that shape well-being are generally of a sort that does not change significantly regardless of era.

Table 8-1 Determinants of General Life Satisfaction in 1985

	Correlation		Coefficient		Coefficient (standardized)	
	r	Sig.	B	S.D.	β	Sig.
Gender (male = 0, female = 1)	.150	**	.346	.047	.169	**
Age (25–59)	.046		.004	.002	.042	
Education (years)	.036		.011	.009	.030	
Household income (logged)	.151	**	.212	.031	.139	**
Upper white (I + II), (reference)						
Lower white (III)	.023		−.068	.065	−.026	
Self-employed (I + Vab)	−.011		−.027	.071	−.009	
Skilled manual (V + VI)	−.053	**	−.101	.070	−.036	
Non-skilled manual (IVc)	−.077	**	−.191	.068	−.074	**
Agricultural (VIIab)	.044		.127	.093	.031	
Unemployed	.053	**	−.077	.077	−.028	
Coefficient of determination (R^2)	.056	**	Adj. R^2	.053	**	

*: p < .05, **: p < .01   n = 2621

Table 8-2 Determinants of General Life Satisfaction in 1995

	Correlation		Coefficient		Coefficient (standardized)	
	r	Sig.	B	S.D.	β	Sig.
Gender (male = 0, female = 1)	.122	**	.223	.061	.107	**
Age (25–59)	.039		.000	.003	.002	
Education (years)	−.013		−.013	.014	−.027	
Household income (logged)	.181	**	.359	.046	.205	**
Upper white (I + II), (reference)						
Lower white (III)	.002		.068	.090	.025	
Self-employed (I + Vab)	.045		.142	.098	.044	
Skilled manual (V + VI)	−.023		.131	.096	.043	
Non-skilled manual (IVc)	−.034		.090	.097	.030	
Agricultural (VIIab)	.019		.269	.152	.048	
Unemployed	.056	*	.198	.093	.074	*
Coefficient of determination (R^2)	.056	**	Adj. R^2	.050	**	

*: p < .05, **: p < .01   n = 1577

Table 8-3 Determinants of General Life Satisfaction in 2005

	Correlation		Coefficient		Coefficient (standardized)	
	r	Sig.	B	S.D.	β	Sig.
Gender (male = 0, female = 1)	.098	**	.234	.045	.112	**
Age (25–59)	-.057	**	-.009	.002	-.082	**
Education (years)	.105	**	.019	.011	.038	
Household income (logged)	.249	**	.431	.035	.249	**
Upper white (I + II), (reference)						
Lower white (III)	.022		-.072	.062	-.027	
Self-employed (I + Vab)	-.057	**	-.192	.076	-.054	*
Skilled manual (V + VI)	-.031		-.011	.074	-.003	
Non-skilled Manual (IVc)	-.083	**	-.122	.070	-.042	
Agricultural (VIIab)	.005		.019	.151	.002	
Unemployed	.017		-.041	.070	-.015	
Coefficient of determination (R^2)	.880	**	Adj. R^2	.084	**	

*: p < .05, **: p < .01   n = 2693

Table 8-4 Determinants of General Life Satisfaction in 2010

	Correlation		Coefficient		Coefficient (standardized)	
	r	Sig.	B	S.D.	β	Sig.
Gender (male = 0, female = 1)	.022		.096	.056	.047	
Age (25–59)	-.075	**	-.007	.003	-.068	**
Education (years)	.140	**	.029	.014	.056	*
Household income (logged)	.235	**	.250	.031	.213	**
Upper white (I + II), (reference)						
Lower white (III)	.012		-.151	.083	-.058	
Self-employed (I + Vab)	-.012		-.094	.101	-.027	
Skilled manual (V + VI)	-.032		-.148	.097	-.046	
Non-skilled manual (IVc)	-.070	**	-.165	.091	-.058	
Agricultural (VIIab)	-.053	*	-.445	.212	-.054	*
Unemployed	-.027		-.105	.087	-.041	
Coefficient of determination (R^2)	.073	**	Adj. R^2	.067	**	

*: p < .05, **: p < .01   n = 1517

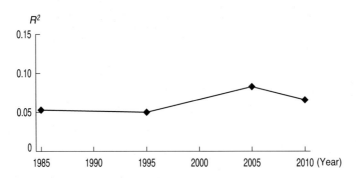

Figure 8-2 Trends in Status-Relatedness of General Life Satisfaction

Comparative Survey Data from 18 Years Later

The following analysis is based on two nationwide mail surveys conducted in 1992 and 2010 by identical research organizations and designed to permit comparisons between different points of time (Table 8-5). My analysis here will focus on the 26–60 age group in common to both surveys.

The 1992 data are from the Second Monitor Survey, which I have already analyzed elsewhere (Kikkawa 1994). The poll was one of the first of its kind to include questions about environmental conservation and health maintenance. The questions were designed to present a trade-off against convenience and comfort when it comes to environmental conservation. Among the statements to which subjects were invited to respond were: "I don't mind sacrificing convenience and comfort in order to conserve energy resources (*Enerugī shigen hogo no tame nara benrisa ya kaitekisa o gisei ni shite mo kamawanai*)," "I don't mind sacrificing convenience and comfort to prevent global warming and the depletion of the ozone layer (*Ondanka ya ozonsō hakai kara chikyū o mamoru tame nara benrisa ya kaitekisa o gisei ni shite mo kamawanai*)," and "I don't mind sacrificing convenience and comfort in order to conserve wildlife (*Yasei dōbutsu o hogo suru tame nara benrisa ya kaitekisa o gisei ni shite mo kamawanai*)." Statements on the subject of health maintenance awareness were framed in terms of a trade-off with economic and temporal costs. They comprised "I don't mind spending time and money to prevent obesity (*Himan o bōshi suru tame nara okane ya jikan o kakete mo kamawanai*)," "I don't mind spending time and money to prevent aging (*Rōka o fusegu tame nara okane ya jikan o kakete mo kamawanai*)," "I don't mind spending time and money to prevent or overcome adult diseases (*Seijinbyō o fuseida ri kokuhuku shita ri suru tame nara okane ya jikan o kakete mo kamawanai*)," and "I don't mind spending time and money to maintain my current level of physical strength (*Genzai no tairyoku o iji suru tame nara okane ya jikan o kakete mo kamawanai*)." In all cases, there were four available answers: "agree," "relatively agree," "relatively disagree," and "disagree."

The SSP-P Survey conducted in 2010 reused the same seven items, albeit slightly rephrased.[8] The list of possible answers was however expanded from four

Table 8-5 Data Descriptions

Title	The Second Monitor Survey	The SSP-P 2010 Survey
Survey period	August in 1992	January and February in 2010
Sampling	Second wave of the nationwide stratified random sampling survey (300 areas)	Area probability sampling from a nationwide master sample
Designed sample	2,022	2,500
Valid cases	1,252	1,385
Response rate	61.90%	55.40%
Research method	Mailing	Mailing
Respondents	Male and female aged 26 to 79	Male and female aged 26 to 60
Organization	Social Research Section in the Schools of Human Sciences, Osaka University (research representative: Naoi Atsushi)	Social Research Section in the Schools of Human Sciences, Osaka University (research representative: Kikkawa Tōru)

to five to include "neither agree nor disagree." The data provided by these two surveys offers insights into how environmental conservation awareness and health maintenance awareness among contemporary Japanese changed over an 18-year period. Below, I will use the social consciousness studies-type regression model to analyze as dependent variables the latent concepts of environmental and health maintenance awareness that were extracted and measured in 1992 and 2010 based on the foregoing questions.

The four questions presented in Chapter 6 regarding authoritarian attitude—the fundamental social consciousness that explains these two concepts—were asked in both of these surveys. Consequently, I will use those results as a scale for measuring these latent concepts (all of the response options were presented in the 5-item agree-disagree format). As to general life satisfaction, I will use the questions asked using the 5-item format about whether the respondens were satisfied or dissatisfied with their all-round lifestyle.

Gender, age, educational attainment, occupation and income were entered as independent variables in an OLS regression analysis. We used a binary variable for gender here where 1 represented male and 2 female, full years for age, and number of years of formal education for educational attainment. Occupation was categorized using five dummy variables relating to employment status and position within an organization: "manager or executive," "regular employee," "non-regular employee," "self-employed," and "unemployed," with "management" used as the reference category. We used yearly household income for "income."

Table 8-6 Deteminants of Environmental Conservation Awareness

	1992			2010		
		model 1	model 2		model 1	model 2
	r	B	B	r	B	B
(Constant)		-1.317 **	-1.091 *		-.937 **	-.600
Gender (ref. Men)	.038	.133	.121	.000	.050	.028
Age	-.018	.003	.007	-.001	.001	.002
Years of education	.175 **	.078 **	.070 **	.136 **	.065 **	.060 **
Occupation (ref. manager or executive)	.027			.041		
Regular employee	-.016	-.066	-.143	.013	-.164	-.138
Non-regular Employee	-.015	-.119	-.187	-.010	-.190	-.154
Self employed	-.012	-.045	-.118	-.029	-.239	-.212
Unemloyed	.029	-.060	-.158	-.005	-.176	-.148
Household income	.081 *	.007	.003	.074 **	.012	.007
Authoritarianism	-.162 **		-.155 **	.001		.019
Life satisfaction	.056		.066	.121 **		.086 **
R^2		.026 **	.047 **		.017 **	.023 **
ΔR^2			.023 **			.007 **
N		726			1,246	

*: p < .05, **: p < .01
Note: One unit of household income is 1 million yen. Cited from Hazama, Hasizume and Kikkawa (2013).

An Era Change in the Determinant Structure

To begin, We conducted OLS regression analyses on both environmental conservation and health maintenance awareness as dependent variables. For independent variables, gender, age, years of formal education, employment status, and household income were entered for Model 1, while for Model 2 these variables were entered alongside authoritarian attitude and general life satisfaction. The data from both 1992 and 2010 were subjected to analyses using these models to consider the influence of authoritarian attitude and general life satisfaction on environmental conservation and health maintenance awareness, and how these relationships had changed over the 18-year period in question.

Using Table 8-6, let us consider the factors that shape environmental conservation awareness. In 1992, there were few factors that had a significant influence on environmental conservation awareness. Examining Model 1, the lone variable shown to exert a significant influence was education; the relationship that can be discerned is one which environmental conservation awareness rises the more years an individual spent in formal education. In Model 2, which

A Hidden Era-Change in Quality of Life Orientations   147

Table 8-7 Deteminants of Health Maintenance Awareness

	1992			2010		
		model 1	model 2		model 1	model 2
	r	B	B	r	B	B
(Constant)		.015	.167		-1.181 **	-.986 **
Gender (ref. Men)	-.169 **	-.254 **	-.259 **	.015	.123	.109
Age	.053	.006	.001	-.073 **	-.007 *	-.006 *
Years of education	.079 *	.030	.039 *	.213 **	.089 **	.087 **
Occupation (ref. manager or executive)	.117 **			.048 *		
Regular employee	.052	-.327	-.196	.044	-.173	-.153
Non-regular Employee	-.061 *	-.371	-.236	-.013	-.244	-.221
Self employed	-.001	-.314	-.188	-.034	-.240	-.220
Unemloyed	-.085 *	-.406 *	-.266	-.040	-.287	-.268
Household income	.087 **	.006	.008	.195 **	.043 **	.039 **
Authoritarianism	.194 **		.188 **	.032		.054
Life Satisfaction	.090 **		.071	.148 **		.063 *
R^2		.034 **	.070 **		.076 **	.081 **
ΔR^2			.039 **			.007 *
N		726			1,246	

*: p < .05, **: p < .01
Note: One unit of household income is 1 million yen. Cited from Hazama, Hasizume and Kikkawa (2013).

incorporated authoritarian attitude and general life satisfaction, the former was seen to have a significant negative effect while the latter had no effects of any significance. Furthermore, the inclusion of these two variables resulted in a significant increase in the value of coefficient of determination (R^2 = .026→.047). These results enabled me to corroborate the outcome of an earlier analysis I conducted (Kikkawa 1994), which indicated that anti-authoritarian attitudes (self-directedness) in 1992 Japan had heightened environmental conservation awareness.

Moving on to 2010, variables exerting a significant influence on environmental conservation awareness were once again found to be scarce. Examination of Model 1 reveals the coefficient of determination to be low (R^2 = .017), and years of education is once more shown to be the lone variable to have a significant positive effect. Model 2, however, presents an appearance entirely different from what we saw for 1992. The authoritarian attitude no longer has the significant effect it did in 1992, while a significant effect for general life satisfaction has emerged. This clearly demonstrates the relationship in 2010 whereby environmental conservation awareness increases under the effect of general life satisfaction. The prescriptive power of general life satisfaction is not nearly as large, however. Based on how small the increment in the coefficient of determination is from Model 1 to Model 2, it cannot be said that the relationship between general life satisfaction and environmental conservation awareness is a strong one.

Table 8-7 permits consideration of the factors shaping health maintenance awareness. In 1992, this attitude associates with numerous factors as zero-order correlations, but when the covariance among independent variables is controlled for the variables that remain significant decrease. The coefficient of determination may not be large in Model 1, but significant effects can be seen for gender and unemployment. The relationships that can be discerned here show health maintenance awareness to be higher among males than females, and among those in management or executive positions than the unemployed. However, the effects of occupation lost their significance in Model 2, which included authoritarian attitude and general life satisfaction. In its place, a significant effect emerged with respect to years of education. Of the two newly added variables, although no significant effect could be seen for general life satisfaction, authoritarian attitude showed a strong positive effect. Furthermore, the inclusion of these two variables brought a significant increase in the value of the coefficient of determination (R^2 = .070), reaffirming the strong prescriptive power of authoritarian attitude.

What about 2010? In Model 1 (coefficient of determination: R^2 = .076) age, years of education, and household income each display significant effects. The younger a respondent, the longer their years of education, the greater their household income, and the greater their health maintenance awareness is. Turning next to Model 2, the effects of age, years of education, and household income declined somewhat compared to 1992, while of the two new variables, general life satisfaction is shown to have a significant effect. Also, the significant effect that authoritarian attitude had in 1992 was gone in 2010. These results make it clear that a relationship had emerged in 2010 such that higher general life satisfaction leads to greater health maintenance awareness. That said, while the effectiveness of general life satisfaction may be significant in view of the increment in the coefficient of determination, it is still not an especially great one.

Based on the foregoing OLS regression analysis, the influence that authoritarian attitude exerted in 1992 on both environmental conservation and health maintenance awareness had by 2010 been superseded by the influence of general life satisfaction. To ameliorate the problem of the insufficient magnitudes of determination produced by these OLS regression analyses, as well as to obtain a more accurate grasp of the change in the effect of authoritarian attitude and general life satisfaction between the two points in time surveyed, we compared parameters by carrying out a simultaneous analysis of the multi-group structural equation modeling (results not shown here). With this we statistically tested the differences in the values of various parameters between 1992 and 2010. That result confirmed the era change implied by the aforementioned OLS regression analysis. Figures 8-3 and 8-4 summarize the causal structure that this study made clear.

Both the environmental conservation and health maintenance awareness that were investigated as dependent variables are indicators of a quality-of-life orientation. Although the 1992 data present an unforeseen inversion structure in which

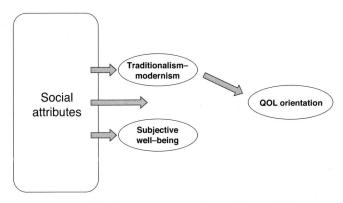

Figure 8-3　Causal Structure of the QOL in 1992

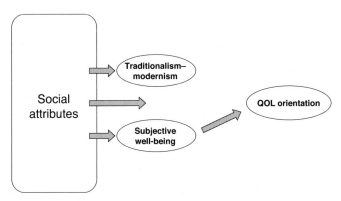

Figure 8-4　Causal Structure of the QOL Orientation in 2010

authoritarian attitude hindered environmental conservation awareness while boosting health maintenance awareness, a causal structure could also be seen. Here, the quality-of-life orientation made its presence known in the form of the traditionalism–modernism axis on which were manifested the influences of various social attributes. However the data for 2010 shows that the route mediated by this axis had lost its significance. In its place, general life satisfaction had come to exert a positive influence on both environmental conservation and health maintenance awareness.

These results can be interpreted as follows. In the 1990s, where quality of life was concerned, Japanese seem to have been influenced by traditionalism–modernism in the sense that an anti-establishment, anti-authoritarian attitude led to environmental conservation awareness while an attitude characterized by order and diligence led to concern for health maintenance. This framework has been lost in the present, however. It has been replaced by one in which individuals with a high degree of well-being (those generally satisfied) orient themselves even more strongly toward improving their quality of life. In other words, over an 18-year period the underlying social consciousness that dictates one's quality-of-life orientation changed from traditionalism–modernism to general life satisfaction (consummatory sufficiency).

From Modernity to Reflexive Modernity

Straying somewhat from the issue of quality-of-life orientation, a more general look at contemporary society suggests that these results can be seen to link with the transition towards individualization laid out in the theory of reflexive modernization. Although the emergence of lifestyles that placed great emphasis on quality of life may have seemed to be a next-stage movement around the close of the twentieth century, that in actual fact was not necessarily the case. It stands to reason that this was because the way in which quality-of-life orientation was adopted rested to some extent on the existing framework at the modern, twentieth century value cleavage implicit in the conflict between tradition (or conventionality) and modernity. But since then contemporary Japanese have gradually ceased to refer to the value system with which the whole of society is endowed as standard for daily behavior, as can be seen from the way in which authoritarian attitude lost its function in society (see Chapter 6). This change can be understood as an expression of the process in which individuals have "disembedded" (Giddens 1991) themselves from the predominant social structure.

Under reflexive modernity, one change expected to proceed alongside the contraction in the influence of the values and norms of the whole society is an expansion of the domain of the individual. This means that each of these individuals must separately recognize and evaluate the living circumstances they are confronted with on their own responsibility; social activities thus become the accumulation of these direct determinations made at the micro level (Bauman 2001; Beck and Beck-Gernsheim 2002). The trend revealed in this research of individuals more strongly committing themselves to improving their quality of life the more fulfilled they are in their own day-to-day lives can be interpreted as the exact embodiment of a society undergoing the process of individualization.

By focusing on quality-of-life orientation—one of the key issues of the contemporary era—our study has successfully pinpointed a change in the eras: at the end of the twentieth century, the anomalous but nonetheless established frameworks of modern society became ineffective and gradually began to be replaced by the frameworks of reflexive modernity. What I hope will be of particular worth is the way in which, by introducing the intermediate term of general life satisfaction to this analysis, we have discerned the early stages of the process of individualization that form the backdrop for the waning of status-relatedness in social consciousness. However, it should be noted that the explanatory power for quality-of-life orientation based on individual consummatory fulfillment does not makes its presence felt as strongly as when that orientation was embedded in the conflict in values of modernity. Additionally, the trends revealed here relating to health maintenance awareness are not as definite as those regarding environmental conservation awareness. For that reason, it will be necessary to carefully ascertain whether the influence of an individual's fulfillment with life will continue to expand with respect to their quality-of-life orientation.

NOTES

1   Chapter 8 is based on the findings of a paper I published recently with two collaborators. I have summarized and revised those findings on my own responsibility to adapt them to the context of this book, and added the results of those analyses I have personally deemed necessary. Please see Hazama, Hashizume, and Kikkawa (2013) for a precise analysis of the results of that research. I would like to express my heartfelt gratitude to my two colleagues, who got ideas from my earlier research and successfully developed them further in the study using more refined techniques.

2   Other components that were also highlighted include residence, income, employment, community, education, governance, general life satisfaction, safety, and work-life balance.

3   There is a large body of work regarding environmental and health consciousness using a wide variety of measures in fields including social psychology, politics, social epidemiology, and public health. However, for the purposes of this book the measures had to be ones in which the same concept was repeated in surveys taken at two different point in time, and moreover had to be ones that enabled us to observe the relationship between authoritarian attitude and general life satisfaction. Thus, only a limited number of measures allowed for analysis. As a result, I am limited to addressing only a subset of various issues of interest when it comes to health and the environment.

4   See Kikkawa (1998).

5   A comparison between two different points in time was not possible as status identification was not included in the Second Monitor Survey. I would like to examine the relationship between status identification and quality-of-life orientation in my future research.

6   In the fields of economics, social epidemiology, and public health, general life satisfaction is itself seen as an index of subjective quality of life. Although its use as a dependent variable is not uncommon, like authoritarian attitude it is treated here as a fundamental social consciousness that mediates between the objective social structure and people's everyday behavior.

7   The positive correlation in 1985 between general life satisfaction and age—where the older someone was the higher their general life satisfaction—had turned into a negative relationship after 2005. However, the connection between these two variables had always been extremely weak and was relatively unimportant compared to the degree of influence other determinants exerted on the degree of satisfaction.

8   For the SSP-P 2010 Survey, the expression "adult diseases" (*seijinbyō*) was revised to "lifestyle diseases" (*seikatsushūkanbyō*).

EPILOGUE
Status Literacy, Consummatory, and Reflexivity

In this book, I have wrestled with the hard-to-grasp character of the social mentality of contemporary Japan. At the end of Shōwa period, sociologists felt that they could get hints about the nature of social consciousness in hands. Getting a clue from them, I was able to reap information in bounteous quantities, even if it was hard to interpret. In this epilogue, I will borrow the resources that sociological theory provides for talking about reflexive modernization to create a single story of the social mentality of contemporary Japan.

The Described Shape of the Social Mentality

The analytical model I have used to evaluate status-relatedness in the social consciousness is what I call the social consciousness studies-type regression model. I will begin here by reviewing the findings obtained in my applications of this model. In my discussion, I will try to avoid the language of survey data analysis and instead speak about this as a study of contemporary Japanese society.

The Mooring of Status Identity (The Quiet Transformation of Status Identification)
In 1985 when talk of a "mass middle class" was rife, aside from the self-evident causality that being economically affluent meant feeling a ready attachment to the upper strata, status identity (via five-level status identification) was not strongly linked to any stratification variables and remained disconnected from the social structure. However, over the next 25 years, educational attainment and occupational status steadily gained influence alongside economic power. Status identity came to be firmly, multiply, and clearly linked to social stratification. This relationship has continued to strengthen down to the present. The improved literacy that Japanese now have when it comes to social strata and class itself constitutes the quiet transformation of status identification.

The Retirement of Traditionalism–Modernism
I used authoritarian conservatism and attitudes toward gender-role segregation as indices in this book to track what became of traditionalism–modernism, which formed a reference axis that had been a primary topic of debate in social consciousness studies. I found that in 1980s Japanese society, the time (new-old) and class (upper-lower) axes overlapped. The pattern in which this was expressed was the higher someone's stratification status, the more likely they could be characterized as "modern." Traditionalism, meanwhile, persisted in the lower strata. This confirmed a construct had formed—the status-relatedness of traditionalism–modernism—that was peculiar to the era.

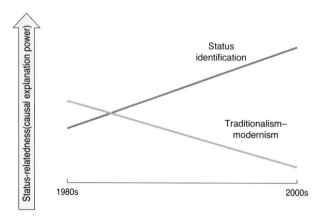

Figure E-1 Changing Trends of Causal Explanatory Power on Two Aspects of Social Consciousness

However, the causal relationship between the social structure and this aspect of social mentality rapidly weakened thereafter. While it still possible to measure someone's place along the traditionalism–modernism axis, it has become difficult to conjecture which social strata have conservative values and which have modern ways of thinking.

Traditionalism–modernism comprises the two "-isms" that together form a reference axis for the debate that figures in the very definition of modern society. For that reason, social consciousness studies in the 20th century regarded the axis to be its unshakable backbone. In 21st century Japanese society, however, it is no longer capable of playing that role.

Contrary Changes
These two changes that occurred concurrently on first glance seem to be headed in contrary directions. Figure E-1 shows in simplified form the changing trends in the causal explanatory power of stratification factors on status identity and the traditionalism–modernism axis.

If the formative effects of social class on social consciousness influence these two social attitudes in the same way, then both should be either rising or falling on the graph. However, the status-relatedness of status identity in fact has been increasing while that of traditionalism–modernism has been dropping. This fact resists simple explanation, such as the change in eras social consciousness is experiencing is due to rising inequality (the rising power of social status) or "the death of class" (the negating of the power of social status).

The Arrival of the Doctrineless Age
Two facts will help us get a grip on this tangled situation. First is the rather passive one that we have not been able to find a new fundamental social consciousness

to take the place that traditionalism–modernism once held. For example, equity and prosocial nature from a logical standpoint appear to be crucial indicators of the state of contemporary society. However, unlike how the case had been for the now-enfeebled traditionalism–modernism axis, these are simply attitudes wafting up from the social structure and do not represent inclinations strongly held by any specific social class. Hence, they cannot be expected to operate in a sociologically useful way as a fundamental social consciousness (an "-ism").

Meanwhile, the younger generations, the university-educated, and women are gradually taking on board a frame of mind accepting diverse ways of thinking. The rules of the game that once made it possible for everyone to position themselves somewhere along the spectrum of a specific doctrine are themselves becoming less certain. A new movement in that consciousness that has been developing since the early 1990s, quality-of-life orientation, shows that the determinative factor is changing from traditionalism–modernism (authoritarian attitude) to personal, subjective fulfillment (general life satisfaction).

Sociological theory about late modernity already predicted the emergence of this paradigm shift following the enfeeblement of the traditionalism–modernism axis that underpinned modern society. There is no alternative but to accept the arrival of the doctrineless age as a fact.

The Consummatory Shift

A more upbeat piece of information provides another handle for getting a grip on the social mentality of contemporary Japan. This is the fact that—regardless of what I pointed out in the preceding section—if you look directly at assertiveness about taking part in (i.e., frequency of) social activities there is a clear gradient based on social status. Specifically, where someone is positioned in society (in terms of age, gender, education, or economic power) has considerable predictive power when it comes to social participation and cultural activities. In short, people are not acting randomly; their social orientations conform with their respective places in society.

Changing focus to inequality, the ways that people perceive it reveals that they tend to pursue their self-interest directly: those in the privileged "majority" favor free competition, while those in the disadvantaged "minority" call for equality and fairness. The state of disillusioned inequality in status identification overlaps here. For that reason, people now determine how something will be to their personal benefit or detriment based on an examination of their own social status that is more dispassionate than ever.

This situation is vastly different from that of 1985, when people—under the illusion that they and their "one hundred million compatriots" were all of the "middle"—acted with reference to the axial principle that something was either traditional (secure) or modern (new). It could also be said that this presents a true picture of the shift to the consummatory orientation—a sociological term that expresses fresh difficulties in trying to understand where contemporary society is heading.

I have treated the consummatory shift as a growing tendency for individuals to consciously identify with their own social positions and yet still make snap decisions about social orientations without the mediation of what some doctrine or principle deems socially desirable. This shift overlaps with habitus in the sense that where someone is situated in society manifests itself not through some doctrine but rather directly in their behavior.[1]

As the foregoing suggests, the findings of this book can be summed up as the increasing clarity of status identity, the declining relevance of traditionalism–modernism, and the consummatory shift in social orientation. This in aggregate might best be understood as a phenotype of quantitative social consciousness studies running through the eras we have been acquainted with, as well as those catalogued by contemporary sociological theory.

Disembedding from the Collective Consciousness

Before moving on to a comprehensive discussion of contemporary Japanese society, I want to review the theories that provided its framework. The notion of reflexive modernity was already introduced in Chapter 3. This concept interprets (first) modern society as having contained vectors that were simple, steady, and could be understood by anybody. The present situation, however, is seen as one where modern society is transforming into its next state—one that is complex, unconventional, and difficult to understand at its edges where the system's rationality has most thoroughly penetrated.

Here, I wish to invoke this perception of society as having entered reflexive modernity to organize the findings from my survey data analysis. Reflexive modernization is a very influential theory in contemporary sociology, and my goal here is to see what evidence quantitative social consciousness studies can provide to increase its power.

Reflexive modernization is spoken of in symbolic terms whose meaning is difficult to grasp. Nonetheless, these terms provide crucial reference points for understanding the currents of the era through which we are now traveling. Accordingly, we need to ascertain the meanings they contain so this discussion is not bogged down in superficial, armchair theorizing. Of the numerous difficult terms involved are three mutually-related concepts crucial for discussing the relationship between society and the individual: "disembedding," "reflexivity (re-embedding)," and "individualization."[2]

"Disembedding" is the term that Giddens has most stressed in reflexive modernization theory. It refers to a social condition that develops in the modernization process whereby people become detached from their local context of intermediate groups and find themselves confronted by a limitless expanse of global time and space. Reflexivity refers to the situation of the contemporary individual who, in this moment, must constantly monitor the conditions they face, adjust their relationship with society, and construct their own identity (Giddens 1991).

In modern 20th century society, we acquired stable identities as individuals through affiliation with such intermediate groupings as social class, family, community, and birth cohort. Naturally, any number of exceptions could be raised, but I ask the reader's indulgence in accepting this as a simple overview. That was the "solid" situation embedded in modern society.

Today, however, we are constantly reconfirming and reevaluating matters on our own responsibility and actively constructing our self-identities as we are forced to deal directly with society in its entirety. The reason this condition is referred to as "reflexive modernity" and not simply "modernity" is because in it we are obliged to engage in the reflexive act of constantly rebuilding our own identities. Under this state of affairs, the individual gets re-embedded in society in a form different from that taken under previous conditions.

"Individualization" refers to the disembedded individual having to confront society in its entirety as a single entity, unlike in the past when the risks and uncertainties were coped with while stably affiliated with a group. Mikami refers to this situation where group identity is weakening and individual identity is becoming distinct as "the demise of the social" (*shakaiteki na mono no shūen*) (Mikami 2010).

However, as I have understood it, the great isolation of the individual from society is not new. One of the issues that social consciousness studies has taken up from the beginning was how the citizens in a modern society manage to establish their own individuality within it given its considerable power. Mass society theory provided the background to this discussion. This 20th century proposition highlighted a state of affairs in which the homogenous, powerless citizen (i.e., individual) had lost the moorings that intermediate groups had provided and was left to cope with elite domination like—in Mannheim's formulation—"a crab without its shell." The "mass" in mass society theory provided a focal point for the debate over the ease with which citizens (individuals) could be mobilized to totalitarianism precisely because of their uniformity. When it comes to the relationship between a powerful society and powerless individuals, there does not seem to be any great difference here with the individualized person in reflexive modernization theory.

Most, including Giddens himself, seem to understand the society of reflexive modernity—the individualized society—to be an evolved form of its mass predecessor. However, it is important to clarify what made them different. Accordingly, I would like to supplement this discussion of changes to the relationship between the collective and individual consciousness across these eras.

It was Durkheim who identified what he called the collective consciousness. The concept refers to how social consciousness exists as a social fact that has externalities and constraints (Durkheim 1895). It explains the standards that society as a whole holds expressed in terms of norms, morals, and what is socially desirable, as well as the influence these have on individuals. The collective consciousness takes what I have referred to as "-isms" (doctrines, ideologies, values) to be social facts, rather than general representations of individual consciousness accumulated through methodological individualism.

This Durkheimian interpretation may be recast into the language of reflexive modernity as follows. In (first) modern society, there was a collective consciousness—an "-ism"—in the "air" of society and society's members were embedded in it. However, as reflexive modernization has proceeded, its existence began to be shaken and its constraints called into question. Individuals became disembedded from the collective consciousness into which they had until then been subsumed. They subsequently examined their own places in society and tried to build connections with it once again in a process called re-embedding. Reflexive modernity can be said to have arrived when this process can been confirmed as taking place.

As the foregoing shows, the mass society conditions of (first) modernity and those of individualization under reflexive modernity can be easily distinguished if we think of the issue in terms of disembedding from the collective consciousness. Under the conditions of mass society, the powerless citizen (individual) is bound by and regularly refers to the collective consciousness (here, traditionalism–modernism) that hangs like a canopy in the airspace above macro society. They think about how conservative they are in their lifestyle, how "rightish" their values are, which doctrine provides the foundation for their daily activities, and so forth.

Thus, the social orientations of the people could once be easily integrated into a single orientation that quite likely also had considerable power. The very existence of a collective consciousness capable of performing actual functions was indispensable to elite domination of the masses. This quite simply was the contiguity between mass and totalitarian society that 20th century theorists feared. To repeat a point I made earlier, mass society theory was a product of the 20th century historical fact of Nazism.

In contrast, with individualization as posited by reflexive modernity, the individuals dispassionately survey their surroundings, constantly reaffirms their shifting social position, and make decisions based on the conditions they face. Moreover, in that moment the individual is no longer subject to the binding force of the collective consciousness and confronts the social system directly. In short, individuals are disembedded from the collective consciousness and re-embedded in the social system in the consummatory.

Thus, the phenomena discovered in this book—increased literacy about social identity, the retirement of traditionalism–modernism, and the shift to the consummatory in social orientation—may all be poured into the mold of theories on the move from (first) modernity to reflexive modernity.

The Social Mentality of the 1980s

While the theory of reflexive modernity may be suitable for my discussion, it is not very accessible. Still, its pedigree shows it permits comparing different eras, positing that a new system has begun to operate that differs from that of (first) modern society. Accordingly, we can gain a more complete understanding of it by considering the contrast between social conditions of the past and those of contemporary society.

Let's reconsider the state of 1985 Japanese society as outlined in Chapter 3. Status identification during this era can be rendered graphically as shown in Figure E-2. There, I present the relationships among the industrial, economic, and stratification system(s) of Japanese society at the macro level; the individual

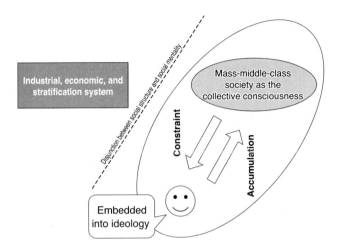

Figure E-2　Status Identification in the 1980s

as the micro-level subject who performs actions; and the collective consciousness (i.e., the social consciousness seen at the macro level). I have already spoken of the industrial, economic, and stratification system as comprising the structure of society—its hardware—and using analytical operations confirmed its existence through the effects that social attributes have on social consciousness. The part of the structure corresponding to society's software is rendered here as a large oval. The processes shown are those of a macro social consciousness forming as the accumulation of individual consciousness, and of the collective consciousness as a social fact influencing individuals' daily lives.

As already discussed, the mass-middle-class ideology—the belief that Japanese society was a homogenous one with everyone collected around the middle strata—during these years held a fixed place within the collective consciousness. Coupled with *Nihonjinron*, it exerted a gravitational pull on status identities of Japanese that tugging them toward society's center. While the collective consciousness that drove this differed from the fascism of the prewar and wartime years, the fact remains that what people were mobilized into by its binding force was again the mass (citizens) of modern society.

However, during this period there was no clearly defined correspondence relationship between the industrial, economic, and stratification system on the one hand and individual status identification on the other. Status identification (middle-class consciousness) of the day had seemingly just wafted into the air. As discussed in Chapter 4, there was in fact no correspondence relationship between mass middle class as an ideology and high-speed economic growth as the actual condition of society; their contemporaneity was nothing more than a coincidence.

Accordingly, the true nature of the mass-middle-class phenomena that lasted

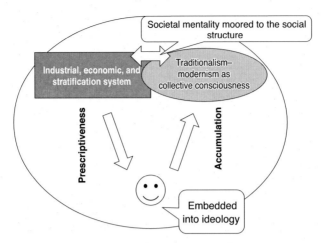

Figure E-3 Social Orientation in the 1980s

until the 1980s cycled back and forth in the social consciousness between the micro and the macro (individual consciousness-collective consciousness); it had come into being with no connection to the actual state of social relationships (where social disparities actually did exist).

Figure E-3 depicts the state of social orientations during this period. We see a robust effect there in that an individual's social attributes defined their social attitudes. Specifically, a stratification-based gradient ran through traditionalism–modernism. In addition to differences in ways of thinking based on birth cohort, the higher someone's stratification status in terms of education, occupational status, economic power, and related factors, the stronger their orientation to self-direction, modernity, and antiauthoritarian tendencies. Conversely, the lower someone's status the greater their tendencies toward conformity, traditionalism, and conventionality.

Furthermore, the form of social consciousness as an accumulation of individual consciousness was consistent with that of the conventionality-modernity duality present in the industrial, economic, and stratification system. This means the actual structure of society corresponded to the general image of the traditionalism–modernism divide. The older generations, the less educated, the hinterlands dwellers, and agricultural or manufacturing workers formed one conceptual set that evoked the conventional; the younger generations, the university graduates, the urban dwellers, and the white-collar workers in core sectors comprised another conceptual set characterized by its considerable modernity. Thanks to that clarity and consistency, Japanese were constantly looking with admiration at this core of the collective consciousness that floated in the air over their society. They could refer to it as an auxiliary line for understanding and adapting to a society in the middle of transfiguration.

As the foregoing makes clear, what made conditions easy to understand during that brief moment of 1985 is the fact that in both hardware and software terms the verticality of stratification status and the conflict over traditionalism and modernism were of the same pattern. Traditionalism quite simply has maintained its magnetic pull and is an important prerequisite of (first) modern society. As Talcott Parsons argued, the individual can remain stably embedded in modern society when a social system is forming rather than rupturing (Parsons 1951).[3]

I may have gone to excessive lengths with my argument in my effort to improve its comprehensibility as social analysis. To be sure, I must say that it is not a fact confirmed by evidence, but rather a picture reconstructed using the fragments of the findings generated by data analysis. However, by supplementing my overall story in this way, I can find the outlines in 1985 Japanese society—my starting point—of those patterns that showed (first) modernity taking its final form.

The Social Mentality of Contemporary Japan

Whatever the case, those patterns have changed completely in the 2010s. First, when it comes to status identification (Figure E-4), we Japanese now take a wide-angle view of where we are in the social structure. This permits more accurately identifying our places within the industrial, economic, and stratification system. Meanwhile, we no longer pay heed to an ideology that proclaims Japanese society to be homogenous and equal.

Over the past 25 years, Japanese have disembedded from the condition of being embedded in the mass-middle-class society. Like it or not, we all are now being re-embedded in a mass-inequality society owing to our heightened literacy in ascertaining differences in our respective statuses (in other words, the stratification structure). I described this in Chapter 5 as the arrival of *a state of disillusioned inequality* that came on the tails of *a state of illusory lebeling*.

As to social orientation, I have spoken repeatedly in this book in terms of sociologists having lost track of where the social mentality is, a state of affairs rendered in Figure E-5. The biggest change is the retirement of traditionalism–modernism, which had formed the core axis of reference for the Japanese social mentality in (first) modern society. The rules of the game in Japan up to the 1980s had been that a person would align themselves along the axis of this or some other doctrine or ideology and decide how to act in daily life on that basis. Someone who could not say precisely which doctrine they supported would be contemptuously dismissed for their lack of judgment as "non-political (*nonpori*)". Incidents of this sort could be seen all the time—not just among intellectuals, but among average university students and working adults as well.

Today's Japanese, however, no longer subscribe to these past rules demanding that they look admiringly upon some ideology floating around and embed themselves somewhere along its spectrum. The social structure and the social consciousness now lack contact with one another at both the macro and micro levels. Under these conditions, it is no longer well understood just who might be authoritarian, prosocial, or have feelings of unfairness. The doctrinally committed (or those committed to an opposing doctrine) of today are ubiquitous in society but with

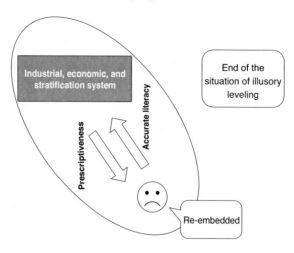

Figure E-4   Status Identification in the 2010s

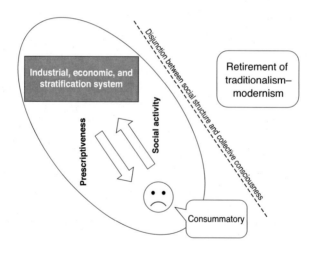

Figure E-5   Social Orientation in the 2010s

their potential latent and subsumed, waiting like some social media-instigated flash mob to emerge. Meanwhile, we engage in our daily activities based on social orientations corresponding to our places in the industrial, economic, and stratification system, and without drawing on the power of some "-ism." The shift to a consummatory orientation indicates how the individual connects with society in this fashion.

In (first) modern society, the vectors of efficiency and development in industry and economy combined with the axis of conflict between traditionalism and modernism to bind the social system together in a simple fashion. Now, however, we have been disembedded from the condition of being subsumed without really understanding it in a large system that had such consistency. Now we understand the industrial, economic, and stratification system, and are re-embedding in it directly. To sum this up simply so there will be no misunderstandings, literacy and the consummatory have combined to produce reflexivity.

My data analysis in this book proves that reflexive modernity arrived in contemporary Japanese society between 1985 to 2010. It occurred in concert with the change of eras loosely defined by the end of the 20th century and start of the 21st, or in the Japanese context more specifically the transition from the Shōwa to the Heisei period.

The Frayed Influence of Social Attributes

Next to consider is what key exactly secures the connection between the social structure and the social mentality when we are re-embedded in contemporary society. The social attributes that once comprised the points at which we were embedded (age, occupation, family, community) are gradually losing the influence they once had as the disembedding process of reflexive modernization proceeds.

However, when it comes to status identity (identification), the influence of social attributes is actually increasing amid these other transformations. Our focus should properly be on the increased literacy of subjective actors first and foremost—their improved knowledge of and ability to accurately interpret status. How these respective social attributes operate is not the issue. Accordingly, we should probe just how much the Japanese population's literacy about issues of class and strata might further improve.

Meanwhile, when it comes to social orientation the fact is, while education, occupation, birth cohort, economic power, and gender may be weakening, they still have a variety of influences. One of these is a point I emphasized early on based on an analysis of data from the 1980s—that Japanese adults demonstrate clear differences in social consciousness that are based on how much education they have (Kikkawa 1998). This structure still persists today, largely unchanged over a quarter century. Moreover, there is a sense in which educational attainment has won by default, so to speak, when it comes to being a determinant of social consciousness—a result of the weakened influence during those years of such factors as occupation and birth cohort.

Another point to scrutinize is that the influence of birth cohort has become scattershot. Whether it works to someone's advantage or disadvantage depends on the situation. There was a generation-based tendency in the 20th century as a relic of past social changes for the young to be more revolutionary and the middle-aged and older to be more conventional. This gradient in the social consciousness that Alex Inkeles sees as modernity (Inkeles 1983) and Ronald Inglehart refers to as the shift from materialism to post-materialism (Inglehart 1990) in fact constituted a generational divide.

In the Japanese case, however, more than 30 years has passed since the era of high-speed growth. With the generation that experienced only the subsequent age of the plateau gradually becoming the majority in the population, the once-clear and simple gradient in the characteristics that defined that era is disappearing. For that reason, generation-based theories of social consciousness today have shifted away from the hypotheses of modernity that were once self-evident. They are turning into a case-by-case affair, dependent on the social attitude being dealt with. This demands that the observer pay much closer attention than before to the details of a situation when discussing it.

Furthermore, the traditionalism–modernism gradient based on birth cohort became less apparent. Concurrently, the overlap in education and cohort effects that was once evident—the younger someone was, the longer their years of formal education—was also becoming less obvious (Kikkawa 2006). To offer some figures for reference, the correlation for amount of formal education and age among both genders in the SSM 1985 Survey showed an overlap of 18.4% ($r = -.429$). In the SSP-I 2010 Survey, the overlap stood at 3.4% ($r = -.185$). The amount of covariation between the two variables has dropped to as little as one-fifth the earlier result. The influence of this transformation casting today—as in the example of prosocial nature—is to generate a heretofore unseen contrast in the social attitudes of an older generation of university graduates and a younger generation without such an education.

As to gender, some slight movement is apparent from 1985 to 2010. It is faintly evident generally speaking that men tend to be embedded in market principles and the status order and calculate their own self-interest in a consummatory fashion, while women tend to be accepting of diversity and abundantly partake in cultural activities. However, as I also noted in Chapter 7, nothing fairly definite can be said for the moment about whether to see this as re-embedding in gender without attempting more time-series analyses of the social consciousness of both men and women.

Other factors such as family and the local community were never indispensable to defining the formation of social consciousness in Japanese society. Factors such as ethnicity and religions that are crucial in other societies likewise are known to have little (though not zero) influence in the Japanese case. Therefore, I believe there is little possibility that such factors have prescriptive power over social consciousness in Japan. Rather, social capital and networks are what draw our attention as powerful sites for re-embedding in this area. While I could not address these factors in this book, we will need to pay close attention to their effects on the formation of social consciousness in the future.

Based on the foregoing discussion, we can see that the interactive relationship between era-specific characteristics and status-relationship that in the 1980s overlapped to define social consciousness is now starting to fray. Put another way, the final aftereffects of high-speed economic growth are causing the overlaps in social attributes to come apart. It is this development that prevents us from coming up with a simple interpretation of the social mentality in contemporary Japan.

Disembedding from Occupation

Finally, I want to emphasize the relevance of studies of the social consciousness based on educational attainment. This is entwined with the question of what happened to the influence of occupational status, which scholars once went so far as to say was the only independent variable in social consciousness studies.

In Japanese (first) modern society, there was little fluidity when it came to careers. People were stuck for a long time in unfavorable jobs, or remained for a long time in favorable ones. Accordingly, when someone who, for example, spent their days in the industrial sector was asked about their identity, they would answer that they were in administration at a building contractor, or ran a small retail shop, or were employed in such-and-such division at city hall, or were a section chief at this-and-that trading company. While there was diversity here in terms of job type, exact industry, position, and company name, all these could be described as forms of occupational identity. Someone's job was the source of their ego, and as such they were embedded in industrial society.

Even today, occupational status is frequently seen on the surface of society as a means by which someone earns their keep. Among the general public, it plays a leading role as an object of ascription and point of reference. Over the past quarter century, however, the careers we pursue now see us making a whirlwind of changes throughout our lives to the companies we work at and the lines of work we are in. Under these conditions, it seems that—compared to the 1980s when people remained in a position based on the custom of lifetime employment—today's Japanese place less emphasis on occupational status as the source of their identities. This denormalization of employment is accompanied by a weakening of commitments to one's job, with people now facing work with a lighter frame of mind. Plainly speaking, it would be difficult for an hourly-wage worker—a *furītā* (a Japanese coinage combining the English "freelancer" and the German "*arbeiter*")—to define how they think about things and their patterns of behavior based on an occupational identity and its associated attitudes given that the conditions under which they live mean they lack such a site of affiliation. The analytical results I presented in this book made it clear that the way occupational status works to form social consciousness is becoming less substantial as conditions become increasingly remote from those assumed by 20th century Marxist class theory.

And so, where is it that these individuals disembedded from occupational status are being re-embedded? To think about this, I will borrow the words of Giddens. In his discussion, Giddens uses the terms "symbolic token" and "expert system" to explain the substantive mechanisms of disembedding. These terms are quite abstract and at first sight may seem quite puzzling. Giddens explains:

> Disembedding mechanisms are of two types, which I refer to as 'symbolic tokens' and 'expert systems.' Taken together, I refer to these as *abstract systems*. Symbolic tokens are media of exchange which have standard value, and thus are interchangeable across a plurality of contexts. The prime example, and most

pervasively important, is money. Although the larger forms of pre-modern social system have all developed monetary exchange in one form or another, money economy becomes vastly more sophisticated and abstract with the emergence and maturation of modernity. Money brackets time (because it is a means of credit) and space (since standardised value allows transactions between a multiplicity of individuals who never physically meet one another). Expert systems bracket time and space through deploying modes of technical knowledge which have validity independent of the practitioners and clients who make use of them. Such systems penetrate virtually all aspects of social life in conditions of modernity—in respect of the food we eat, the medicines we take, the buildings we inhabit, the forms of transport we use and a multiplicity of other phenomena. Expert systems are not confined to areas of technological expertise. They extend to social relations themselves and to the intimacies of the self. The doctor, counsellor and therapist are as central to the expert systems of modernity as the scientist, technician or engineer (Giddens 1991: 18).

While his meaning might be a bit difficult to grasp, we can understand him as saying that abstract systems provide yardsticks that are versatile and general for contemporary society, which is expanding and becoming increasingly complex. Money, Giddens suggests, might be one such yardstick.

Adapting this observation to the context of this book might lead one to believe that people are disembedding from occupational status and re-embedding in economic power. Unlike occupational status, economic power—the outcome of individual labor—is distributed continuously and changes incessantly. It is difficult at first glance to imagine that individuals might have their identity in this status and engage in their daily activities on its basis. However, it could make sense if the story were such that fluctuations in occupational status have Japanese keeping track of however many thousands or tens of thousands of yen they earn annually and see *that* as their connection to society rather than working "a job equivalent to section chief at a major company" or "as an automobile mechanic." Giddens argues that money is turning into a fastener of sorts that ties us to society through acts of consumption. This is because it comprises one corner of the economic and financial system that has gone beyond time and space to achieve universality.

Until now, economic status has been the object of a certain amount of attention of everyone from economists to the general public, and spoken of in terms of wealth or poverty. I have taken the logarithmic value of annual household income nearly throughout the whole of this book to be an indicator of economic power. Its influence on the social consciousness is a fact and growing increasingly certain. In this sense, the fact of our re-embedding into economic power and hence the economic system can be seen as one correct facet of the current realities.

However, I certainly do not believe that the social mentality of the Japanese people in the years ahead will be decided solely by blunt economic determinism. This is because in contemporary Japanese society, there is one thing that is an even better fit for the role of receptor of re-embedding as *symbolic token* and shaper of the social order as *expert system*. This, it almost goes without saying, is education.

Re-embedding into Education

Educational credentials were once thought of simply as a means for obtaining occupational status. During the Shōwa period for example, if someone (a man) could get a lifetime job—regardless of whether the position required at least a junior-high education or a university one—once they entered the work force neither they nor the people around them would refer back much to the name of their alma mater. The moment the individual obtained stable employment and was embedded in industrial society, the mediating role that the education attainment played for acquiring status was largely over.

However, as I've noted, a change occurred over the two-plus decades of the Heisei period so far. The fluidity of employment has resulted in individuals needing to rewrite their résumés countless times in their lives. Today, opportunities for job applicants to provide more information about their alma maters, degrees, and certifications have increased, serving as deciding factors that provide evidence of their capabilities. Such opportunities are becoming increasingly important. Under these conditions, the individual repeatedly makes use of their educational background after they've entered the work force. As a *symbolic token* indicative of their social status and life opportunities, that background becomes the objective of unending reflexive monitoring.

There are still other values incidental to the name of someone's undergraduate alma mater or the graduate degree they obtained that cannot be reduced to functional ones, such as how it might relate to work or income. For example, for someone who has no plans to write up their résumé again (say a full-time housewife or retiree), their educational background is tantamount to deadwood or the residue from some substance that has lost its potency. Even so, contemporary Japanese do not speak in such blunt terms about their alma maters. On the other hand, some think about their educational background with heavy negative thoughts. They have lifelong complexes about their own poor attainments if they completed only compulsory education, or feel excessively inferior about not having a university degree. In sociology of education, this is called the effects of the symbolic value of credentials. The symbolic value of educational credentials to a large degree governs the state of one's social consciousness; these credentials produce a gradient in the social mentality of adults. Given such broad implications, education is quite simply a *symbolic token* that provides a point for identity to re-embed in society.

Education has been rooted in society from the start with the function of forming academic knowledge and professional literacy. That being the case, it is dramatically easier to understand how *expert systems*, even more than money, provide the bedrock for order in global society—today's advanced information society. In that light, if we substitute "educational attainments" for "expert system" in the above-cited passage from Giddens then his meaning becomes crystal clear.

Based on this, it is evident that in contemporary Japanese society, now in the state of full-blown reflexive modernity, education as both *symbolic token* and *expert system* has become a point of re-embedding following the disembedding from occupational status.

Why, then, has the importance of educational credentials above all as a determinant for social consciousness manifested itself in contemporary Japanese society? To explain this precisely here I would need to double the length of this book, but fortunately I have already written about the mechanism involved elsewhere. In short, I explain that this is because contemporary Japan has reached the stage of a mature credentialist society (Kikkawa 2006) and become a society of educational disparity completely dissimilar from any other one (ibid. 2009). However, given the magnitude of importance that this linchpin of education has assumed, continued and further expansion of this research stream may well yield new and important insights as to the nature of the social mentality in the 21st century and beyond.

Concluding Remarks

The broad trends I have examined from 1985 to the present denote changes in the social environment that we could not simply alter on our own. Just as we cannot avoid the cold spells, powerful storms, or scorching heat that pressure patterns inevitably produce, we have no choice but to make do and accept these trends that develop through the ages. All we can do is provide as many people as possible accurate information about the risks and benefits that may be present in Japanese society today so that they can deal with them appropriately.

The biggest risk factor given this history is that it is no longer clear if someone can create potent currents in social orientation by directing their appeals to one or another social class. Presently, it is extremely difficult to control Japanese society at will. In fact, for most of the past decade Japan's political leaders have tried to define certain political flashpoints as the single issues of essential focus, whether it be reforms to the postal system, the issue of U.S. military bases on Okinawa, or nuclear energy policy. Even when they have momentarily been able to ride the winds blowing through the times, they no longer seem capable of winning stable support by aligning themselves with some doctrine deeply rooted in the social structure.

Put another way, however, this also means there is no fear either of Japanese being mobilized by some simple, powerful force, because they no longer have a social mentality that is easily aroused like that of 20th century mass society. The fact that each member of contemporary Japanese society is a constituent subject of democracy capable of monitoring current conditions without illusion is our current society's greatest strength. At the very least, based on the trends that social survey data show, there are no apparent omens that the foreboding form of one of the "-isms" that wreaked havoc in the 20th century is drawing new breath.

I believe the greatest driving forces these conditions have produced, over the quarter century I have taken the measure of in this book, are the facts that we Japanese are now more literate about the systems and state of our society, and that many of us can now understand and accept that conditions are relative. Perhaps this change can best be expressed by saying that we have become more self-directed.

Behind the gentle but still tremendous advances that contemporary Japanese have made in this direction lies the fact that the level of the education (of adults) we used to grasp the key to the social mentality grew by an enormous degree. We have gone from the situation seen at the end of the Shōwa period (1985) where only 13% of the population were university graduates and more than half had been educated under the prewar schooling system, to one in which there is a 50-50 split between people who did and did not graduate from a university. That shift put Japan on the road to being one of the world's leading higher education societies. On this point, too, we cannot overlook the influence of the educational attainments (the public education system), which now govern social mentality.

The citizens (individuals) of the Heisei period have become somewhat more sophisticated than the citizens (mass) of the Shōwa. For that reason, they are cautious but they are also autonomous; for better or worse, their movements are hard to forecast precisely. This means that, at a glance, they may seem to be apathetic, to be becoming more conservative, or even to be fickle. But the reality is not that simple. That in and of itself is what is so hard to comprehend about the social mentality of contemporary Japan.

NOTES

1 Intrapsychological processes of this sort are in a black box when it comes to survey data analysis research. Accordingly, the consummatory shift for the moment remains a speculatively-derived tentative proposition.

2 When it comes to the reflexive modern society, the issues that are debated range broadly and include globalization, increased risk, intimacy, and gender. Here, however, I have focused my thinking on the relationship between the individual and society.

3 While I have had traditionalism–modernism in mind in this book, the hierarchical differences in culture—high-class culture for the upper strata and mass culture for the lower—are integrated into the social system and function in the same way.

Afterword

Many readers may be familiar with the Hollywood movie *Back to the Future*. In it, Michael J. Fox played a high school senior named Marty who was able to travel through time and space using a time machine made out of a modified DeLorean (a once-hailed American brand) sports car. It was a hit in the late 1980s, and spawned two sequels.

Marty's voyage through time began on a certain day in 1985. The period to which he traveled in the first movie was 30 years before to 1955 when his parents were adolescents. In *Back to the Future II*, which came out in 1989, Marty traveled 30 years into the future. These movies have become objects of especially deep contemplation for me, who is of the same generation as Marty. What I noticed was that the future to which Marty traveled corresponds roughly to the present when I am writing this.

Using this hit movie series as a point of reference may be a bit of an awkward fit, but the story I've told in this book is one in which we've traveled from the near future of this second movie back to 1985 and then returned. In university lectures around that time, my sociology professors looked back at postwar Japanese society from the vantage point of the 1980s. They spoke in terms of *Nihonjinron* and the mass-middle-class theory, topics that have also come up in this book. They were looking at exactly the same time period from the same standpoint as the first *BTF* movie. If that is the case, then perhaps the story I am telling in place of Shōwa-era sociologists should properly be labeled "Social Consciousness Studies Part II" for how it takes up the same central theme but with the era on which it is focused moved forward to the next generation. The time machine that we used here might therefore be thought of as the vehicle of survey data analysis. That kind of thinking gave me the idea for this book.

There is an American couple who are old friends of mine. Both scholars, they have visited Japan numerous times since the 1970s and observed its changing face. On one of their more recent visits, this couple happened to mention that "Japanese have become nicer." I'm not sure what modern rationalists who experienced the full bloom of youth in the 1950s and eventually developed an attraction for Eastern culture felt was "nicer." However, as someone who actually experienced the same period in his own life, I certainly get a palpable sense that the social mentality of today's Japanese is of a higher quality than it was before. While I must offer my regrets to the Japanese of the Shōwa period to whom I owe so much, I do not want to go back to the society of those times.

Since the start of the 21st century, Japanese sociologists have spoken of obstructiveness and of concerns about the future when it comes to the social structure. Of course, we must not be unreflective or irreverent about the mountain of issues that face us. Yet, there indeed is also an aspect to the state of the Japanese soul that has become "nicer." This is so whether we are speaking from personal feeling or quantitative fact.

It is with these sorts of considerations that I have tried here to give future generations an accurate sense of what the trends of these eras were really like, beneath all the talk that tends to be negative. Essentially, I consider the very fact that most Japanese can serenely share a theory about their times that is anything but simple, and is spoken of in terms of complex and intricate tendencies and in a partially positive (or partially negative) way, to be a sign of how much Japanese society has grown.

This book turned out as well as it did thanks to the efforts of Shikama Yūsuke in Yuhikaku Publishing. I offer him my deepest thanks for the pithy and rapierlike stimulation he provided when I tended to fall behind, as well as for the aptness of his ideas. I would also like to thank my students and the other younger folk around me for encouraging me to see things in new ways. I hope that with this book I have offered them something in return.

Toru Kikkawa
Spring 2014

Works Cited

Adler, Nancy E., Elissa S. Epel, Grace Castellazzo, and Jeannette R. Ickovics. 2000. "Relationship of Subjective and Objective Social Status with Psychological and Physiological Functioning: Preliminary Data in Healthy White Women." *Health Psychology* 19(6): 586–592.

Adorno, Theodor W., Else Frenkel-Brunswik, Daniel J. Levinson, and R. Nevitt Sanford. 1950. *The Authoritarian Personality*. New York: Harper & Brothers.

Aoki Tamotsu. 1990. *Nihon bunka ron no henyō: Sengo Nihon no bunka to aidentiti* [The transformation in 'theories of Japanese culture': Post-war Japanese culture and identity]. Tokyo: Chūōkōron shinsha.

Bauman, Zygmunt. 2001. *The Individualized Society*. Cambridge: Polity Press.

Beck, Ulrich, and Elizabeth Beck-Gernsheim. 2002. *Individualization*. London: Sage Publications.

Bourdieu, Pierre. 1979. *La distinction*. Paris: Éditions de Minuit.

Cabinet Office of Japan. 2014. *Kokumin seikatsu ni kansuru yoron chōsa* [Public Opinion Survey Concerning People's Lifestyles], <http://www8.cao.go.jp/survey/index-ko.htm>, last accessed 01/15/2014.

Doi Takeo. 1971. *Amae no kōzō* [The anatomy of dependence]. Tokyo: Kōbundō Publishers.

Durkheim, Émile. 1895. *Les règles de la méthode sociologique*. Paris: Presses Universitaires de France.

Erikson, Robert, and John H. Goldthorpe. 1992. *The Constant Flux: A Study of Class Mobility in Industrial Societies*. New York: Oxford University Press.

Eysenck, Hans J. 1954. *The Psychology of Politics*. London: Routledge and Kegan Paul.

Fromm, Erich. 1941. *Escape from Freedom*. New York: Holt, Rinehart and Winston.

——. 1980. *Arbeiter und Angestellte am Vorabend des Dritten Reiches*. München: Deutsche Verlags-Anstalt.

Giddens, Anthony. 1990. *The Consequences of Modernity*. Cambridge: Polity Press.

——. 1991. *Modernity and Self-Identity: Self and Society in the Late Modern Age*. Stanford: Stanford University Press.

Hamada Hiroshi. 2012. "Senkei ketsugō moderu wa kagakuteki setsumei tariuruka: Kaisō kizoku ishiki kenkyū ni okeru keiryō to sūri no yūgō" [Can a linear combination model be scientific explanation?: Integration of mathematical sociology and empirical social research in class identification study]. *Riron to hōhō* [Sociological theory and methods] 27 (2): 259–276.

Hamaguchi Eshun. 1977 (reprint 1988). *Nihon-"rashisa" no saihakken* [Rediscovering Japanese-ness]. Tokyo: Kōdansha.

Hara Junsuke. 1988. "Kaisō ishiki kenkyū no kadai to hōhō" [Issues and methods in strata consciousness research]. In *1985-nen shakai kaisō to shakai idō zenkoku chōsa hōkokusho 2: Kaisō ishiki no dōtai* [Report on the SSM 1985 Survey 2: Trends of strata consciousness]. SSM 1985 Survey Management Committee:

1–18.
Hayashi Chikio. 1988. *Nihonjin no kokoro o hakaru* [Measuring the mentality of the Japanese]. Tokyo: Asahi Shinbun Publications.
Hayashi Yūsuke and Satō Yoshimichi. 2011. "Ryūdō-ka suru rōdō shijō to fubyōdō: Hi-seiki koyō o meguru shokugyō kyaria no bunseki" [A fluid labor market and inequality: An analysis of occupational careers related to non-regular employment]. In *Nihon no shakai kaisō to sono mekanizumu: Fubyōdō o toinaosu* [Japanese social stratification and its mechanisms: Reconsidering inequality], eds. Seiyama Kazuo, et. al. Tokyo: Hakutō shobō: 35–60.
Hazama Hiroshi. 1971. *Nihonteki keiei: Shūdan-shugi no kōzai* [Japanese-style business management: The merits and demerits of collectivism]. Tokyo: Nikkei Publishing.
Hazama Ryotarō, Hashizume Yuto, and Kikkawa Tōru. 2013. "Kankyō hogo ishiki, kenkō-iji ishiki no kitei yōin no jidai henka" [Changes in the determinants of environmentalism and healthism]. *Shakai to chōsa* [Advances in social research] 11: 70–84.
Hidaka Rokurō. 1960. *Gendai ideorogī* [Contemporary ideology]. Tokyo: Keisō shobō.
Hout, Michael. 2008. "How Class Works: Objective and Subjective Aspects of Class since the 1970s." In *Social Class: How Does It Work?*, eds. Annette Lareau and Dalton Conley. New York: Russell Sage Foundation: 25–89.
Imada Takatoshi. 1987. *Modan no datsu-kōchiku: Sangyō shakai no yukue* [Deconstructing the modern: The future of industrialized society]. Tokyo: Chūōkōron shinsha.
———. 1989. *Shakai kaisō to seiji* [Social stratification and politics]. Tokyo: University of Tokyo Press.
Inaba Keishin. 2008. *Omoiyari kakusa ga Nihon o dame ni suru: Sasaeau shakai o tsukuru yattsu no apurōchi* [Disparities in altruism that diminish Japan: Eight approaches to establish a corporative society]. Tokyo: NHK Books.
Inglehart, Ronald. 1990. *Culture Shift in Advanced Industrial Society.* Princeton: Princeton University Press.
Inkeles, Alex. 1983. *Exploring Individual Modernity.* New York: Columbia University Press.
Ishida Hiroshi and Miwa Satoshi. 2011. "Shakai idō no sūsei to hikaku" [A description and comparison of trends in social mobility]. In *Gendai no kaisō shakai 2: Kaisō to idō no kōzō* [Contemporary stratified society: The structure of stratification and mobility], eds. Ishida Hiroshi, Kondo Hiroyuki., and Nakao Keiko. Tokyo: University of Tokyo Press: 3–20.
Kaibara Ekiken. 2005. *Yōjōkun.* Translated by Matsuda Michio. Tokyo: Chūōkōron shinsha.
Kanbayashi Hiroshi. 2010a. "Kōdo keizai seichōki no kaisō kizoku ishiki: Sengo Nihon ni okeru kaisō ishiki ni kansuru nōto (1)" [Status identification in the era of high-speed growth: Note on social identification in postwar Japan (1)]. *Tōhoku Gakuin Daigaku Kyōyō Gakubu ronshū* [Tohoku Gakuin University Faculty of Liberal Arts review] 156: 25–54.

---------. 2010b. "Chū Ishiki no Hōwa to Senzai Suru Henka: Sengo Nihon no kaisō kizoku ishiki ni kansuru nōto (2)" [Saturation and latent changes of the "middle" status identification: Note on status identification in postwar Japan (2)], ibid. 157: 1–22.
---------. 2011. "Chūryū ishiki to Nihon shakai: Kaisō kizoku ishiki no jidai henka to sono imi" [Middle-class consciousness and Japanese society: The temporal change of stratus identification and its meaning]. In *Nihon no shakai kaisō to sono mekanizumu*. Tokyo: Hakutō shobō: 151–184.
---------. 2012. "Sō-chūryū to fubyōdō o meguru gensetsu: Sengo Nihon ni okeru kaisō kizoku ishiki ni kansuru nōto (3)" [Discourses on the "mass middle class" and inequality: Note on status identification in postwar Japan (3)]. *Tōhoku Gakuin Daigaku Kyōyō Gakubu ronshū* 161: 67–90.
Kawakami Norito, Hashimoto Hideki and Kobayashi Yasuki, eds. 2006. *Shakai kakusa to kenkō: Shakai ekigaku kara no apurōchi* [Health and social disparity: A social epidemiology approach]. Tokyo: University of Tokyo Press.
Kido Kōtarō. 1970. *Shakai ishiki no kōzō* [Structure of social consciousness]. Shinyōsha.
Kido Kōtarō and Sugi Masataka. 1954. "Shakai ishiki no kōzō" [The structure of social consciousness]. *Shakaigaku hyōron* [Japanese sociological review] 4 (1-2): 74–100.
Kikkawa Tōru. 1994. "Gendai shakai ni okeru ken`i-shugiteki taido shakudo no yūyōsei" [Relevance of the authoritarian attitude scale in contemporary society: As an analytical perspective of the "conservationist" and "health conscious" attitudes]. *Soshioroji* 39 (2): 125–137.
---------. 1998. *Kaisō kyōiku to shakai ishiki no keisei: Shakai ishiki ron no jikai* [Stratification, education, and formation of social consciousness: The magnetic field in social consciousness studies], Kyoto: Minerva shobō.
---------. 1999. "Chū ishiki no shizuka na henyō" [Changes of the determinant of class identification in Japan. *Shakaigaku hyōron* 50(2): 216–230 (English translation: Kikkawa Tōru, 2000,"Changes of the Determinant of Class Identification in Japan," *International Journal of Sociology*, 30-2: 34–51.).
---------. 2000. "Taishū kyōiku shakai no naka no kaisōishiki" [Strata consciousness in mass education society]. *Nihon no kaisō shisutemu 3: Sengo Nihon no kyōiku shakai* [Stratification system in Japan 3: Educational credentials in the postwar stratification system]. Ed. Konodō Hiroyuki, Tokyo: University of Tokyo Press: 175–195.
---------. 2001. *Gakurekishakai no rōkaru torakku: Chihō kara daigaku shingaku* [Local tracking system in an educational credentials society: College advancement from rural areas]. Kyoto: Sekai shisōsha.
---------. 2003. "Keiryōteki monogurafu to sūri-keiryō shakaigaku no kyori" [Distance between numerical monograph and mathematical sociology]. *Shakaigaku hyōron* 53 (4): 485–498.
---------. 2006. *Gakureki to kakusa fubyōdō* [Education and social inequality: Contemporary educational credentialism in Japan]. Tokyo: University of Tokyo Press.

———. 2008. "Kaikyū-kaisō ishiki no keiryō shakaigaku" [Quantitative sociology of class-strata consciousness]. *Kōza shakaigaku 13 Kaisō* [Sociology of social stratification: Sociology in Japan 13], eds. Atsushi Naoi and Fujita Hidenori. Tokyo: University of Tokyo Press: 77–108.

———. 2009. *Gakureki bundan shakai* [Society of educational disparity]. Tokyo: Chikuma shobō.

———. 2011. "Kaisō ishiki no genzai to yukue" [The current state of strata consciousness and the future]. *Gendai no kaisō shakai 3: Ryūdōka no naka no shakai ishiki* [Values and attitudes in a time of destabilization: Contemporary stratified society 3], eds. Saitō Yuriko and Misumi Kazuto. Tokyo: University of Tokyo Press: 63–78.

———. 2012. "Sōchūryū no yoron to seron" [Public opinion and social sentiment of mass middle class]. *Mita shakaigaku* [Mita journal of sociology] 17: 13–27.

———. 2013. "Yutaka na shakai no kakusa to fubyōdō" [The economic gap and inequality in an affluent society]. *Do! soshiorojī, kaiteiban* [Do! sociology, revised edition], eds. Tomoeda Toshio and Yamada Mamoru. Tokyo: Yuhikaku Publishing, 125–148.

———, ed. 2007. *Kaisōka suru shakai ishiki: Shokugyō to pāsonariti no keiryō shakaigaku* [Stratifying social consciousness: A quantitative study of work and personality]. Tokyo: Keisō shobō.

———, ed. 2009. *Shokugyō to kazoku to pāsonariti ni tsuite no dōitsu paneru chōki tsuiseki chōsa* [Long-term follow-up panel survey on occupation, family, and personality]. Kagaku kenkyūhi hojokin kenkyū (KAKENHI) hōkokusho [Grant-in-aid for scientific research report].

———, ed. 2012. *Chōki tsuiseki chōsa de miru Nihonjin no ishiki henyō* [Transformation of attitudes in Japan: Based on a long-term follow up survey]. Kyoto: Minerva shobō.

——— and Fujihara Sho. 2012. "Class Awareness in Japan and the U.S.: Expansion and Stability." *Riron to hōhō* 27(2): 205–224.

——— and Takayasu Nakamura. 2012. *Gakureki, kyōsō, jinsei: 10-dai no ima shitte oku beki koto* [Education, competition and life: Relevant tips for teenagers]. Tokyo: Nihon Tosho Center.

——— and Makoto Todoroki. 1996. "Gakkō kyōiku to sengo Nihon no shakai ishiki no minshuka" [School education and democratization of social consciousness in postwar Japan]. *Kyōiku shakaigaku kenkyū* [Journal of educational sociology] 58: 87–101. (English translation: Kikkawa Tōru and Makoto Todoroki, 1998, "School Education and Democratization of Social Consciousness in Postwar Japan," *International Journal of Sociology* 28-1: 92–108.).

Kim Myungsoo. 2012. "Shakai ishiki" [Social consciousness]. In *Gendai shakaigaku jiden* [Encyclopedia of contemporary sociology], eds. Ōsawa Masachi, Yoshimi Shunya, and Washida Kiyokazu. Tokyo: Kōbundō: 562–563.

Kishimoto Shigenobu. 1978. *Chūryū no gensō* [The illusion of "middle class"]. Tokyo: Kōdansha.

Kitayama Shinobu. 1998. *Jiko to kanjō: Bunka shinrigaku ni yoru toi kake* [The self and emotion: An inquiry based on cultural psychology]. Tokyo: Kyōritsu shuppan.
Kobayashi Daisuke. 2008. "Kaisō kizoku ishiki ni tsuite no kiso bunseki: Jiten hikaku no tame no chūiten [A basic analysis of status identification: Points of attention for time comparisons]. In *2005-nen SSM Nihon chōsa no kiso bunseki: Kōzō, sūsei, hōhō: 2005-nen SSM chōsa shirīzu 1* [Basic analysis of the SSM 2005 Survey: Structure, trend and method], eds. Miwa Satoshi and Kobayashi Daisuke. SSM 2005 Survey Management Committee: 111–126.
Kohn, Melvin L. 1969. *Class and Conformity: A Study in Values*. Chicago: University of Chicago Press.
Kohn, Melvin L. and Carmi Schooler, with the collaboration of Joanne Miller, et al. 1983. *Work and Personality: An Inquiry into the Impact of Social Stratification*. New York: Ablex.
Kondō Katsunori. 2010. *Kenkō kakusa shakai o ikinuku* [Surviving a society of health inequalities]. Tokyo: Asahi Shinbun Publications.
Kōsaka Kenji. 2000. *Shakaigaku ni okeru fōmaru seorī: Kaisō imēji ni kan suru FK moderu* (Formal theory in sociology: The FK model for images of stratification]. Tokyo: Harvest-sha.
Lipset, Seymour M. 1959. *Political Man: The Social Bases of Politics*. New York: Doubleday and Co.
Mamada Takao. 1990. "Kaisō kizoku ishiki: Keizai seichō, byōdōka to 'chū' ishiki" [Status identification: Economic growth, equalization and middle-class consciousness]. In *Gendai Nihon no kaisō kōzō 2: Kaisō ishiki no dōtai* [The stratification structure of contemporary Japan: The transformation of strata consciousness], ed. Hara Junsuke. Tokyo: University of Tokyo Press: 23–45.
Manabe Kazufumi. 2004. "Tsū-bunka hikaku chōsa oyobi kokusai hikaku chōsa no hōhōronteki kadai: Chōsa no dōkasei no mondai o chūshin ni" [Methodological problems in cross-cultural and international comparative surveys: Focusing on equivalence]." *Hōgaku kenkyū* [Keio University journal of law, politics and sociology] 77 (1): 504–538.
Marx, Karl. 1859. *Zur Kritik der politischen Ökonomie*. München: Franz Duncker.
Mikami Takeshi. 2010. *Shakai no shikō: Risuku to kanshi to kojinka* [Thought in society: Risk, surveillance and individualization]. Tokyo: Gakubunsha.
Mills, C. Wright. 1959. *The Sociological Imagination*. New York: Oxford University Press.
Ministry of Internal Affairs and Communications, Statistics Bureau website. Jinkōkōsei http://www.stat.go.jp/data/kokusei/2010/kouhou/useful/u01_z24.htm, last accessed 01/15/2014.
Misumi Kazuto. 1990. "Kaikyū kizoku ishiki" [Class identification]. In *Gendai Nihon no kaikyū kōzō 2: Kaisō ishiki no dōtai*: 71–95.
Mita Munesuke. 1965. *Gendai Nihonjin no seishin kōzō* [The structure of the contemporary Japanese mentality]. Tokyo: Kōbundō.
———. 1968. "Shakai ishikiron" [Social consciousness studies]. *Shakaigaku kenkyū nyūmon* [A primer on sociological study], eds. Watanuki Jōji and

Matsubara Haruo. Tokyo: University of Tokyo Press: 189–220.
——————. 1976. "Gendai shakai no shakai ishiki" [Social consciousness in contemporary society]. In *Shakaigaku kōza: Shakai ishikiron* [Sociology lecture 12: The theory of social consciousness], ed. Mita Munesuke. Tokyo: University of Tokyo Press: 1–26.
——————. 1979. *Gendai shakai no shakai ishiki* [Social consciousness in contemporary society]. Tokyo: Kōbundō.
—————— (as Maki Yūsuke). 1981. *Jikan no hikaku shakaigaku* [A comparative sociology of time]. Iwanami shoten.
——————. 1993. "Shakai ishiki" [Social consciousness]. In *Shin-shakaigaku jiden* [New encyclopedia of sociology], eds. Morioka Kiyomi, Shiobara Tsutomu, and Honma Yasuhei. Tokyo: Yuihikaku Publishing: 592–594.
Miura Atsushi. 2005. *Karyū shakai: Arata na shakai shūdan no shutsugen* [Lower-class society: The emergence of a new social category]. Tokyo: Kōbunsha.
Miyajima Takashi. 1983. *Gendai shakai ishikiron* [Contemporary social consciousness studies]. Tokyo: Nippon hyōronsha.
Mori Naoto. 2008. "Sōchūryū no shisō to wa nan datta no ka: Chū ishiki no genten o saguru" [What was the ideology behind the mass middle class society? Uncovering the origins of the middle consciousness]. In *Shisō chizu 2* [Map of philosophy 2], eds. Azuma Hiroki and Kitada Akihiro. Tokyo: NHK Publishing: 233–270.
Murakami Yasusuke. 1984. *Shin chūkan taishū no jidai* [The age of new mass middle class]. Tokyo: Chūōkōron shinsha.
Murakami Yasusuke, Kumon Shunpei and Satō Seizaburō. 1979. *Bunmei to shite no ie shakai* [The *ie* society as a pattern of civilization]. Tokyo: Chūōkōron shinsha.
Nakane Chie. 1967. *Tate shakai no ningen kankei: Tan'itsu shakai no riron*. [The human relationship in the society of vertical order: A theory of the homogeneous society], Tokyo: Kōdansha. (English translation: Nakane Chie, 1973, *Japanese Society: a Practical Guide to Understanding the Japanese Mindset and Culture*, North Clarendon: Tuttle Publishing).
Naoi Atsushi. 1987. "Shigoto to ningen no sōgō kankei" [The interaction between work and human beings]. In *Hataraku koto no imi—Meaning of Working Life: MOW no kokusai hikaku kenkyū* [What it means to work (Meaning of working life): An international comparative study on the meaning of working], ed. Misumi Jūji. Tokyo: Yuhikaku Publishing: 103–144.
Naoi Michiko. 1979. "Kaisō ishiki to kaikyū ishiki" [Stratum identification and class identification]. In *Nihon no kasō kōzō* [Social stratification in Japan], ed. Tominaga Ken'ichi. Tokyo: University of Tokyo Press: 365–388.
——————. 1988. "Shokugyō kaisō to ken'i-shugiteki kachi ishiki" [Occupational status and authoritarian value consciousness]. In *1985-nen shakai kaisō to shakai idō zenkoku chōsa hōkokusho* 2: 225–242.
——————, ed. 1989. *Kaji no shakaigaku* [The sociology of housework]. Tokyo: Saiensu-sha.
Nishiyama Tetsuo. 2013. "Gendai ni okeru kagaku-chi to nichijō-chi no kōryū ni

tsuite" [On the interactions between scientific knowledge and the knowledge of daily life]. In *Kagakuka suru nichijō no shakaigaku* [The sociology of making daily life scientific], ed. Nishiyama Tetsuo. Kyoto: Sekai shisōsha: 13–52.

Oda Teruya and Kōji Abe. 2000. "Fukōheikan wa dono yō ni shōjiru no ka: Seisei mekanizumu no kaimei" [How a sense of unfairness is generated: An explication of the mechanism at work]. In *Nihon no kaisō shisutemu 2: Kōheikan to seiji ishiki* [The stratification system in Japan 2: Sense of fairness and political consciousness], ed. Umino Michio. Tokyo: University of Tokyo Press: 103–125.

Odaka Kunio. 1967. "Yasuda Saburō-kun ni kotaeru" [A reply to Yasuda Saburō], *Shakaigaku hyōron*, 18 (2): 109–113.

Organization for Economic Cooperation and Development. 2013. "OECD Better Life Index" <http://www.oecd-ilibrary.org/economics/how-s-life-2013_9789264201392-en>, last accessed 02/15/2016.

Oguma Eiji. 1998. *Nihonjin no kyōkai: Okinawa, Ainu, Taiwan, Chōsen shokuminchi shihai kara fukki undō made* [The boundaries of the Japanese people: Okinawa, Ainu, Taiwan and Korea from colonial rule to reversion movements]. Tokyo: Shinyōsha.

Ojima Fumiaki, ed. 2001. *Gendai kōkōsei no keiryō shakaigaku* [A quantitative sociology of today's high school students]. Kyoto: Minerva shobō.

Ōtake Fumio. 2010. *Kyōsō to kōheikan: Shijō keizai no hontō no meritto* [Competition and the sense of equity: The true merits of a market economy]. Tokyo: Chūōkōron shinsha.

Ōtsuka Hisao. 1949 (reprint 1968). *Kindaika no ningenteki kiso* [The human foundations of modernization]. Tokyo: Chikuma shobō.

Parsons, Talcott. 1951. *The Social System*. New York: Free Press.

Pedersen, Peter David. 2006. *Rohasu ni kurasu* [Living a LOHAS life]. Tokyo: Business-Sha.

Putnam, Robert D. 2001. *Bowling Alone: The Collapse and Revival of American Community*. New York: Simon & Schuster.

Rokeach, Milton. 1960. *The Open and Closed Mind*. New York: Basic Books.

Saitō Yuriko. 2011. "Yori yoi shakai o meguru toi: Shakai kaisō to kōkyōsei, seigi" [Questions about a better society: Social stratification, publicness and justice]. In *Nihon no shakai kaisō to sono mekanizumu*: 225–254.

Saitō Yuriko and Ōtsuki Shigemi. 2011. "Fukōheikan no kōzō: Kakusa kakudai to kaisōsei" [Structure of the sense of unfairness: Stratification and expanding social disparity]. In *Gendai no kaisō Shakai* 3: 219–232.

Sandel, Michael J. 2009. *Justice: What's the Right Thing to Do?* New York: Farrar, Straus and Giroux.

Satō Kenji. 2011. *Shakai chōsa shi no riterashī: Hōhō o yomu shakaigakuteki sōzōryoku* [Understanding the history of social research: Sociological imagination to examine methodology]. Tokyo: Shinyōsha.

Satō Toshiki. 2000. *Fubyōdō shakai Nihon* [Japan as an unequal society]. Tokyo: Chūōkōron shinsha.

———. 2009. "Kaisō kizoku no imiron: Jiseiteki kindai ni okeru kaisō ishiki" [The semantics of status identification: Social psychology in reflective

stratified societies]. *Shakaigaku hyōron* 59 (4): 734–751.
Seiyama Kazuo. 1990. "Chū-ishiki no imi" [Middle class identification in postwar Japan]. *Riron to hōhō* 5 (2): 51–71.
——————. 2004. *Shakai chōsahō nyūmon* [Introduction to social research]. Yuhikaku Publishing.
Seligman, Martin E. P. 2002. *Authentic Happiness: Using the New Positive Psychology to Realize Your Potential for Lasting Fulfillment*. New York: Free Press.
Shiobara Tsutomu. 1994. *Tenkan suru Nihon shakai* [Japanese society in transition]. Tokyo: Shinyōsha.
SSM 1975 Survey Management Committee. 1976. *1975-nen SSM chōsa kōdo bukku* [The codebook for the SSM 1975 Survey]. SSM 1975 Survey Management Committee.
SSM Torendo Bunseki Kenkyūkai [SSM trends analysis study group]. 1983. *1995-nen SSM chōsa: 1980-1981-nendo sai-kōdingu kōdobukku* [The SSM 1995 Survey: The codebook for re-coding the 1980 and 1981 studies]. SSM torendo bunseki kenkyūkai.
SSP Purojekuto [SSP project]. 2013. *SSP-W2013 1st: Kōdobukku oyobi kiso shūkeihyō* [SSP-W2013 1st: Codebook and basic report]. SSP Purojekuto website, <http://ssp.hus.osaka-u.ac.jp/pdf/SSP-W20131st.pdf>, last accessed 01/15/2014.
Sudo Naoki. 2009. *Kaisō ishiki no dainamikusu: Naze, sore wa genjitsu kara zureru no ka* [The dynamics of status identification]. Keisō shobō.
——————. 2010. *Nihonjin no kaisōishiki* [Status identification in Japan]. Tokyo: Kōdansha.
Sugino Isamu. 2012. "Ryō to shitsu no kyōtsū no junkyo mondai" [Shared standards of quantitative and qualitative studies]. In *Shakaigaku o tou: Kihan, riron, jisshō no kinchō kankei* [Inquiring sociology: The tense relationship among model, theory, and evidence], eds. Yonemura Chiyo and Sudo Naoki. Tokyo: Keisō shobō: 124–157.
Tachibanaki Toshiaki. 1998. *Nihon no keizai kakusa: Shotoku to shisan kara kangaeru* [Economic discrepancies in Japan]. Tokyo: Iwanami shoten.
Tanioka Ken. 2012. "SSP-I 2010 ni miru kakusa shakai no kaisō kizoku ishiki" [Status identification in an inequality society: Based on an analysis of SSP-I 2010 data]. *Tōkei sūri kenkyūsho kyōdō kenkyū ripōto* [Joint study report of the Institute of Statistical Mathematics) 287: 145–157.
Tarōmaru Hiroshi, Sakaguchi Yūsuke, and Miyata Naoko. 2009. "*Soshioroji* to *Shakaigaku hyōron* ni miru shakaigaku no hōhō no torendo 1952–2008" [Trends in sociology methods as seen in *Soshioroji* and *Shakaikagaku hyōron*, 1952–2008). Tarōmaru Hiroshi website, <http://tarohmaru.web.fc2.com/documents/journal.pdf>, last accessed 01/15/2014.
Todoroki Makoto. 1998. "Ken'i-shugiteki taido to gendai no shakai kaisō" [Authoritarian attitude and contemporary social stratification]. In *1995-nen SSM chōsa shirīzu 6: Gendai Nihon no kaisō ishiki* [SSM 1995 Survey report series 6: Strata consciousness in contemporary Japan], ed. Mamada Takao. SSM 1995 Survey Management Committee. 65–87.

———. 2000. "Han-ken'i-shugiteki taido no takamari wa nani o motarasu no ka" [What does the rise in the anti-authoritarian attitude imply?]. In *Nihon no kaisō shisutemu* 2: 195–216.

———. 2008. "Ken'i-shugiteki taido to shakai kaisō: Bunpu to senkei kankei no jiten hikaku" [Authoritarian attitude and social stratification: Temporal comparison of distribution and linear relationship]. In *2005-nen SSM chōsa shirīzu 8: Kaisō ishiki no genzai* [SSM 2005 Survey report series 8: The current state of strata consciousness], ed. Todoroki Makoto. SSM 2005 Survey Management Committee: 227–247.

———. 2011. "Kaisō ishiki no bunseki wakugumi: Kachi ishiki o chūshin to shite" [The analytical frame of strata consciousness: Focusing on values]. In *Gendai no kaisō shakai* 3: 79–91.

Tōkei sūri kenkyūjo [Institute of Statistical Mathematics]. 2013. *Nihonjin no kokuminsei chōsa* [The study of Japanese national character], <http://www.ism.ac.jp/kokuminsei/table/index.htm>, last accessed 01/15/2014.

Tomoeda Toshio. 2010. "Datsu-umekomi" [Disembedding]. In *Shakaigaku jiten* [Encyclopedia of sociology], ed. Nihon Shakaigakkai Shakaigaku Jiden Kankō Iinkai [Japanese Sociological Society *Shakaigaku jiten* publication committee]. Tokyo: Maruzen: 208–209.

———. 2013. "Shakaigaku no hōhō: Shakai o kagaku suru" [The methods of sociology: Applying science to society]. In *Do! soshiorojī, kaiteiban*: 1–21.

Tomono Norio. 2006. *Kōdō keizaigaku: Keizai wa kanjō de ugoite iru* [Behavioral economics: Economy is driven by emotion. Tokyo: Kōbunsha.

Umino Michio. 2000. "Yutakasa no tsuikyū kara kōhei shakai no kikyū e: Kaisō ishiki no kōzō to henyo" [From chasing affluence to seeking justice: The structure of and changing trends in strata consciousness]. In *Nihon no kaisō shisutemu* 2: 3–36.

———, ed. 2007. *Ningen kōdō to seisaku: Haikibutsu o meguru sūri-keiryō shakaigaku* [Human behavior and politics: Mathematical sociology environmental problems]. Kagaku kenkyūhi hojokin kenkyū (KAKENHI) hōkokusho [Grant-in-aid for scientific research report].

Umino Michio and Saitō Yuriko. 1990. "Kōheikan to manzokukan" [Equity and satisfaction]. In *Gendai Nihon no kaikyū kōzō* 2: 97–124.

Watanuki Jōji. 1986. "Shakai kōzō to kachi tairitsu" [Social structure and value conflicts]. In *Nihonjin no senkyo kōdō* [Japanese election behavior], eds. Watanuki Jōji et al. Tokyo: University of Tokyo Press: 17–37.

Yamada Mamoru. 2010. "Saikiteki kindaika" [Reflexive modernization]. In *Shakaigaku jiten*: 210–211.

———. 2013. "Kojinka suru shakai to shinmitusei no wana" [Individualization and the intimacy trap]. In *Do! soshiorojī, kaiteiban*: 25–50.

Yamamono Shichihei. 1983. *"Kūki" no kenkyū* [Essays on "atmosphere"]. Tokyo: Bungeishunju.

Yamazaki Masakazu. 1984. *Yawarakai kojin-shugi no tanjō: Shōhi shakai no bigaku* [The birth of soft individualism: Aesthetics in a consumer society]. Tokyo: Chūōkōron shinsha.

Yasuda Saburō. 1973. *Gendai Nihon no kaikyū ishiki* [Class consciousness in contemporary Japan]. Tokyo: Yuhikaku Publishng.
Yoda Takanori. 2010. *Kōdō keizaigaku: Kanjō ni yureru keizai shinri* [Behavioral economics: Economic mood driven by emotion]. Tokyo: Chūōkōron shinsha.
Yoneda Yukihiro. 2007. "Sangyo shakai ni okeru pāsonariti keisei" [Personality development in industrial society]. In *Kaisōka suru shakai ishiki: Shokugyō to pāsonariti no keiryō shakaigaku*: 49–76.
Yoshizaki Tatsuhiko. 2005. *1985-nen* [1985]. Tokyo: Shinchosha Publishing.
Zheng Yuejun, Yoshino Ryōzō, and Murakami Masakatsu. 2006. "Higashi Ajia shokoku no hitobito no shizenkan, kankyōkan no bunseki: Kankyō ishiki keisei ni eikyō o ataeru yōin no chūshutsu" [An analysis on the attitudes toward nature and environment in East Asia: Main factors in the formation of environmental consciousness]. *Kōdō keiryo-gaku* [Japanese journal of behaviormetrics] 33(1): 55–68.

Index

SUBJECT INDEX

A
Altruism   122
Analytical monograph   **36–39**
"The angels' share"   **39–41**, 85, 93
Authoritarianism (Authoritarian attitude, Authoritarian conservatism)   15, 27, **98–109**, 113–116, 139–151, 153–155
The Authoritarian Personality   99

B
Baby boomers (Japanese), *see Dankai no sedai*
Behavioral economics   4–6
Better Life Index   137
Bourgeoisie   69
"Bubble" (economy) years   **48**, 86, 138

C
Class identity   **70**
Collective consciousness   **17**, 156–160
Consummatory   130–132, 149–150, **155–162**
Contemporary social consciousness studies   **13–21**
Contextualism   **58**
Conventional (Conventionality)   **12–13**, 30, 97–98, 103, 150, 156, 160
Cultural activities   126–134
Cultural consumption activities   126–131, 155
Cultural psychology   22
Cultural reproduction   125
Culture   8
———— sociology of   **16–23**
———— status-relatedness of   126

D
Dankai no sedai   56
Disembedding   **156–167**
Diversity, acceptance of   **123–125**, 131–135
Doctrine (*see also* "-ism")   8–9, **122–132**, 154–163

E
Education   10–12, 37–38, 49, 83–89, 103–104, 110–114, 130–134, 164, 169
———— re-embedding in   **167–168**
Education society   12, **168–169**
Elections, frequency of voting in   127–130
Emotions and feelings   **9–10**
Environmental conservation awareness   138–151
Equity   41, 117–120
Ethos   **8–9**
"Exotic Japan"   **57–59**, 62
Experience and frequency of foreign travel   129–131
Expert system   **165–167**

F
Face-to-face interview   **32–34**, 40, 72, 80, 102–103, 107
Faith in percentages   **33**
"Farewell to the Mass Middle Class"   66
Fascism   98–99
Five-level status identification   **65–72**, 81–85
Fubyōdō shakai Nihon   66, 79

G
Gender-role segregation, attitudes toward   109–115
General life satisfaction   139–150
General Social Survey (GSS)   42, 70, 79–80, 88

H
Habitus   8, 17, 125–126
"Hardware"   13, **25**, 27, **41**, 87, 101, 126, 159, 161
Health maintenance awareness   138–151
High modernity   51

I
Ideology   **8–9**, 159–161
Illusory leveling, state of   **91**, 161
Individuality   **7–9**

Individualization **150–158**
"Inside-outside role" attitude 109–111
Interested party 33, 122, 132
"-ism" (*see also* "doctrine") 8–9, **123–125**

J
Japanese National Character Survey 33, 35, 60, 79
Justice 118–119

K
Kohn-Schooler study **100**

L
Library visits, frequency of 126–130
Life of the People Survey 33, 65–66, 76–77
Lifestyle of health and sustainability, *see* LOHAS
"Literacy" xiv, 91, 158–167
LOHAS 139
Lower-class society **69**, 78

M
Marxist class theory 13–14, 69, 165
Mass inequality **83–92**, 161
Mass middle class xiii, 19–22, 30–32, **61–62**, 65–80, 81–83, 87–93, 159–161
Mass society theory 13, 17, 62, **157–158**
"Master-subordinate role" attitude 109–112
Mathematical sociology 22
Mechanism of Escape 7, **99**
Meritocracy 113, 133
Methodological individualism **17–18**, 158
Middle-class consciousness **66–67**, 76–77, 159
Modern (modrnization) **12–13**, 52, 58–61, 97
Modernism, *see* Traditionalism–modernism
Modernity xii, **97–98**, 138, 150, 156–158
"Museums visit" 126–130

N
Naive realist reflection assertion **80**, 93
National Survey of Social Stratification and Social Mobility, *see* SSM Survey
Neoliberal perception of inequality 121–122
New middle mass 89
Nihonjinron 22, **57–62**, 159, 171

O
"One hundred million-strong mass middle class" **62**
Ordinary least squares (OLS) regression analysis **36–39**
Organization for Economic Cooperation and Development (OECD) 137
Orientation 8, **31**

P
Personal interest, *see* Interested party
Population pyramid 55–56
Positive reevaluations of the uniqueness of Japan's culture **57–59**
Postwar social consciousness studies **12–13**, 20–21
Premium goods, frequency of purchase of 128–131
Prosocial nature 122–123
Psychologization xi
Public opinion statistics **32–36**

Q
Quality of life orientation (QOL orientation) 138–149
Quantitative social consciousness studies 3–6, 10–23, **25–43**
Quiet transformation of status identification 37, **86–88**, 93, 153

R
Re-embedding 20, **156–158**, 163–167
Reflexive modernity xii–xiii, 6, 31, 50–51, 98, 150, **156–158**
Response distribution 31, 35, 42, 67, 75–80

S
Second Monitor Survey xvi, 144–145
Self-direction 41, **100–102**, 113, 115, 140, 147, 160, 168
Show cards **72–73**
Social attitude (s) **8–11**, 15, 19, 26–27
Social capital 126, 164
Social character 8–9
Social consciousness studies v, xi–xv, **3–23**
Social consciousness studies-type regression model **37–41**
Social epidemiology and public health 6
Social fact **17–18**, 157–159
Social mentality **xi–xiii**
Social psychology **4–9**

Social structure   25
Sociological imagination   28
"Software"   xi, **27**, 101, 126, 159, 161
SSM Survey   xvi, 16, 19, 48, 52, 65–80, 102–103, 107, 115, 119
SSP-I 2010 Survey   xvi, 32, 48, 67, 83, 109, 120
SSP-P 2010 Survey   6, 107, 144–145
SSP Project   iii, xvi, 48, 63
SSP-W 2013-1st   xvi, 74
State of disillusioned inequality   92, 155, 161
Status identification   **30–31**
Status-relatedness   **14–15**
Stratification and Social Psychology Project, *see* SSP Project
Stratification consciousness studies   18–21
Stratification, Education, and the Formation of Social Consciousness   iii, 10–12
Structural equation modeling   38, 148
Subjective well-being   138–149
Subjectivity   **8**
Symbolic token   **165–167**

T
Theory of Japanese uniqueness, *see Nihonjinron*
Traditionalism, *see* Conventionality
Traditionalism–modernism   xvi, 30–31, **60–61**, 97–115, 153–164

U
Unfairness, feelings of, *see* Equity

V
Value judgment   9, 119
Value orientation   **8–9**, 33
Volunteer and NPO   129–130

W
Work and Personality   **100–103**, 106, 113, 115

NAME INDEX

Adorno, Theodor   10, 99
Aoki Tamotsu   57–63
Bauman, Zygmunt   50, 150
Beck, Ulrich   50, 150
Bourdieu, Pierre   8, 16, 125–126
Durkheim, Émile   7, 16–17, 157
Fromm, Erich   7, 98–99
Giddens, Anthony   50, 98, 150, 156–157, 165–168
Hamaguchi Eshun   58–59, 63
Hayashi Chikio   52, 60
Hidaka Rokurō   12–13, 15, 22
Hout, Michael   80
Imada Takatoshi   52, 82
Inglehart, Ronald   163
Inkeles, Alex   163
Kanbayashi Hiroshi   72, 76, 79, 86–87, 90
Kido Kotarō   15–16, 20, 22, 27, 37, 99
Kishimoto Shigenobu   82
Kitayama Shinobu   22
Kohn, Melvin   41, 100–101, 115
Mannheim, Karl   8, 157
Marx, Karl   11, 14, 19, 27, 101, 135
Merton, Robert   7
Mikami Takeshi   51, 157
Mills, C. Wright   28
Mita Munesuke   xv, 12–23
Miura Atsushi   78
Miyajima Takashi   13–22
Mori Naoto   71, 78, 92
Murakami Yasusuke   57, 89
Naoi Atsushi   100, 102, 145
Naoi Michiko   80, 92–93, 106
Nishiyama Tetsuo   xii
Odaka Kunio   18, 21, 23, 69, 72
Oguma Eiji   63
Ōtsuka Hisao   12
Parsons, Talcott   161
Sandel, Michael   119
Satō Kenji   16, 23
Satō Toshiki   66, 72, 79–80, 91
Schooler, Carmi   41, 100–101, 115
Seiyama Kazuo   23, 41, 80, 93
Sudo Naoki   77, 79–80, 86, 90, 93
Todoroki Makoto   100, 104, 106, 113–116
Tominaga Ken'ichi   23, 79
Tomoeda Toshio   51–52
Watanuki Jōji   61
Weber, Max   7–8, 97
Yamada Mamoru   51
Yasuda Saburō   8, 16, 18, 21, 23, 66, 69
Yoshizaki Tatsuhiko   52